kitchen table, mashed potatoes castles, parents droning, bed-time, lights out, silence, thinking, other kids playing late on the street, turn on transistor radio, tinny, pressed to ear under blankets, a voice sings, scratchy, addresses universe on behalf of 8 year old spirit, recognition of something greater, promise made: "Someday, someway, somehow I wll be involved with music when I grow-up."

and then the challenge. how to hold this contract steady within oneself across the years—serving and protecting it or sacrificing it to the dogs/gods.

— JANE SIBERRY,
on why most people are in the
music business and why there is such variety

The best way to prepare yourself for the music industry is to get educated. Go to school, get well rounded. You don't necessarily need to know everything about the music business, but you need to know about how business is done. And be prepared to understand that your music is about to become a business.

— SEAN "PUFFY" COMBS,
CEO of Bad Boy Entertainment

I feel the most important education in the music business is the one that you give yourself.

— CHRIS SCHWARTZ,
CEO and Founder of RuffHouse Records

# *the* REAL DEAL

## HOW TO GET SIGNED TO A RECORD LABEL FROM A TO Z

### DAYLLE DEANNA SCHWARTZ

BILLBOARD BOOKS
An imprint of Watson-Guptill Publications/New York

Senior Editor:  Bob Nirkind
Book and cover design: Bob Fillie, Graphiti Graphics
Graphic production: Ellen Greene

First published 1997 by Billboard Books, an imprint of Watson-
Guptill Publications, a division of BPI Communications, Inc.,
1515 Broadway, New York, NY 10036

ISBN 8230-7611-3

**Library of Congress cataloging-in-Publication Data**
Schwartz, Daylle Deanna.
      The real deal: how to get signed to a record label from A to Z/
   Daylle Deanna Schwartz.
         p.    cm.
      ISBN 0-8230-7611-3
      1. Popular music—vocational guidance—United States
   2. Sound recording industry—United States.    I. Title.
   ML3795.S244    1997
   780'. 23'73—dc21                                        96-49874
                                                              CIP
                                                              MN

Manufactured in the United States of America

First printing, 1997

1 2 3 4 5 6 7 8 9 10 / 99 98 97

This book is dedicated to my parents with much love. To my father, Bob Herman, who has always encouraged me to be an independent, self-sufficient woman; who brought my rap records into stores and talked them into taking them on consignment; and who proudly touted my accomplishments in the music industry while others thought I was nuts. To my mother, Ruth Herman, who was one of those who thought I was nuts for running a record label, yet supported me anyway; who wanted me to take a more traditional route for women but loved me anyway; and who finally sat in on a music business class I was teaching and came up to me afterwards with so much pride saying, "I never understood what you were doing and that you knew so much. You should write a book." Here it is, Mom!

## ACKNOWLEDGMENTS

There are many people who contributed to the fruition of this book. I want to first thank my wonderful sister, Carla Herman, for buying me a computer (when I was too stubborn to give up my word processor), without which I may not have had the patience to finish this book. Second, I want to thank my terrific, enthusiastic, and very smart agent, Sheree Bykofsky, of Sheree Bykofsky Associates, Inc., for being totally supportive from the beginning to the end of this project and for spending so much time watching out for my best interests. Second A, I want to thank the best editor I could ever hope to work with, Bob Nirkind, for teaching me a lot more than I've ever learned in a writing class, and for being thoroughly a pleasure to work with on every level.

I want to thank Janet Rosen at Sheree Bykofsky Associates for recognizing the potential of my book, and for doing a terrific job working with the editorial content of my book proposal. I want to thank my friend, publicist Sherri Rosen, for continually hounding me to take the time to finish my book and get it published.

Where do I begin to thank all of the wonderful industry people whose support and knowledge helped shape *The Real Deal?* The music industry is known for being an unsupportive, cutthroat business. Yet these people have completely proven otherwise, making my research a pleasure!

I'll start with those who took the time to share their knowledge and experience with my readers. These people make the music industry worth being in. Since there are so many, I'll thank them in alphabetical order to make it easier. Thank you, thank you, thank you to Jerry Ade, Dave Ayres, Karin Berg, Marilyn Bergman, Gail Boyd, Kirk Burrowes, Peter Ciaccia, Johnny Clegg, David Cohen, Sean "Puffy" Combs, Chuck D, Wendy Day, Jeff Fenster, Julie Flanders, Wendy Goldstein, Chris Jones, Alex Kochan, Adam Kornfeld, Peter Leeds, Micheline Levine, Julie Lipsius, Linda Lorence, Kenny MacPherson, Deborah-Mannis Gardner, Shirley Manson, Karen Matheson, Rose Noone, Shannon O'Shea, Joy Pederson, Mark Pitts, Gladys Pizarro, Frances Preston, ?uestlove, Phil Ramone, LeAnn Rimes, Erica Ruben, Chris Schwartz, Debbie Schwartz, Stormy Shepherd, Jane Siberry, Diane Stagnato, Jeannie Stahlman, Stan Soocher, Steve Ward, Sandy Wilbur, and Karen Yee. The music industry is a wonderful place when you attract the positive people!

I also want to thank Pat Baird (BMI), Lauren Iossa (ASCAP), Lori Lousararian (Rogers & Cowan), Glenn Manko (RuffHouse Records), Amy Morris (Geffen Records), and Chamaine Thomas (Ujama Music, Inc.) for their wonderful cooperation and support in helping me get information requested. I appreciate your taking the time to assist me!

Many people went out of their way to prove there are very supportive people in the music industry. A very big super-special thank you to Larry Rudolph, Wallace Collins, Arnie Goodman and Jeff Epstein (DiscMakers) for their friendship, and for going the distance with me over many years with continued support of my educational endeavors, both my book and my seminars. Thank you Phoebe Snow and Kathy Baylor, for your friendship, and for sharing your wisdom and your continued encouragement. Thank you Bob Grossweiner, for your time, knowledge, and resources. Thank you Jane Blumenfeld, for your friendship, enthusiasm, refreshing vision about the music industry and for being Jane Blumenfeld! And last but not least, thank you Terrie Williams, for your continuous support over the years, and for showing by example that we can be caring, supportive, and spiritual in the industry. I whole-heartedly appreciate my industry friends and love you all!

On a personal level: I want to thank God and the universe for all my blessings. Thank you to my best friend in the universe, Ellen Penchansky, for her continuous belief in my ability to accomplish anything I chose to do, even when she didn't understand what I was doing! Thank you to Tracy Bowen for his unwavering faith and long distance encouragement. Thank you to my friends Terry Hacker and Judy Wong for being there from the beginning and hanging in with me for many years with support, shoulders to cry on, and encouragement. Thank you Eva Rex-Vogel for helping me to find my way.

And last but not least, I want to thank my lovely daughter, Tami Schwartz, for accepting an unconventional mother, for enduring being the daughter of "The Rappin' Teach," and for giving me the greatest encouragement of all!

# CONTENTS

# INTRODUCTION

P eople are always coming to me for advice on how to get signed to a record label. Sometimes they're so confused by what others tell them, they can't make good decisions for themselves. Everyone in the music industry has an opinion. Ask five different industry people how to approach a specific situation and you may get five conflicting points of view. It's hard to know who to pay attention to. Trying everything can set you up for what I call the *yo-yo effect*, being yanked back and forth as you grab at any suggestions for getting ahead. You're advised to "do this" so you rush to try it. Then someone else recommends another option and you hurry to try that too. Heeding everyone's advice can get exhausting and frustrating, with little getting accomplished. You can burn yourself out by expending all of your energy following the wrong advice.

How can anyone know who to listen to? As a teacher of music business classes and a consultant for start-up labels and artists/ songwriters, I regularly hear misconceptions about the music industry. I was hampered by them myself when first breaking into working in music. While there's no formula for getting a record deal, the wrong advice can keep you from trying all of your options. It can hold you back, set limitations on what you can do to get signed, and even create opportunities for you to get ripped off. This book will tell you the real deal about how you can maximize your chances of attracting the best record deal possible.

## HOW DO I KNOW WHAT I'M TALKING ABOUT?

My entry into the music industry came from a very different place than most. I used to be a school teacher in New York City, and guarantee that anyone reading this knows more about music than I did in the beginning. I didn't even know what a CD was! There were few female rappers back then, and no white ones to speak of when my students dared me to make a rap record. They laughed at me, saying a white woman couldn't rap. I became determined to break their stereotypes; to show them they shouldn't let things like their sex or race stop them from doing what they believed in.

I eventually learned how to rap by hanging out in the streets, going to clubs, listening to the rap shows on the radio, and literally living and breathing hip hop. I got ripped off big time, swayed by everyone's promises. There were a lot of misconceptions about the music industry in the streets where my lessons began. In the beginning I believed everybody because I wanted to believe the exciting things that were being said. My passionate highs dropped to disheartening lows as I went from excitement (because someone had souped me up, blowing up my bubble), to downright depression (because someone else burst my bubble). It was an emotional time—one of much learning, growing, and toughening my stance. But I survived.

When I made my first rap cut, the kids in school were sold. I got nicknamed "The Rappin' Teach" and picked up a lot of media attention. But still no deal. I didn't have a clue then what I was doing. The kids thought I was good and were furious when they heard how people jerked me around. This is a heck of an industry. Many insiders will tell you anything you want to hear at that moment so you'll kiss up to them. At first I kissed, so desperate was I to learn what to do, and to get the record deal I felt was deserved.

But the people in industry sent me a message that no one believed a white woman could succeed in rap, even though they knew I was good.

The kids decided I should get revenge, and felt some of the specific people who had jerked me around should have their tires slashed, their houses spray painted, and any other nasties they could think up. If I wouldn't do it myself, there were volunteers to do the dirty work for me. However, I truly believe it's healthier to use the energy behind your anger to do something positive for yourself. So instead of slashing people's tires, I opened Revenge Productions and through it, Revenge Records, which was intended to be a vehicle for me to put out my own material. That was the beginning of my positive revenge!

I learned by trial and effort and got taken advantage of many times. My knowledge was so limited back then that I had to depend on others for everything. But I worked very hard, determined to prove my point. At music seminars I felt like a nonentity but continued to network like crazy. People would read my tag and walk away with their noses in the air. What a lousy feeling! But that's the way it can be in this industry. Be prepared for it. It may never get better. A strong belief in your talent and a thick skin can help you get through those times of feeling like a nobody.

My efforts began as a lesson to my students about how to avoid letting stereotypes stop them from achieving their goals. But all of a sudden I had a viable record label. I was signing artists, and selling lots of records. Major labels were making deals with me for my artists. Best of all, I was finally earning one of the hardest commodities to attain in this business—respect. A lack of respect is something you have to be prepared for, at least at first. Respect is something to be earned. And the dues can be high. In the beginning I was laughed at and humored because I'm friendly, but definitely not taken seriously. I was just "Teach" to most people.

Ignoring the skepticism, I focused on making a success of my label. After my first major deal, people started seeing me in a different light. When I began being asked to speak at national music seminars, I recognized that respect was there. And when I broke POWERULE ("Smooth," "Brick in a Wall"), my most visible act, the respect factor increased. I got extensive airplay for both of their videos. That was a big deal. Now people not only talked to me at seminars once they read my tag, they coveted me to the point where I almost wished to be back in anonymity.

## FROM TEACHER TO RAPPER TO TEACHER

I learned from my mistakes, and you can learn from my mistakes too! Since I'm a real teacher, people have always come to me for advice about making it in the music industry. My former students would send me their friends and relatives because they believed, as one put it, "Schwartz will tell you the real deal about the music business." Much of the informal advice I gave came from the lessons I learned while running Revenge Records, and from the information I picked up from seminars and books in order to expand my own education. The rest came from *on the job training*. I was the paid manager of an alternative rock band for two years. I successfully shopped material. I learned from my successes. I learned from my failures as well. It's said that experience is the best teacher. My experiences were certainly lessons you cannot learn in school.

In 1990 I put together a formal seminar called "How to Start & Run Your Own Record Label." After pressure from satisfied students, I also started teaching "Producing For a Living," "Marketing Your Music," and most currently, "How To Get a Record Deal From A to Z." I still teach these sessions regularly and get people attending my private full day seminars in New York from all over the country, as well as from overseas. I also travel to other cities to lecture in educational programs. They all want to learn from the ex-"Rappin' Teach."

I put this book together because I've found a great need for simple, qualitative facts about getting your product heard and marketed. It's an offshoot of my ever-popular classes, which are known for starting with the assumption that nobody knows anything and working up from there. People are often embarrassed to ask simple questions, assuming they should have the answers already. Most of the seminars I attend and the books I read assume that people already know some of the basics. But there are no real sources of getting those basics. Thus I've put my classes in a book. No matter what level you're on, there should be information here for you. I've tried to include all of the things, from A to Z, that come up in my classes and during consultations. If you're going to try and knock yourself out for your music, you'll need all the help you can get.

Both creative and professional industry people consistently give the same piece of advice to those trying to break into the music business: "Educate yourself as much as possible about all aspects of this business." You don't have to be a lawyer, manager, etc., but you do need to have some idea of how the business itself is run. That's why I've included information in this book on publishing and recording royalties as well as some specifics about recording contracts that I feel are particularly important. Even a little knowledge can go a long way in keeping you from getting ripped off. Back in the 1950's, for instance, some of the famous doo-wop singers received no royalties from hit songs they wrote. These writers signed away various songwriting rights without understanding what they meant. Over the years, many popular artists who've written their own songs have opted for the quick deal, a pretty lump of cash at the beginning with nothing on the other end. The record label got most of the money. Why? Ignorance.

## THE IMPORTANCE OF LEARNING THE BUSINESS

A large number of musicians who are ripped off are young people, often without a lot of money. Most are hungry for a deal. A label might offer what seems like a huge chunk of change at the time—$5,000, $10,000, or even $25,000 as an advance. To a kid desperate for a deal, that could seem like a lot. Often without the benefit of a lawyer or manager, artists sign contracts on their own, clueless as to the amount of money and/or control they're giving away. It's usually too late when they finally see how much money the label is making off of their album, and how little they are getting.

When I'd just started rapping, I met a man who turned out to have written some of the biggest, most memorable hit songs of the 1950's. This man was living on the fifth floor of a run-down tenement building in Harlem. He had one room and was sharing a bathroom. During the day he pumped gasoline to earn a living. He told me that his record label got all the money from his songs. Forty years ago he signed whatever they offered because he was so excited about the deal. By the time he learned what songwriting royalties were, he'd signed all of his rights away. This man's classic songs are still sung today and yet he makes nothing from them. He encouraged me to learn as much about the business as possible.

Soon after meeting the doo-wop writer, I talked to a guy who was in one of the first rap groups to go platinum. He and his friends had nothing when they were offered a deal. They couldn't afford a lawyer. He told me he was so anxious to sign and get the $15,000 advance that he didn't want one anyway. His whole group was wooed by what seemed like a large advance and some good money for doing shows. So they waived all rights to any other potential income, including songwriting royalties, merchandising, and much more. He told me they got "stupid money," a large sum up front that blinds you to being smart about other considerations. "Stupid money" is given fast, and because you think it'll keep coming in (which it doesn't), it's spent quickly on unnecessary luxuries. Then the cash flow stops. Although this group had many hit records, they're now struggling to survive. The member of the group who I met warned me to learn the business.

Learning as much as you can about the business end of the music industry can only help your career. You don't need to be an expert, but it's important to have some basic knowledge at the ready. I've taken a course in auto mechanics with no intention of working on my car. But my knowledge has saved me a lot of money when I discuss my car's problem with the person at a repair shop. As a result, I often know what to check first, before going in for a major overhaul. The same is true with a record deal. It's useful to be able to talk to your lawyer with some understanding of what's being said. It helps you to ask the right questions, and challenge the wrong answers. It's also important to understand how deals are made so you don't try to market your music with too much idealism.

## GETTING A DEAL TAKES WORK

It's up to you to work to get a deal. Rarely will someone come to you before there's been an initial effort on your part. Talent is not enough. Great material is not enough. Dynamic image is not enough. The artists who make it in this business are the ones with talent, material, and image; they're the ones who want it bad enough to do almost anything it takes to get the attention of someone who can be instrumental in getting them a deal. Sitting home waiting to be discovered won't cut it, no matter how much talent you have. Learning as much as you can about all aspects of the music business and doing all you can to reach as many people as possible offers the best shot at success.

I meet musicians all the time who tell me they've written hundreds of great songs. When I ask them what they do with these songs, the replies are variations of "One day someone will discover me and then something will happen." They stay in their home studios continuing to write, probably because they don't know what else to do. Then there are the musicians who jump at a chance to play out, even for free; there are those who run to open mikes; there are those who cultivate contacts in the industry at every opportunity. These people want to get a deal for their music so much that they'll hustle and network and keep paying dues until they get what they want. IF they have the talent to match their drive, they'll get their deal.

In order to survive, a musician must develop a coat of armor. This is a tough industry. Promises can take you on an emotional seesaw ride, like the one I used to be on. The high is exhilarating when success is dangled in your face. Anticipation can raise the adrenaline. But the lows can come very quickly when promises are unfulfilled and the bearer of those promises doesn't even return your calls. That ride can destroy. Musicians burn out all the time because disappointment makes them lose heart.

When I first started rapping, someone would pull my chain and get me all excited, promising me a deal shortly. I'd be ready to scream with anticipation. Then they'd just disappear, and my excitement would turn to depression. Luckily someone pointed out to me that I'd crash if I continued on that seesaw. Now I try to stay mellow through the good and the bad. I only get excited when the deal is signed. You can't take people seriously until they come through. Take everything people say with a grain of salt. It's healthier.

There are plenty of things you can do to give yourself the best shot at achieving success in the music industry. Time and time again I hear young musicians speak with misconceptions as to how to go about getting a record deal. In this book, I've included and dispelled many common misconceptions that I've heard regularly from people in my classes. These are myths that people hear and believe that keep them from exploring every avenue possible to getting a deal. Having learned this industry the hard way, I'd like to share the knowledge I've gained both from my own experiences and from the numerous industry professionals I've interviewed while writing *The Real Deal* in order to present different perspectives. Take the tools in this book and apply them to whatever genre of music you're working in. The rest is up to you!

# PART ONE

# GETTTING PAST THE MYTHS

## CHAPTER 1

# UNDERSTANDING WHAT IT TAKES TO MAKE IT IN THE MUSIC BUSINESS

MYTH:
*You need a lot of luck to get a record deal,*
*and that's not in my control.*

There are no pat rules for getting ahead in this crazy business. One of the main components is *luck*. While some say that's something we have little control over, I believe most of us make our own luck by being out there. Networking, getting exposure for your act or material, and working hard increases your probability of having *good luck*. When I started in the music industry, people told me I was very lucky to succeed in the ways I did. That's nonsense! I created my own luck by networking my butt off, talking to everyone I met, showing respect to everyone I encountered, and never taking "no" for an answer. Had I listened to what others with more experience had told me, I may never have succeeded. I worked hard to put my music out there and I owned any luck that came my way because of it.

There are many factors that can enhance your chances of attracting luck. They may seem obvious, but becoming conscious of how you handle each one can make a difference. Taking an active role in getting you and your music out there on as many levels as possible is much better than waiting for luck to come to you. The key words I emphasize in my classes are *buzz, visibility, relationships, perseverance, talent, patience, belief, knowledge,* and *balls.* These terms represent different ways of increasing your potential for attracting good luck.

## BUZZ

*Buzz* seems to be the catch-word of the music industry these days. You'll hear it over and over at seminars: "If you want a record deal, you have to create a buzz." Record labels are always listening for the buzz. But what does creating a buzz on your act mean? It means that people are taking notice of you, for any of a number of reasons. It can be because your act is getting radio play or club play. People may be noticing you because you're doing a lot of gigs to larger and larger groups of fans. You may have gotten a review for your demo, or a write-up on your act. Your band is doing well on the college circuit. Or your privately-released CD or tape may be selling well in record stores.

Having a buzz means that something is happening that's calling attention to your act. And the ability to get attention is what labels are looking for. Throughout this book I'll present various tactics for generating that all-important buzz. Begin by trying as many ways as possible to develop a story about your act. The more directions a buzz is coming from, the more seriously the labels will take you.

## VISIBILITY

Visibility definitely can help create a buzz. The more people you meet or who see you play out, the more familiar you become to those in the industry. Visibility enhances your luck. Being lucky enough to be at the right place at the right time is easier if you put yourself in as many places as possible. It's logical. The odds of meeting the right people are more favorable as contacts increase. The more you're out and about, the more people you can meet who might be helpful. The more times you play your music in public, the more people may hear and love it. Sitting home complaining that no deals are forthcoming is counterproductive. Having a great act and hit material is not enough. Opening yourself up to the largest number of possibilities will create the most opportunities for luck to work with you.

You can also develop your visibility by appearing at industry functions. You can perform or hang out at clubs that play your music, attend seminars, crash industry parties, etc. Showing your face around helps industry people get familiar with you. It's the beginning of networking. It keeps you in the thick of music-related socialization. You may not meet the people you feel you need, but it helps you to become a known entity. As you develop your presentation and get closer to being ready for a deal, you won't be a total stranger in music circles. Even a little visibility can help.

## RELATIONSHIPS

Success in the music industry can hinge on developing relationships with people you deal with on all levels. A consistent piece of advice given by industry pros at music seminars is to *build relationships* with the people you work with and with those who can be crucial to advancing your career. When people know and like you, there's a greater chance of receiving help. Getting friendly with as many people in the industry as possible can't hurt. This is a people-oriented business. Technology may help it function, but it's the people who make the decisions.

What does building a relationship mean? It doesn't mean you have to become buddies with everyone you meet. It doesn't even necessarily mean anything on a personal level. It does mean developing a level of confidence and trust between yourself and others. It does mean creating a good rapport. It does mean creating a level of comfortable interaction between yourself and the other person, making yourself seem easy to deal with. Building a good relationship does not mean you ever have to meet in person. Phone relationships can suffice. I've built great relationships with people I've never met face-to-face.

Building a relationship means that when you work with the person there will be some mutual respect. It means that when you call these people, they *may* take your call. It can be hard to reach people by phone in the music industry, even when they know you well. But without a relationship, it can be next to impossible. Building a good relationship can create productive and successful interaction between yourself and others. It's the ground level of working your way up in the music industry. It's the top level of being a success.

Building a good relationship also involves establishing boundaries that increase the comfort level of interactions. People are more likely to want to deal with someone who's professional and reliable, and who's not a pest. For example, I have a relationship with a top entertainment person. There are many times I want to call for a favor but don't. She knows I don't abuse her courtesy, so when I ask for something I always get a response. If she can't help me, I thank her anyway. Doing things for people without having a "price tag" attached can strengthen a good relationship. You don't want people to avoid taking your calls because you're too pushy, abrasive, etc. They shouldn't feel you only come to them because you want something.

Before you have a record deal, good relationships with people may mean they'll help you get your foot in the door, secure live performances, and keep you in mind for other activities that can further your career. They may introduce you to other people who might be helpful. A good relationship can mean the difference between you or someone else being chosen to fill the one slot left at a charity show. If a person knows you are cooperative and pleasant to work with, choosing you may seem more appealing.

After you get a deal, good relationships can help you receive the maximum cooperation from the people at your label. If you work well with everyone, they'll give you a more enthusiastic push. It can mean the difference between a label giving your CD a half-hearted nudge when it's released, or everyone working it hard. Some artists are known for being difficult to work with. I've had some on my label that I didn't feel motivated to push as hard as I might have. The ones I got along with, whom I didn't feel a constant tug of war with, were those I went the greatest distance for.

What can you do to build good relationships? One very important factor is showing a respect for the other person's time. When you call, for instance, be prepared. Say what you need to and don't keep the person on the phone too long. In addition, remember to say "thank you" if you get help, whether it was successful or not. "Thanks for trying" can make someone more amenable to try again. Finally, don't be a pig. Learning to ask is important, but prioritize your needs and ask only for what's necessary. Free tickets to a gig can wait if you know that person can hook you up with someone who can help your career.

## PERSEVERANCE

Getting a record deal is often a combination of having a marketable act and managing to get the attention of the right people. So much of the road to success can be construed as luck, but as I've already said, the more hard work you put into getting out there, the more potential for luck you'll have. Perseverance is another important quality that industry people recommend developing in order to market your act successfully. If you have the talent and don't quit, you'll get there eventually! If you're not prepared to hang in, don't waste your time.

As I've already indicated, this isn't a business consisting only of the sweetest people. You may hear promises up the yazoo and then see nothing materialize. You must persevere! People aren't good at returning phone calls in this business. You must persevere! Someone may be your best buddy one day and forget you the next. Get used to it! There may be many disappointments. You must persevere! There may be times you pay someone for a service you don't receive. You must persevere! You may be ignored, disrespected, or kicked in the face. Welcome to the music industry—home of the stoutest of heart! You must persevere! Or, you must choose another career. The music biz ain't easy.

## TALENT

Many A & R people have told me that "the cream always rises to the top." Unfortunately many musicians don't have enough talent and good material to make that trip. Throughout the book I will emphasize this: *It is critical to understand that you've got to be very good to have the best chance at a deal.* Many musicians just don't know if they have the talent. There are plenty of good solid musicians around. But only a few have that special something that sets them above the rest. If you actually do have the talent and material, someone will eventually find you if you keep yourself on the music scene.

I go to hear live music regularly. There's a lot of talent out there. There are many acts I listen to and enjoy very much. It's rare that one jumps out at me, though. When that happens, I know they'll get a deal if they hang in. That's what A & R people are looking for. They want the big hit. They want something that sounds better than all the good solid musicians they hear. I rejoice when seeing a band that motivates me to say "they've got it." You can't just have *some talent* to have a good shot at a recording contract. The talent, including your songs, must shine like a neon sign to the people at a record label. They should see "hit" written across your forehead.

A good example occurred when Women In Music, Inc. (a non-profit organization offering support services for music industry people) had a Pitchathon in New York. Songwriters were offered the opportunity to pitch songs to an A & R person with a panel of knowledgeable industry people commenting on each song. One after another the songs were played. They were all good, and there were kind words for many of them from the panel. Then came a song by two guys who I'd always thought had the talent. When the song was done, I was thrilled to hear my sentiments echoed from someone on the panel—"That's a hit!" The song leapt out over all the other songs. It was perfect for the market. That's the kind of talent necessary to rise above the others. Sometimes people struggle for years, not understanding they just don't have what it takes.

## PATIENCE

I once heard a musician complain that her friend shouldn't be lamenting over her disappointments because she'd only been performing her music for a few years. You have to be prepared to pay your dues. You have to be prepared to wait until the time is right for you to get that deal. It could take many years. Those with patience can get the deal. Time usually makes a smart musician more savvy about the industry. It gives you time to develop your act to perfection, and to learn from your mistakes. Be prepared for the long haul or don't waste your time.

Patience helps you to deal with all the characters who will take their time fulfilling promises. Even well-meaning people can keep you dangling for a while. This business keeps everyone busy, so it may take longer to get around to you than you'd like. Sitting tight can be very hard to do, but it's essential while waiting until the time is right and the people are ready to help you. You cannot allow your spirits and your belief in yourself to falter. When your act is developed fully, your songs are perfect for the current market, and people are noticing you're ready for a deal, there'll be a deal if you've stuck around for the long haul.

## BELIEF

One thing that's definitely true is that *you* have to believe in yourself!! No matter what anyone else thinks, you have to know your material is the absolute greatest. If you don't have 1,000% complete faith in what you're doing, it's not worth the effort to try to market it. Your own enthusiasm can attract attention or provoke curiosity. A subdued pitch for your music won't excite anyone. Many musicians called me when my record label was active. I had little interest in those who described their music as "okay," "pretty good," or "you'll see for yourself." The ones I wanted to hear were those who said their music would blow me away, or similar enthusiastic versions of that concept. Most of them didn't impress me, but their enthusiasm got me to listen nonetheless.

Believing in your music increases your confidence—a quality

industry people like. If you find yourself apologizing that you could have done a better job in a better studio, wait until you have the money to go where you can get the quality you want. It's worth it. Don't sell yourself short by not putting your best foot forward. Respect yourself and your music by setting high standards. In the long run, this will earn you the respect of others. People do get deals with demos that aren't the best. But you want to max out your chances.

## KNOWLEDGE

I've already stressed the importance of educating yourself about all aspects of the music industry. No matter what kind of music you're working with, the basic information in this book will be valid. What I must also emphasize is that you have to know your own genre of music well. This is something you have to do for yourself. I can tell you about doing live performances, but *you* have to know what venues are appropriate for your music. I can tell you how to get press coverage, but *you* have to know the publications that cover your genre. I can tell you to hang out and network in clubs, but *you* have to know which ones. Regardless of what you're doing, the more you live and breathe it, the more you'll know about it and the better the chance you'll have of finding an open door. The more you read about it, listen to radio stations that play it, go to live performances, join organizations, etc. the more contacts you'll make and the more knowledgeable you'll be.

When I was working with rap music, I listened to the rap shows as much as I could. In private I mainly listened to rock. But for a while my focus was on the music I was trying to market. I went to rap shows and rap clubs. This enabled me both to develop an ear for exactly what style was popular and to make valuable contacts. I read magazines that focused on rap music and knew the names of the reviewers, writers, and main editors. I went to seminars with an emphasis on hip hop. I got to know it so well that I was eventually asked to speak on hip hop panels. I did the same thing when I was trying to do dance music projects, and also when I worked with an alternative rock band. Immersing yourself like a sponge in your own genre gives you an edge.

## BALLS

If you want the best shot of getting a deal, you need to develop balls. It takes balls to ask for what you need. It takes balls to get up on stage and perform for an audience who don't know your music. It takes balls to speak highly of your music when others may doubt you. It takes balls to tell someone they have to sign you because you'll make them a lot of money. It takes balls to hang in when the going gets tough. Not quitting can be the hardest thing you do. Either develop balls or do your music as a hobby.

# PART TWO

# FINDING THE KEY PLAYERS FOR YOUR CAREER

## CHAPTER 2

# SEEKING THE RIGHT PERSONAL MANAGER AT THE RIGHT TIME

MYTH:
*It's important to have a manager right away,*
*even if it's not someone with lots of experience.*

Some call a manager a glorified baby-sitter. When artists signed to my label opted to wait for management, I informally assumed that position. They called with all their personal problems as well as all their business problems. I often did feel as though I was baby-sitting. But being a real manager is a whole 'nother animal.

### THE ROLE OF A PERSONAL MANAGER

A manager orchestrates all aspects of your career. Manager Peter Ciaccia (PC Management) has worked in the music business in a variety of areas for fifteen years. When I asked Ciaccia what his definition of a personal manager is, he replied:

> Someone that can take the client that they're working with and cover a lot of ground for them. A manager winds up being everything to the acts . . . the A & R per-

son, the publicist. A manager has to make good judgment calls for the band. He is the liaison between the artist and the record company. When a band is unsigned, he works with them from the beginning to find a home for them. He's out there selling the band, selling the image and music of the band. He has to have a good sense of what the market calls for, what would interest people, and how to get to the people. He creates a realistic buzz about the band . . . he has to be tied into the street.

Some managers actually help to financially support artists until their money begins to come in. Managers may also invest in developing artists and their material. If you can find someone who believes enough in your project to invest in it, you might want to give them a try. They'll then have a vested interest in you besides time. I've been told it's quite common for managers to put money up either for music production or to get the act out and playing in order to break the band.

A manager is usually the person who shops your tapes, representing you in obtaining a record deal. A manager also helps you make decisions about the direction of your career, which label to sign with, etc. Once a deal is signed, a manager acts as liaison between you and your record label, making sure the terms of your contract are met. In addition, a manager is the one to insist the label gives your record good promotion and marketing, in general, to make sure the label treats you right. Peter Leeds (Leeds Davis Management), who managed Blondie almost from the beginning through their *Parallel Lines* hit album, told me that "A manager is like a hub in a wheel. Around the hub there's lots of spokes. The spokes would be all of the different aspects of the record company personnel."

A manager advises you as well on all aspects of the production of your songs and on the people you work with (producers, lawyers, agents, etc.). If you're lucky, your manager will have a good ear to give you creative guidance with your material. Finally, a manager is responsible for contacting talent agents to get you booked into live appearances, hopefully for a profit. He or she makes sure the arrangements are fair, the tour support reasonable, the transportation available, and that everything else goes smoothly. How can someone with no experience hope to do all of the above properly? According to Peter Ciaccia,

> A person should not just jump into managing a band without fully understanding what it means to manage a band and manage a business. That's the primary point . . . it's a business. You have to be quick enough on your feet to make business calls. You have to know what goes down in this business, from record contracts, to publishing contracts, to budgeting tours, to wiping people's noses. That's really what managers do. To jump in there thinking "I just want to do it" without understanding the background of it is a mistake. I think if someone really wants to seriously get into management, the first advice would be to get yourself situated somewhere in the music business to learn as much as you can about different aspects of the business. You will get a good sense of what the business is all about.

## HOW A POOR MANAGER CAN DAMAGE YOUR CAREER

A good manager can steer you to the greatest heights of success. A bad manager can be the cause of your career's demise in no time flat. Because a manager represents you as an artist and presents an image of you through their representation, it's best to have a very professional, knowledgeable, and experienced person working on your behalf.

Although you may be anxious to acquire a manager, getting just anyone willing to take on an unknown artist is not necessarily going to help. The cold hard truth is that the very good managers often don't want to represent artists until they have something going for them. It's usually better to wait until you get to that point in your career. If you sign a long term contract with someone just starting out, you may be stuck with a representative speaking for you who can do more harm than good. Patience is essential. I've heard of instances where artists lost record deals because the labels didn't want to deal with their seemingly inexperienced manager. I asked Peter Ciaccia how signing with the wrong manager can actually hurt an artist.

> You have to really understand this business is made up of a lot of relationships and contacts. From inexperienced to experienced, a manager can screw an artist up just by not being available; by being kind of standoffish with people who are trying to deal with the band. Young baby bands need nurturing and a manager needs the time for that. It's a 24 hour job.

Arnie Goodman, General Manager of Viceroy Records, told me that inexperienced managers can try too hard. "Sometimes, calling too much can blow the deal, especially if the management sound too desperate." Peter Leeds feels that many managers don't understand how much effort has to be put into getting a band out. He also believes that if he can't get his acts to do what needs to be done, then he's not doing his job properly. He said, "I've been talking to managers who are morons and idiots. They don't understand . . . They're afraid to talk to their act. The manager and the artist need to have a good rapport so that the manager doesn't wind up being too intimidated to go to the artist and say something the artist doesn't want to hear.

Once I had an artist (whom I shall refer to as Lisa) on my label whose producer/mother's boyfriend became her manager, much to my dismay. When a major label offered me a production deal, we were all thrilled. However, just before we signed the contracts I got a call from the label telling me the deal was off. Lisa's manager had gone behind my back to try to negotiate some points directly with the label. What he did was considered unethical and the label decided not to deal with an artist who had such unprofessional representation. I sadly dropped this very talented artist from my label.

I've since heard other horror stories about how this manager continued to do stupid things which ruined other opportunities for Lisa. Today she's still unsigned.

## WHAT TO LOOK FOR IN A PERSONAL MANAGER

If you have a manager in mind, talk to that individual and see how you get along. See what their game plan for your career might be. Pay attention to their enthusiasm, or lack of it, for your music. Your manager doesn't have to love it, but it helps. Interview the potential candidate as you would anyone who was going to work for you. Don't act like they're doing you a favor. If you believe in yourself, others will too. Your manager should see you as a good source of future income.

Many people are dying to be managers, but much fewer know what the job entails. They think they can just learn as they go. WRONG!!!! Being a manager doesn't necessarily come naturally. It's not just about trying to make appointments with A & R people. It's much more than hanging out at clubs to schmooze with industry people. Being a manager involves carrying yourself in an appropriate manner. Being a manager involves being familiar with industry protocol. Being a manager means knowing as much about the music you're working with as possible.

According to Peter Ciaccia,

> A young band should suss the manager out by asking about the manager through other sources. If he's a young and upcoming manager, it doesn't mean he's a bad manager. Check around, check his credentials and see who knows him. Have many conversations with the manager to see if he's intelligent and articulate enough to express what the act is looking for, or at least to guide the act to something.

Being a manager is a big commitment. Many think it's something that will be lots of fun. It may not be so much fun when the stress and hard work get intense. A manager needs to be available. One cannot *manage* when it's convenient. Sometimes there may be nothing to do. Other times it may feel like a never-ending, thankless job. It all goes with the territory.

Mark Pitts (Mark Pitts Management), who manages artists such as rap star Notorious B.I.G., says that a good personality is an asset if you're going to network with people in the industry. He believes the most important thing when choosing a manager is feeling a good vibe. "The vibe has to be right. That's something that's all in your heart."

Peter Leeds warns that, "one of the things that too many acts do that hurt them is they take their best friend to be their manager." A friend may not be as objective as necessary. A manager must have enough savvy to make the correct decisions for the artist. The artist must have enough respect for the manager's judgement to readily go along with those decisions. Leeds believes that "A manager has to communicate with the band and make decisions. So many people make decisions by not making decisions." Soon after Blondie got signed, Leeds kept them on the road for over a year straight. He says, "We just kept going. And I never asked their permission. I just told them where they were going." A friend or inexperienced manager may not have the ability to do that.

It's also important to assess the candidate's personality and attitude. Recently I spoke to an A & R person with a top label who said that if the artist's manager rubs her the wrong way from the beginning, she's less likely to sign the artist. She told me about a group she's signed with a manager who's very pushy and talks much too much. She said she'd do a lot more with the group if she didn't have to go through this individual. Instead, she passes over them with opportunities because she doesn't feel like putting up with the manager's annoying ways. She feels bad about neglecting the group but knows there's lots of talent around. She simply can't be bothered having to put up with a manager who gets on her nerves. Your manager is the person who deals with the record label, so if their personality annoys you, think again. And if they don't know exactly what they're doing, think how that will look to the people at the label.

## WORKING WITH AN INEXPERIENCED MANAGER

An inexperienced, yet driven person who wants to manage you should not necessarily be passed up. Someone who wants to work with your band because they believe in your music, who seems ready to work their ass off for you, should definitely be considered. You just have to be more careful.

Arnie Goodman started off as a manager. He was asked to manage rock group Savoy Brown because they were friends, and they knew he was a hard worker. He learned the business by working in it and acquired experience dealing with labels under fire. Having been there himself, he's not averse to choosing an inexperienced but potentially good manager. He recommends getting "somebody who will be hustling and not worrying about how much money you may make. Everyone has to start someplace. A manager needs drive. The main thing is they have to be hungry."

Manager Shannon O'Shea (SOS Management), who manages the band Garbage, says "The problem with management in general is there is no training process or it's very difficult to get training. A lot of bands may find a young manager with not a lot of experience but . . . who has the hunger and drive and is prepared not to see a huge amount of income initially." She points out that if an inexperienced manager can get the ball rolling for the act, they have the potential of joining a larger management company. Approaching a company when the band has momentum is easier. O'Shea says that

> Young managers can get pushed aside once the success starts happening because they get out of their depth. Then the band will end up going to a major management company and what can happen there is they can get lost in the system. But if they do a deal where they put their guy in a bigger company or under a major manager who can then oversee the next plateau . . . they know this guy is going to be on their side . . . and if he needs advice or somebody to make the phone call to kick somebody's ass, he's got that available to him or her. That way [the band] keeps people who are loyal to the band and in it for the right reasons.

I found it a relief to know this option exists, although it isn't as easy as it sounds. But if you have a green manager who does work with you to get things happening, and management companies approach you, try to get your manager placed within that company. If you're a manager, keep an eye out for this possibility.

If you have a potential manager in mind who's inexperienced, ask lots of questions. Ask why that individual wants to be a manager and what she or he sees as their main responsibilities. Find out what contacts they have and how they intend to use them. Set up various scenarios that might arise and ask how they would handle them. Make sure that you respect their judgement.

## HOW TO FIND A MANAGER

Most managers tell me that they'll find you. Those who are looking to pick up new acts have their feelers out. They go to clubs looking for artists to manage. If you're playing out and getting attention, a manager may approach you. If you're approached, many managers will accept tapes with a press kit. Include any write-ups you've gotten, even from small publications. Shannon O'Shea says,

> I would try to gain as much local press as I possibly could ... reviews of what they're doing. Try and get radio interested, even if it's local college radio. Get as much local support as you can get so you get a nice package together. Maybe you can get quotes from a radio station. Then you've something to go to management with and go 'Look.' Management are going to want to know that the band is willing to work, and if they can do this on their own, well then they've got what it takes. If you've been doing gigs, include a listing of those too. Mention the size of your following, if you have one. Anything showing activity in your career would be of interest to a potential manager. Managers want to see that you are working hard. They want to work with acts who have already developed a foundation.

Most managers will want a photo included in your press kit. If they like what they see and hear, they'll come hear you play.

One way to find a personal representative is to ask around for the names of managers working with artists in your genre of music. When you go to clubs, get names from other artists. If you want to know the manager of a signed artist, call the public relations department of the record label and ask for the name of that artist's manager. Sound professional and you'll often get what you've asked for. Also, check out directories of managers that list whom each represents. If you're out and about in the industry long enough, you'll find a manager.

To catch the interest of the managers you approach you need a creative tactic. One that shows how hard you're working is the best. According to Shannon O'Shea,

> What I would do is send a fax through to . . . someone on a mid-level who's going to be less busy and more open to what they have to say. Send them a short fax . . . maybe attach a one-page cut–and–paste of best reviews and just bullet-point it. Tell them what you've accomplished locally . . . just do a short, hard pitch that's the bottom line stuff, that's really positive, and say that you'll be sending a package shortly. On the envelope you want to put "expected material," unless you happen to get lucky and speak to the guy on the phone who does request it. Then you put "requested." Remember that everybody has this big box in their office, particularly labels but managers as well, and it's full of tapes they've got to listen to. So you need to separate yours by [what you write] on the envelope so the assistant knows they're expecting it and to push it through. Otherwise it can sit in a pile. And be a little patient. Appreciate that people are busy and it may take time for them to get back to you. Don't hound people, because they'll think 'the artist is going to be driving me crazy.' Pursue the manager as you would work with them.

Be patient about finding a manager. Sure it would feel better in the short run if the guy down the block who knows more about the industry than you do could manage you for the time being and take some of the pressure off. But in the long run, waiting for the right manager to represent you is usually the best way to go.

## SIGNING WITH A MANAGER

Although management agreements can be for as short as six months, most are for a three-to-five-year period. How can you tie yourself up for that length of time to a person who may not do the job they're supposed to? You can usually protect yourself to some degree by having a clause in your contract stipulating a minimum amount of money you must earn in the first two years. If that amount isn't reached, you can terminate your management contract. You can also have an option for a release if your manager doesn't get you a deal with a good label in that two year period. But that's still two long years of dealing with someone who may keep you from getting where you should go.

Try to sign a contract for the shortest amount of time possible. If nothing has happened with your career during that time, chances are you'll want to try with someone else. Nevertheless, I've heard musicians say they'd rather have their manager committed in writing to a longer period of time so that it gives this individual more time to develop them to their fullest potential. But they might also ignore you during that time. If you're doing well at the end of that period, your manager will want to renew anyway.

### WHEN YOUR MANAGER DOESN'T WORK ALONE

When you sign with a manager who has partners or works in an agency, you have to protect yourself if there's only one person you want representing you. After all, what happens if your manager goes to another agency or just isn't available anymore? How can you avoid getting stuck with someone else in the firm you don't like? You need to have your attorney put a *key man* clause in your contract which specifies that this particular manager is personally representing you and if he or she isn't available, you have the option of terminating your contract. Some established companies won't go for this. Then it's your choice whether to sign or try to find someone else who you know you can count on.

## HOW FAR SHOULD A MANAGER REPRESENT YOU?

Some managers actually ask for a *power of attorney*. This means they have the power to act in your behalf for almost everything. It's amazing how many people will give managers the right to sign their names on contracts. With a power of attorney a manager can also cash your checks, hire and fire people who work for you, and more. If this is in your contract, find out specifically from your own attorney what you're giving away. Most of those things you can really do yourself. You may want to give your manager a power of attorney for very specific circumstances, but only with your permission in advance.

## PAYING A MANAGER

Managers only get paid when you do. Depending on their contract, they're usually entitled to reimbursement of expenses made on your behalf. For all the services they perform, personal managers tend to get between 15% to 25%, and on rare occasions 30% of your gross earnings. Having spoken with many artists, I've found that 20% is the most common rate.

With few exceptions, managers get their percent off the top, before any expenses are paid. In the case of a recording advance, managers who are fair, and artists who are smart, will agree to the manager taking their percentage after recording costs are paid. Your lawyer will have to work out the finer points and include reasonable exceptions and deductions from this *gross income* for you.

# CHAPTER 3

# UTILIZING THE SKILLS OF A TALENT AGENT

## MYTH:
*I don't need a talent agent if I have a manager*

lthough a manager and an agent work together, they are two different and distinctive members of your team. Talent agents are primarily concerned with your ability to earn an income from doing live performances. Managers orchestrate the entire picture of your career. Therefore, you'll probably have a manager before you sign with a talent agent. As a result, a manager often assumes both roles in the beginning. Nonetheless, once your potential for paid performances develops, an agent should be added to your team.

A manager is not an agent. Your manager should be able to concentrate on managing your career while your agent concentrates on getting you paid appearances. Your manager should work with your agent to get you the best bookings possible. While your manager can make suggestions to your agent or push to get you on a good tour, he or she should not directly be doing the booking. That's not their job.

## THE ROLE OF A TALENT AGENT

A talent agent plays a limited, though essential and potentially lucrative role in your career. The agent's main responsibility is to book you for live appearances. Playing live can help you, no matter what level you've reached. When you're just starting out, it can help build your following. When you're signed, your performances can be both a great source of income and a big help in selling your records. Alex Kochan, president of Artists & Audience Entertainment, representing an impressive roster of acts such as Guns 'N Roses, Nine Inch Nails, Live, and Paul McCartney, feels that the word *agent* is misleading to many. He recommends that you "Throw all the caricatures out the window. We're not movie agents. We're not like television agents. 'Agents' is really the wrong word for us. The stereotype of an agent probably does more harm than help."

A good agent has strong relationships with the various people who bring talent into clubs, as well as with tour promoters. At the beginning of your career, a talent agent can get you into the smaller clubs where your following can be developed. Once you have a large following or a record deal, hooking up with an agent who works with name artists in your genre of music may help you to get booked onto a tour as an opening act. Check with different agencies and see what acts are on their rosters.

Jerry Ade, president of Famous Artist Agency, representing talent such as Salt-N-Pepa, Deborah Harry and LL Cool J, says

> I tell every artist to choose somebody to be on your side. You have one record company, you have one manager, you have one mother, you have one agent. When you put a cohesive team together, and they all work in unison with one another as a team, you are more apt to be successful than if you are fighting a variety of different influences in a variety of different ways. You've gotta be consistent to present a unified force.

Your team should work together towards your best interest. The main goal for everyone on your team should be furthering your career. When you reach the level where larger agents are interested in representing you, Alex Kochan advises an artist to

> Look for somebody that you can trust because essentially the agent represents you and not the manager. Although the agent will do all of the work through the manager, you want to have somebody that you actually trust to do the right thing for you, the band, as opposed to the right thing for the manager. When there's success, staying on track and being able to present an opinion about what's right for the band becomes awfully difficult. You want to have an agent that has an independent view, that's not the record company's view, that's not necessarily rubber stamping the manager's view. That way they're a real member of the team as opposed to somebody's 'yes man.' If an agent is the expert for the live touring business that you hire, then you want to get what you're paying for. You want to get their expertise. You don't want to just have it blocked, suppressed, or written off by some pre-packaged formula idea of artist development that the record label may have. Because the record company is selling records. They're not selling tickets . . . There are different approaches that are needed for both, although they intersect along the way.

## DIFFERENT TYPES OF AGENTS

Talent agencies come in all sizes. They range from larger operations, such as Famous Artist Agency and Artists & Audience Entertainment, to small regional agencies that can do a good job of booking acts into clubs and other local venues. Regional agencies, which exist in every corner of the country, run the gamut in size. They both book acts into venues that pay expenses only as well as those that pay thousands of dollars for a gig. There are also people like David Cohen, who acts as a personal representative for music, comedy, and novelty acts through his New York-based company,

Dancing Bear. Cohen gets his roster of acts into colleges throughout the United states, including Alaska. Which type of agent would be right for you?

Jerry Ade says it's critical to be selective about choosing your agent. "There are many different areas of music . . . agents have specialties as attorneys and doctors. It's important to find somebody who works in the area you are working with."

Unless you have a record deal, signing with a large agency is unlikely. Ade says "bigger companies can't afford to take no-name artists that don't need to be moved around the world. That's where a regional agency has significance. It has the ability and lack of expenses to go out there and work." He points out that big companies in big cities have a big overhead and need to get acts that can bring in money to offset their expenses. Regional agents can work out of their home, or have a small office. Their expenses can be kept to a minimum, so they can afford to work more with artists who aren't bringing in the big bucks. They can take more time developing artists who show themselves to have potential.

Adam Kornfeld, a booking agent with QBQ Entertainment, representing top acts such as Billy Joel and Metallica, books venues that range in size from clubs to stadiums. He says

> If it's a regional band with a regional CD out locally, meaning like in a four-or-five-state region, I would definitely [recommend looking] for some of the regional booking agencies around the country, who know every little nook and cranny and every little Main Street bar that does shows. Once the record goes national, picked up by a national label, [the artist] will want representation on the national or international level, which is what I do.

There are regional booking agents who are able to help a young artist on a grassroots level. Jeannie Stahlman has been called a grass roots agent. Through her company, Mercury Rising Entertainment in New Jersey, she books a variety of unsigned artists into clubs that range from small ones necessary to developing a following, such as The Bitter End in New York City, to larger ones like the Tin Angel in Philadelphia, where her acts play to packed houses while opening for more well-known artists. Stahlman says she works with these so-called baby bands because she loves it. Although she earns her living booking bands, she assured me she's not doing it for the money. There are easier ways to earn a better living. Being an agent on the grassroots level is a tough job.

A small regional agent is probably more effective to you at the beginning of your career than when you've got a successful record. Regional agents usually know about their region and have those all-important relationships with people who book the venues. Once your career warrants it, you may need to move to a bigger agent who'll be able to get you into the venues more appropriate to the next level of your career.

## ACQUIRING AN AGENT

Ideally, your manager should be the one who helps you choose your agent. Most larger agencies won't show an interest in signing you unless you can present them with a good reason—such as having a record out on a good label. Or, you may get signed if you put out your own CD and it's selling well. Having a large following can be evidence that your act is a good draw in concert.

You should also let an agent know about any publicity, radio, club play, etc. that's creating a buzz for your act. Your manager should be handling this, if you have one. In addition, an agent should be kept informed of any specific regions where your record is doing well. If you have a following somewhere, let them know about it. While they might not book you on a national tour so fast, they may at least book you in the area where you're getting a response.

I wish I had an easy answer as to how to get an agent. I don't. Agents aren't that hard to locate. Every October *Billboard* publishes *Billboard International Talent and Touring Directory*, which is a great source for U.S. and international talent. It includes booking agents, facilities, services, and products. *Performance* and *Pollstar* are also great resources if you want to learn more about touring. These publications, which are gotten by subscription only, are filled with a plethora of concert business information covering activities both in the U.S. and abroad, including up-to-date news briefs, box office statistics, an extensive listing of tour schedules for all genres of music, and much more. In addition, both *Performance* and *Pollstar* have a series of directories that they sell for a reasonable price. The directories include listings of artists and their booking agents, as well as a variety of information such as major concert promoters, nightclubs, fairs, festivals, or theme parks booking touring artists. Most are listed in the resource section in this book.

As a new artist, you'll probably have to start off with regional agents. There's good money to be made with established ones and there are many of them. Ask around in venues where you'd like to play and find out who books for them. Talk to artists who are further along in their careers than you and see who they use. You may have to do a lot of research but the rewards can be worth it. Call or drop into the Student Activities office at colleges and see if anyone has the name of an agent. Jeannie Stahlman says that

> an artist is ready for an agent when they are performing and have some audience that will come to see them. In New York they eat you for breakfast if you don't have an audience. I really feel there's an enormous amount of talent out there. It's funny how that's become the easy part when that used to be the hard part. Now there's so much talent that it becomes 'do you have an audience?'

Diana Stagnato is an agent with Cellar Door Entertainment, based in Washington D.C. with an office in Virginia Beach. She books bands from New York to Key West, Florida, concentrating on the Washington D.C., Maryland, and Virginia areas. Cellar Door gets bands into a variety of venues, from college-type bars to blues restaurant bars, from large to small clubs, from original rooms to cover rooms. Stagnato says

A lot of bands who do original music that want to play a lot need to do some covers as well. The bands that become very popular right away doing all originals are the ones that come out of colleges, because then they have a following. It's very difficult for a band to get together and do all original music if they don't have a fan base. They often will do covers as well. Once they become popular people will listen to their originals too. Bands have to understand that. Sometimes they can get a good gig opening for someone or in a small room where they can build a following and not make a lot of money. But an agent is looking for bands that make money since your income is a percentage of what they make.

Some bands will do covers for the money and originals for their fans. Stagnato mainly works with bands in her area. She says it's not always easy to put a band from out-of-state in a local club since most of the clubs want bands that will draw. "It depends on the club," she says. "Some clubs are healthy clubs and there's going to be people there no matter who plays because the club is fun and does well. Those are usually near colleges or on the water." According to Stagrato, the only bands that aren't from the region who do well are those who do covers for an audience that wants a lot of modern rock or party music. That's why Stagnato prefers local bands.

Once you've got a buzz going, try calling a small agent in the region where you've developed a following and work out from there. You may have to do your first gigs for little money, but it's a foot in the door. Once you establish yourself, better gigs will come. Most artists have to work their way up with agents.

Working with regional agents involves building those all-important relationships. Agents like working with acts that have proven reliable. They like knowing you can draw people. They prefer acts that are pleasant to deal with. Prima donnas don't go over well with agents (or anyone else, for that matter), unless they're making so much money the agent has little choice. Jeannie Stahlman says

> If I listen to your tape I will hear whether you're good or
> bad. When I come see you I'll know how you perform. It
> may seem like the least important but first and foremost
> I want to know what kind of person you are. It's easier
> for me to work with a nice person. I don't want to deal
> with a person who will scream and yell at me if they're
> not getting what they want.

David Cohen is also concerned about working with people with
whom he gets along. He says he wants acts who are cooperative
and have stage presence as well as stage personality and original
technique. It's important, he insists, to know "whether I can be
friends with them." Cohen wants acts that are recommended,
preferably by one of his other acts. The Dancing Bear roster is small
and selective, and his acts are supportive of one another. Cohen
says that colleges "either want the solo or musical duo acts, or they
want the cover bands. That's it."

Every agent has their own way of choosing bands, but those easy
to work with seem to be a favorite choice. Stormy Shepherd of
Leave Home Booking in Hollywood, California books an assortment of bands from unknown acts to well known ones such as L7.
She says "I have to love their music. They don't need a following to
work with me."

In order to attract an agent, Shepherd recommends trying to get
booked on a bill with bands represented by an agent with whom
you might want to get signed. Offer to play for free if necessary.
Wendy Day, president and founder of Rap Coalition, an organization that offers support for hip hop artists trying to break into the
industry (with offices in New York, Chicago, and Los Angeles),
says there are not many agencies who will represent unsigned rappers. She recommends making friends with people in clubs that
book hip hop acts. Day says, "I would introduce myself on a business tip. Set up an appointment with the club. People respect people who take the initiative." If you keep in touch with them, they

might let you open for a known artist. Day says that even if you play free, you'll be performing in front of consumers rather than just your friends. If you do well, it can lead to more bookings, which can lead to getting an agent.

Diana Stagnato likes bands to send her a promo kit with a good bio and well-shot photos. If they have a CD it's a plus. If they're an original band, they need a following. Stagnato says

> If I feel what they've sent me is good and they're polite and have a good attitude, I'll put them in a few rooms. If they do good and the clubs want them back I'll keep working with them. I'm looking for bands that have a professional attitude, that are realistic, that will try to promote their shows, that will do a good job and who realize that agents are people too.

Since Adam Kornfeld works for a large agency, longevity is more of an issue for him. Whereas regional agents may have a larger turnover and can usually find new local acts to book into their clubs, larger agencies want acts signed to national labels who can be developed on the touring circuit. Kornfeld says

> In a business sense for signing new acts, [I look for] the potential to be an artist that will have a long touring career. I always have to be into the music, because that's what it's all about to begin with. That's why I'm in the business. But of course since I am a booking agent, [I am looking for] the viability of this artist to have a touring career that will hopefully climb the ladder and move from the club circuit up to larger venues.

Although Alex Kochan also finds it preferable to sign an act that already has a major deal, he'll occasionally sign a band before they get a record deal. He'll consider a band that has put out a private CD, and is "already in the track to sign at a major label but doesn't have the deal yet." Kochan is motivated by a great live performance. He says

A few bands come along that are just such compelling performers that you have to get involved immediately. Whether there's a deal or not in place is irrelevant. You just see these bands as incredible performers and it's just a matter of time before they get a record deal. We've had a few like that. We look for incredible performers who have that something magic that happens between them and their audience; we look for that at every level.

You often don't have a choice as to who will represent you at the beginning of your career. Most artists are happy to work with an agent who will get them gigs. It's not as critical to be selective when you're dealing with small regional booking agents because you can always go to another if you're unhappy. When you're at the point of selecting a larger agent who may want to represent you exclusively, David Cohen suggests

The real key issue is when you have an agency that is willing to sign you, you'd better make sure that whoever your signing agent is has the true belief in you and really has the desire to push you, and the ability to do it. I sit down with my artists and ask them 'what do you want and what do you need?' If I don't feel that I can achieve that, I tell them to seek other representation. If we're within the ballpark of it, I tell them 'this is what you have to do.' It may require an outlay or some promotion. The original music acts on the college market are there to sell product, get exposure, build a mailing list, etc.

Diana Stagnato says

I basically try to find the best bands out there that want to work with me and that I want to work with and we make a game plan. Some want to play every weekend, some only want to do the A rooms, some want to stay in their area, some want to travel. I feel that being a good agent you're trying to get the band what they want.

You may try working your way up with regional agents. Start by booking your own tour. Once you've got the following, approach a small agent. After you've proven yourself by doing some successful gigs, ask for a reference to other agents, either those who book larger venues or gigs out of their region. If you've developed a nice relationship, your first agent may help you, as long as it doesn't conflict with their gigs. When your act gets bigger, don't forget the agents who gave you your start. Do some gigs for them occasionally, even if you've gone beyond their level. It cements a long-term relationship and shows appreciation.

## AGREEING TO TERMS WITH AN AGENT

Most larger national and international agents will try to get you to sign an agreement giving them an exclusive commitment. This means they handle all bookings for you. In such an arrangements, if someone calls you directly, you must have them call your agent—even if your agent had nothing to do with attracting the booking. Sometimes you can avoid signing an exclusive, especially with a smaller agency. The more the agent wants you, the more you can negotiate for a deal that's not exclusive. If you're signed to a big deal with a major record label, this may allow you to call more shots. In the case of agents who only work regionally, or in one specific area such as colleges, you can generally use more than one.

Most agents will want you to sign with them for at least three years. You'll want to keep your agreement to a maximum of one year. The hotter your act, the more flexibility you'll have in terms and length of commitment. If you must sign for more than a year, have a clause added in the agreement stipulating that if your agent doesn't generate earnings of at least X amount of dollars in a year, you can be released from your contract. Why be stuck with an agent who isn't booking you? Most of them won't object to a reasonable bottom line figure because if they aren't making money with you, they won't care about keeping you anyway.

Finally, most agents take 10% of your concert fee. They aren't entitled to anything else, in most cases. Don't sign away any of your publishing or record income either because it isn't ethical. Some regional agents will ask for a flat fee if you're doing low paying gigs to build a following. Otherwise they may only get a few dollars for their efforts. Agents usually have nothing to do with anything in your career except for the live appearances they book for you.

## BEFORE YOU ACQUIRE A TALENT AGENT

When you're still building your foundation and haven't yet found an agent, your manager can represent you in booking gigs. These are usually instances where appearances get you exposure and build your act a following. If you don't have a manager, a friend who knows how to hustle and has some street savvy can speak for you with the clubs. If circumstances merit your manager representing you because you don't have an agent, it's a conflict of interest for them to take an agent's fee as well. They're already getting their percentage as a manager.

An artist with talent who's willing to work hard should be able to eventually find a good agent. As Jerry Ade says

> I have found no artist who couldn't grow if they kept working. It's very hard to understand that, but I find a rock band or a jazz band or a black band can find their way in this business and have a career if they're willing to never quit working. They have to be talented and I take for granted that's there. But if they're willing to work hard they can build some kind of life for themselves and make a substantial living. There's hundreds of jazz artists that most wouldn't be familiar with that can go gross a million dollars a year and tour the world and have a pretty nice life-style because they never quit. I've found rock bands with substantial regional followings that can gross an enormous amount of money and maybe never make it to that next level. Because they are willing to keep trying, they keep working. Hard work pays off in this business and it's rarely forgotten.

## CHAPTER 4

# HIRING THE APPROPRIATE ATTORNEY

## MYTH:
*Someone I know isn't a music attorney but wants to represent me. She'll be good because I trust her.*

EVER!!!!!!! You absolutely, positively, unequivocally should not allow yourself to be represented by anyone who is not a music/entertainment attorney. Unless an individual specializes in this field they'll rarely understand the specifics of a recording agreement. People get screwed in deals all the time because they allow a well-meaning friend or relative to represent them. Most of these individuals aren't capable of handling music contracts, which are quite specialized. I've had too many artists come to me to complain after they got screwed over by a label because of a bad contract. They couldn't understand why their father/aunt/best friend/etc. had let them sign such an unfair agreement. It happens all the time.

### REASONS FOR HIRING AN INDUSTRY PROFESSIONAL
I actually get a lot of attorneys coming to the seminars I teach. They want to work in the music field BUT don't know enough about it. It can take years of learning, plus the on-the-job experience of negoti-

ating deals. According to Larry Rudolph, Esq. of Rudolph and Beer, an entertainment law firm in New York City, "a lawyer does not learn how to be an entertainment lawyer in law school." He says that classes in entertainment law are more general, and don't train anyone to be a music attorney. You have to learn entertainment law and practice it. A seasoned veteran is a better representative.

Beware of people saying they're *sort of* a music attorney. That usually means they aren't one, but are trying to be. The music business can be exciting. Practicing other kinds of law can be tedious, even boring, according to some of the lawyers who come to my classes with the intention of switching to the entertainment field. These *nouveau entertainment lawyers* need practice and seasoning before they are capable of representing you effectively.

Don't be someone's guinea pig, even if they give you a much better rate. The cost may be higher in the end if you get less than you should in the deal. One of the acts on my label had a non-entertainment litigator turned music attorney represent them when I was getting them a production deal on a bigger label. This lawyer continuously screwed up the negotiations, causing us to lose one deal and almost another. The act would have faired much better with a music attorney. Theirs was actually being coached by friends. When I was recently putting together a major seminar and someone I highly respect recommended this lawyer to be on the panel, I winced. She asked why. When I told her, she laughed and said that he had told her he was awful when he first started in music. Now he's excellent. But it took years to get there.

There are so many different conditions in a music-related contract that it boggles the mind. It takes a lawyer devoted full time to music to truly understand all the ins and outs. While other types of attorneys may understand the basic contract, they probably won't know what figures are considered favorable by record industry standards. There's a lot of give-and-take in negotiating a record deal and certain concessions are expected—but only to those who know them. There are always conditions and clauses in a contract that the label can remove as a trade-off for something else. To a seasoned music attorney these trade-offs are routine. To an attorney inexperienced in the music business, it can be a foreign negotiation. When you get an artist contract from a record label, it'll obviously favor that label. A lawyer must know what a label will typically give on and what you'll have to accept.

According to Wallace Collins, Esq., a New York City-based lawyer specializing in entertainment, copyright, and trademark law, "An entertainment lawyer will navigate you safely through the minefield that is the music business. Recording and publishing agreements can be extremely complicated and proper negotiating and drafting requires superior legal skills as well as a knowledge of music business practice."

It's hard enough to negotiate an equitable deal even with a music attorney. Don't sell yourself short by using someone who will not give you the best possible representation. As Larry Rudolph says, "If you need brain surgery, would you go to a foot doctor? So if you need a music contract negotiated, don't go to a real estate attorney." Get one who specializes in what you need.

**WHEN YOU NEED A MUSIC ATTORNEY**

Once you decide to move ahead with your goal of getting signed to a record label, you need to know which attorney will represent you. This doesn't mean putting someone on a retainer or paying before it's necessary. It means shopping for a lawyer while you're not under pressure, which gives you the best chance of finding a lawyer who you truly feel good having represent you.

Musicians all too often wait until they have an A & R person on the phone offering them a contract before beginning their search. That's not the right time, because you then might have to settle for whomever you can get quickly. You should have your representation in place before you approach anyone for a deal.

Once you've found an attorney you respect, let them know you'd like their representation when you have a deal. Establish the specifics of their fees. Ask if it's all right to give their name as your representative. Don't give a lawyer's name to a label until you've let that individual know you'd like them to represent you.

You still shouldn't have to pay anyone a fee at this point. Some attorneys want a retainer up front to cover any quick representation you may need, or for time spent on the phone while you're in preparation. Policies vary from attorney to attorney. I've never had a problem finding one who didn't expect payment before they gave representation. Give yourself time to shop around.

## HOW TO SELECT YOUR ATTORNEY

The best way to find an attorney is through recommendation. Ask around. It's not hard to get some names. Just don't settle for the first one you meet. See if you can get a low- or no-cost consultation to feel him or her out. When you have time you can take your time. You want to get the right attorney for your needs. Wallace Collins, who was signed to Epic Records as a recording artist before he became a lawyer, recommends meeting with several candidates to find out which one makes you feel most comfortable.

What do you need to know about a potential legal representative? You need to know how they base their fees. You need to know their attitudes. You need to know how they feel about your music. You need to get a feel for their personalities. After all, you don't want to have an attorney who rubs you the wrong way, or whose personality doesn't seem favorable for influencing someone during contract negotiations.

Some attorneys are more into the music itself, knowing everything that's happening in the music scene. They actually go to clubs to see bands and network as much as possible. Others prefer to stick to the business, reading trade magazines to keep abreast of what's going on. These individuals don't worry as much about the music, as long as they know the going rates for an album deal. Neither approach is right or wrong, but you may feel more comfortable with one or the other.

It's always nice (though not essential) to find an attorney who believes in you. Such an individual may work harder in your favor, or perhaps help get you an intro to that A & R person you want to reach. Enthusiasm can go a long way, and can especially work in your behalf when your legal counsel is dealing with a label. Larry Rudolph recommends finding one "who you vibe with . . . who you feel comfortable with personality-wise . . . who will work with you on their fees and who believes in your talent."

Attorneys who believe in you may be more flexible with regard to their payment. If they feel you have strong potential, they may take you on as a client as sort of an investment. They'll keep track of their time but not charge you for everything at the beginning, assuming they'll make it up when you hit big. Having your attorney behind you can also be motivational. It's always nice when your lawyer likes you enough to come down to see your gig.

In selecting an attorney, you'll want to find out what your prospective legal representative thinks are the most important conditions of a contract when negotiating a deal, i.e., where their priorities lie. Some may be more concerned with an advance, while others may focus on a video, a large promotional budget, etc. See if their intentions are the same as yours. You also want to find an attorney whose fees you can afford.

## ATTORNEYS' FEES

Attorneys' fees have a wide range of difference. According to Larry Rudolph, the average is anywhere from $175 to $350 an hour. You'll probably find top attorneys charging more and younger ones with less experience willing to do it for less. That's a lot of bucks, but like it or not that's what they get. Many lawyers are now charging a flat fee of 5% of the advance on your first album to negotiate an artist agreement.

There are variations in the way attorneys bill. You can use two different people for the same amount of time at the same hourly rate and pay one a lot more than the other. Some are more flexible than others as to what they'll bill you for. That's one reason it's so important to shop for the right lawyer for you, and for your budget.

One thing you want to find out is whether you'll be on the clock every time you speak with your attorney, or if they're flexible about billing for their time. I've actually used a lawyer who charged me for the few minutes it took when I called to see if he received something I'd sent. He'd add all the minutes and bill for that time. Many music attorneys aren't like that. As I've already said, if they believe in you, they may be more agreeable to working with you within your budget. If they feel you have a good future, they may be more realistic in the present, hoping you'll still retain them when your career is doing well. This doesn't mean they'll work for free. But it can mean your bills won't be as high.

Don't expect as much flexibility from a well-known attorney with lots of celebrity representation. Generally the more well-known the attorney is, the higher the fee. Make sure you shop around. Never feel you have to settle. If you believe in yourself, make them believe too. And always remember, your legal counsel is working for you.

## CHANGING YOUR ATTORNEY

If you don't like your attorney, you can always get another. It's not usual to sign a contract with one saying you must exclusively use them for a given amount of time. Unless you're in the middle of a negotiation that needs the continuity of the same person, or if will cost too much to have a new lawyer start proceedings all over, you can get a new one if the old one isn't working for you. You'll just have to make a financial arrangement for the time already put in.

## WHEN YOU CAN'T AFFORD LEGAL COUNSEL

When you can't afford an attorney, you must be sure to put everything in writing. Handshake agreements are out. Period! I can hear most of you thinking "But . . . But . . . But." Too many people get in trouble because they think they're the exception to the rule. You may be thinking, "But she's a very good person." "But he's my best friend." "You don't understand. I can trust him with my life." Trust him with your life but don't trust him to do something with your career without at least putting it in writing. It's always better safe than sorry. When you work with someone, no matter who, it's always best to keep it on a business level. Keep the personal stuff at home. I don't care who it is you're working with—not even your mother, spouse, best lifelong friend or child. Otherwise you may lose your relationship with this individual in the long run.

People forget promises when a big deal is imminent. They may not be purposely looking to screw you, but they're going to look out for their own best interests. They may actually believe they never said you could have points on their record. They may not mean to have a fuzzy recollection of what had been agreed upon. They may actually think that their way is the best for everyone concerned. But where you're concerned, you want to be responsible for your best interests. Be careful! Have everything you agree upon in writing.

If you're a producer, manager, or songwriter make sure you have everything specified on paper before you put one dime into an artist. I once made this statement in a class and Lou, who was participating, blanched. After the class he told me he was producing a singer and had already recorded an album. He then went on to praise what a good person the singer was and how much he trusted her. Lou said he was trying to get a contract together but had been lax. I tried to contain my response when he told me he'd already made a video of the single. All this was without a written agreement. I told him to rush to a lawyer the next day and get one. Two months later Lou called to say the singer had never signed the contract and was using his material to shop a deal on her own. So much for trust.

Sometimes a record label will put pressure on one party to do a project in a different way, one which may eliminate you. Fear of blowing the deal may cause them to blow you off. For example, if you're producing for your friend the label may want to bring in their own producer. In most cases, no matter what the deal between you and the artist, you're out! A written agreement could force them to at least make a financial arrangement with you. Some people you work with may claim they never understood the terms of what you agreed upon. It doesn't matter. An agreement is an agreement. Make sure it sticks! Your best insurance policy is to put it in writing.

People get greedy. I've worked on projects with very close friends who almost literally stabbed me in the back to get a contract with a major label directly instead of through me. These were people I swore I could trust, who I went back years with. They insisted they were just watching out for themselves, nothing personal. I've had two artists try to break their contract with my label in order to sign directly with a major instead of going through my label. They couldn't do it because our contract was valid, but boy did they try! These were people I'd have trusted without a contract had it not been for my lawyer. This industry changes people. Don't take chances. I'll keep repeating myself. *Make sure everything is in writing.*

If you can't afford a lawyer, at least put your arrangement in writing. Prepare a letter of agreement between yourself and the other party, spelling out specifically what they'll do for you in exchange for specifically what you'll do for them. For example, if you promised your friend three points for producing a song, be specific about what it's three points of. Is it only what he worked on or the whole album? This needs to be down in writing. Be as specific as possible about whatever he's going to do for you in exchange for what he'll get from you. When you have your letter of agreement ready, make two copies and make sure that both of you sign it. Each of you should keep one copy. I'm told getting it notarized isn't necessary, but it can't hurt.

According to Wallace Collins, "a simple contract may not necessarily require extensive involvement by lawyers. A contract can be as basic as a letter describing the details of your arrangement which is signed by both parties to the agreement." While Collins acknowledges that an oral agreement is binding, he emphasizes how much easier it is to prove if all the terms are written down.

I strongly recommend that you have a real contract from a lawyer if you're investing money in an artist, whether as a producer or to put that individual's material out on a record. If your goal is to get a deal for the artist you're working with, you must have a formal contract or you may stand to lose if you do hook up the deal. If you act as middleman for the artist, you'll need that person locked up in writing with you if you want your fair place in the deal. I've had too many of my students call me crying that they'd taken the artist into the studio and the artist left them afterwards because there was no contract. No contract, no profit! Get it in writing.

A label won't give you a production deal if you don't have a good contract with your artist. In a production deal, the contract is between you and the label. The artist is still signed to you under the terms of the original agreement. So the label must make sure your agreement with the artist is legal and binding, and that you have at least a reasonable commitment for albums that must be recorded. If you don't, the label may not want to bother, especially if it feels the contract can be broken by the artist. Otherwise, the artist could up and walk away. Or the artist can sign directly with the label and leave you cold. Don't invest money in anyone without protecting your investment. And the only real protection you can have is a binding contract.

The old expression says "you're better safe than sorry." Listen to it. Handshakes don't usually stand up in court, although technically any agreement is supposed to. But you can't prove a handshake. Words on paper are less likely to be misconstrued. Of course, while a formal contract is the best way to go if you can afford it, a letter of agreement is still written proof. Please, put everything in writing!!

### MAKING USE OF LEGAL RESOURCES

If all this legal stuff sounds very expensive, be aware that in many cities there are organizations which offer a variety of legal services. The one I've dealt with in New York City is called Volunteer Lawyers For the Arts (VLA). It's a non-profit organization for people involved in the arts. They give free legal advice via their telephone hotline. You can call them and ask specific questions. The calls are usually answered by interns, but if they don't know the answer they'll take your number and call you back after they've spoken to someone with experience. They'll also give recommendations for music attorneys. If your income is low enough, they will even give you free representation if you need it.

In addition, if you have access to New York City, the VLA has a wonderful legal library you can use for free. You can make copies of anything you find there for the price of using their copying machine. They also sell inexpensive books as well as books containing sample contracts. There are organizations like this all over the country. Each has specific services offered. Many are free. I've listed many of them in the resource section at the back of the book.

You don't want to just get a record deal. You want to get a deal that gives you the greatest potential to make money and have a good career doing your music. Having the right attorney watching out for your best interests can help you reach that goal. Having everything written down in a legal and binding manner will protect your rights and give you the best chance of getting what you're entitled to.

## CHAPTER 5

# USING A PRODUCER TO ENHANCE YOUR RECORDING

MYTH:

*I don't need a producer. I can write my own songs.*

I hear many artists say they don't need a producer. Some make the mistake of letting their egos convince them they can orchestrate the whole recording process themselves. Some don't trust anyone else to make decisions for them. Some don't want the expense of paying a producer and/or giving up a share of their royalties when they get signed by a record label. Many musicians think that they don't need a producer because they don't fully understand what the role of a producer is, and its importance.

### THE PRODUCER AS PROJECT DIRECTOR

A producer is not necessarily a songwriter. A producer is not an engineer. A producer is someone who oversees the production of a recording, making sure all the players are in place, the studio is right, the song is working, and the budget is adequate.

A producer is the manager of the recording session, directing the players of a production. This individual works with the songwriter and artist, making sure the project goes as planned. In the purest sense, a producer is the person who sets up the budget; organizes the project and chooses the studio, engineer, editor, and session players; and makes sure the end result is what is should be. When I asked producer Phil Ramone about the producer's role, he answered, "To understand like a director what is musically going on in front of you."

In reality, with the influx of small, and often in-home studios, a producer may be all of the above, including songwriter. Several producers may be used for one album, with each working on as few as one track. For smaller projects, producers aren't always the ones who set up the budget. They may just come in and work for an hourly rate or a flat fee, depending on what's individually agreed upon.

Producers are often given points on the record when it's released. The going rate averages from two to four points. A producer with an impressive track record may want more. This is all arranged in the beginning, before you go into the studio. If you do hire a producer, make sure everything is in writing from the get-go. This way you avoid disputes in the future.

A producer doesn't need to know how to write songs, but must have a good ear in order to work with the creative people. A producer must be objective. He or she needs to make suggestions for revisions of a song, and know when it's finished. A producer usually has the final say on a project.

## THE PRODUCER'S ROLE IN PRE-PRODUCTION

The producer plans what will go on in the studio before getting there. A good producer will meet in advance with the artist, songwriter, musicians, and any other members of what should be thought of as a team and specifically decide what will be done in each session. The producer makes sure everyone is prepared.

The producer should continue this planning from session to session. Meetings and discussions out of the studio don't cost anything. Figuring out your next step in a room that costs at least $50 an hour isn't economical. Planning ahead saves much wasted time when arriving in the studio, and in this case the time equals money.

Essentially, these are the activities that a producer traditionally is responsible for:

- Preparing a production budget
- Making most decisions about production
- Having a good ear for music and taking responsibility for knowing when the project is finished
- Knowing how to choose a good production team
- Being a diplomat when there's a dispute, i.e., the engineer and the artist disagree on something or the songwriter wants to add something that just won't work
- Letting the engineer know what needs to be done, and what their limitations are, i.e., not giving creative input if it's not asked for
- Knowing where the trends in music are going and being ahead of them
- Motivating everyone to be as creative and productive as possible
- Understanding the artist's needs when doing the vocal tracks and knowing when they've had enough
- Treating each artist as an individual and understanding their particular needs and the best way to get a good vocal

## THE EXECUTIVE PRODUCER'S PART IN YOUR PROJECT

An executive producer is the person financing the project. When I do a project for my record label, I'm the executive producer because I'm paying the expenses. The executive producer usually has the final say as to whether a project is finished since the money's coming out of their pocket. Sometimes they suggest a musician they want to use, or an engineer to do the mix. But usually the producer is in charge of most things and the executive producer doesn't get too directly involved.

## WHY YOU NEED A PRODUCER

First and foremost, you need a producer because it's hard to be impartial about your own music. It's always good to have another set of trained ears when working on a song. Kicking ideas around with someone who knows what they're doing can make putting down tracks in the studio more productive. It's hard to be the producer of your own material. Phil Ramone agrees that a producer must be objective: "I highly recommend an independent producer. Billy Joel and Paul Simon are perfectly capable of producing themselves. You need one soul in the room who can say 'no'." A producer can be more detached in their decision making than the songwriter.

Kirk Burrowes, the General Manager of Bad Boy Entertainment, agrees that a separate producer is important

> because [a project] needs the objectivity and it helps you give the best you can give because sometimes you might not know all you can do and you can stretch your potential by having someone else be involved to push you to new limits. Choose someone you're comfortable with, that you think is going to bring out something in you that you to that point have not been able to tap into.

A good producer can step back and decide what's working and what needs to be changed. This individual should have more skills in the studio than you do, and should be compatible with you and the team working on the project. A producer should like working with your music, and should be experienced with the same genre. A producer is someone who will listen to your concept, and make sure it goes in the right direction. You can't be everything. If songwriting is your forte, focus on that. If several of you are collaborating on the song *and* you all have very good ears, a separate producer might not be as essential.

As Ramone told me, a producer can also take on the role of the heavy. This can mean making decisions that are right for the project but may be uncomfortable for you. For example, a producer can ask your well-meaning friends, who come to the studio and then distract you, to leave. I once was producing and had to insist someone leave during a session. He was a very close friend of my two artists but was clowning around. We were wasting studio time that was paid for. The friend was very angry that he couldn't stay and my artists acted annoyed until he left. Then they thanked me, saying he was distracting them too much, but they didn't want to be the ones to ask him to leave. A producer needs to intervene in all situations where decisive action must be taken, whether the decision will be well received or not.

# PART THREE
# PREPARING YOUR PRESENTATION

**CHAPTER 6**

# USING CONSTRUCTIVE CRITICISM TO GET WHERE YOU WANT TO GO

MYTH:
*Everyone tells me my music is
fantastic, so I know it's a winner!*

Practically every musician who called my label, Revenge Records, prefaced their pitch by saying that *everyone tells them their music is fantastic.* They also told me they were sending out a demo that would blow me away. I must sadly say that most of these demos were rated G for garbage. A & R people tell me the same thing. A large percentage of material they receive isn't worth listening to, in their opinions. Yet the artists sending them insist they're getting positive feedback from others. I find it sad when I see how much money is put into packages that are sent to labels. These demos are filled with someone's hopes and dreams. What a shame that everyone didn't help them out by telling them the truth.

My A & R staff for Revenge Records was the general public. I used to bring my boom box to school yards and play material for the kids there. They were the ones who bought the music I was putting out. While I was able to recognize that the quality of many of those demos was poor, the kids were able to identify samples that were played out, beats that were not happening, and vocals that were unintelligible. So how come *everyone* didn't know the tracks weren't working?

It's really important to get constructive criticism. How can you learn from your mistakes otherwise? I love it when people whom I respect give me suggestions for improving my work. Why shouldn't it be the best possible? In getting input from others, though, be sure to go to people who will give you truthful, objective feedback. Being objective about your own material is difficult, especially when you're being souped up by *everyone*. Learning not to get carried away by the enthusiasm of those who aren't the best critics can be even harder. So who can you turn to for an objective analysis of your material?

## WHERE NOT TO GO FOR AN OBJECTIVE CRITICAL EVALUATION

Usually *everyone* is your friends, family, neighbors, etc.—people who know you on a personal level. Most people naturally go to those who like them to get opinions. And most people don't like to give negative opinions to someone they like. As a result they don't always tell the whole truth, or they sincerely want to like your material a lot because they like you. Usually we approach friends with enthusiasm about our latest work, expecting enthusiasm in return. Looking at a friend saying "so, do you like it?" does not encourage an objective critical evaluation.

This doesn't mean your friends are liars. They just may not want to criticize someone they like, figuring that if it's really no good someone else will tell you. After all, we don't always like friends who aren't positive about our work. I'm that way. As a songwriter, I too like to get feedback. But deep down I only want praise. When I play a song for someone who starts to criticize it, I don't like that person anymore. It's just human nature. It's not that I'll hate the person but I will have some resentment for them, if only for a little while. I (unfairly I admit) find myself asking *how dare this person criticize my wonderful material!* It must come across in my attitude because my friends tell me they love everything I write, even when they may not. I have to go elsewhere when I want honesty.

There are also times when people sincerely think that what they hear is good—from you! Often friends and loved ones know you so well they just don't see you first as a musician. So when you produce something that's not half bad, they honestly are impressed since they may not have expected anything. They praise you to the hilt for a song that isn't going to cut it in the same way with an A & R person who doesn't know you at all. Manager Peter Leeds calls it *The Emperor's New Clothes* syndrome.

> Artists take their music and they play it for their mother and their sister and their best friends, none of whom know the difference between a good and a bad song. More importantly, even if they didn't like it they would not tell them because they don't want to hurt their feelings. In *The Emperor's New Clothes* they were afraid of what the emperor would do. In this case it's more like 'maybe he or she won't like me if I tell them this song sucks.' The artist is bolstered into thinking that something that's not good, is good. That creates a vicious circle.

When I started rapping, I was very proud of what I was doing. I'd never rapped before and what I heard in the studio sure sounded legitimate to me. I played my first tracks to the high school kids I was teaching and they raved about them. Boy, were we wrong! Now nobody can pay me enough to hear them. It's embarrassing just thinking about how awful my rapping was, yet I proudly played it and the kids responded with sincere enthusiasm.

Teenagers can be very critical, yet my students were really excited. How can that be? Because they expected a white woman to sound like a total fool and I didn't. I was far from good at that point, but for their teacher I was fantastic. So off I went playing my awful tapes to everyone. Eventually, with the help of a new producer, I did get a good style of rap. That was when I realized how bad I was at first. And it also made me very aware of how hard it is to get an objective opinion from people who believe in you. They're not the ones to judge your material.

## WHERE TO GO FOR AN OBJECTIVE OPINION

Before you mix your demo, try to get objective opinions from people who know music, such as DJs, people working in record stores, etc. These people love music and are usually happy to hear your material if approached in a respectful way. If you're friendly you'll find much cooperation. Sometimes you have to play up to people's egos to get them to listen to your tape and give their *expert's opinion*. But these individuals usually know what's selling and in what direction music is going so it's good to ask them for advice. When your record is out, you can thank them for their feedback, which may make them want to push it more. If it becomes a hit, they can brag that they gave you advice at the beginning.

The best way to get an objective opinion from anyone, especially an industry person, is to avoid telling them it's your personal tape. Say it belongs to a friend, someone you may work with, etc. Get rid of the personal obligation attached to the tape. They'll be a lot more honest. Also, criticism is easier to take when you're anonymous. It can be embarrassing to have your music put down. I can even agree with negative comments if the evaluator doesn't know it's my material.

I always equate creating music with a pregnant woman. The future mother is carrying life just as you're carrying the life of an idea, which you give birth to in the studio. Having your idea come to life on a tape is euphoric. It can, especially for an unseasoned artist, sound fantastic even when it's not. That was what happened to me. Just hearing what had been in my head sound like real music was incredible, perfect. When a mother gives birth to a baby, she almost always thinks it's beautiful, perfect. I see more babies than not that are red, wrinkled, lopsided, and/or funny looking. Yet I always tell the mother what a beautiful baby she has. It works the same with your music, which is in a way your baby. Your idea has come to life and while you proudly wait for a response to it, no one wants to tell you your baby is ugly. So if you want honesty, don't tell those whose opinions you seek that it's your baby. You can tell them later on when it's a hit!

## LEAVE YOUR EGO AT HOME

You have to accept the fact that you don't know it all. You've got to be open-minded to criticism and suggestions. This doesn't mean changing whatever everyone tells you, but it does mean accepting that you may not always be right. If the same suggestions are given by several people, however, they should at least be considered. It might make your material even better. It might be something you didn't hear because you were too immersed in your original ideas. It's so hard to be objective about your own material. Even managers fall so in love with the music they're working with that they can lose their objectivity.

It's easy to get so caught up in an idea that you lose sight of the market. Trends change so fast it's hard to keep up. What was working when you were in the studio may not sell today. It's something you have to accept. Listen to what others tell you, whether you like what they say or not. Don't act on everything you hear, but accept that others may have a better idea. If one person after another tells you the music isn't current or cutting it, pay attention. Play it for more people in stores and if the opinion is the same, be prepared to make some changes. If you're working on a trendy style of music, be ready to work fast. Don't spend so much time in the studio that it's not happening anymore by the time you finish. Try to stay on the cutting edge of what's selling so you can get in on the beginning, not come in on the tail end.

## CHAPTER 7

# RECORDING THE DEMO THAT GETS YOU NOTICED

MYTH:
*A & R people will act as visionaries if they hear a song
that has potential, even if the quality isn't good.*

Put your expectations in your product, not in an A & R person. A & R people get huge numbers of tapes each week. A producer who has spoken at my seminars tells of how his friends in A & R give him cartons of demo tapes they don't want every time he sees them. It would be nice if A & R people had time to use their imagination to recognize the potential beyond the poor quality of a demo tape, but it doesn't usually happen that way. They may work to make a great product sound even better, but they often can't be bothered with something that doesn't strike them immediately.

Most A & R people don't have time to give each tape more than a few initial seconds of a listen, unless the track hits them and makes them want to hear more. Most don't have the time to analyze raw material to determine how to make it sound good. There's too much polished material already available. If your tape doesn't blow them away, chances are you won't get a deal. When doing A & R for Universal Records, Kathy Baylor, who has been a talent scout for Midnight Songs, Inc., a publishing company, says she often listens to demos from musicians who don't have the money to make a good recording. "I can listen past that because of my publishing background, but many other A & R people don't."

Many A & R people are up on music, and have an excellent ear. But others aren't as knowledgeable. They may hear what you give them and nothing beyond. According to Steve Ward, an independent producer and owner of Mu Music International Recording Studio in New York,

> A & R people are not necessarily experts on music, nor do they understand music like a musician. Their talent lies in determining what will sell. Therefore you want to leave as little to their imaginations as possible. They may not be able to hear the finished product as you do. You want to get to the point where the A & R person has little doubt that you can be a success. A finished quality gives them a better sense of how serious you are.

Kirk Burrowes of Bad Boy Entertainment acknowledges that not all A & R people have the vision to see beyond a poor quality demo, but says

> If people whose ears have vision are listening to it they will still be able to pick it up. It's person by person when it comes to something like that. There might be someone who feels if it didn't come with a marked case, a picture and a bio, they don't want to consider it. I think that's sometimes wrong, because most of the talent that makes it big, that succeeds, is raw talent . . . that probably was not really developed and prepared to be a star, but became one because they had that raw talent, that raw magic.

It can be a matter of luck whether you get to an A & R person who appreciates the raw talent. Don't leave your fate in someone else's hands. Make sure your demo is produced well enough for the A & R person to hear your vision.

## RECORDING YOUR DEMO

It's best to give A & R people as finished a product as possible. A great majority of tapes I've received for my label are of very poor quality, i.e., too much noise in the background, vocals I can't understand, muddied tracks, etc. They're not pleasant to listen to. I often get an accompanying note saying what could be done with the material if I sign them. But even if I can see their vision, I have little evidence they can pull their plan off. I've signed only artists to my own label who provided quality demos because it's the only guarantee the project can be brought to its full potential. I may remix or edit, but the end needs to be in sight before I invest money in it.

Many will argue this point, but I believe that if you make a demo as clean and good as possible, it has a better chance of standing out among the others when an A & R person listens. Competition is bad enough without defeating yourself. And no matter how good and clean and produced to the best of your ability your material is, present it as a demo. Don't call it a finished product. Let the A & R person envision how much better it can be with money behind it! That could make it even more appealing.

### MIXING YOUR DEMO

If possible, use a reasonably good studio to record your demo. Finding one that suits your needs isn't always easy. Steve Ward recommends asking for credits. Let them play you something recorded there. According to Ward, "One of the problems a musician faces is the technology to make recordings has become cheap. The hard part is finding someone who knows how to use the equipment."

If you can't afford to do your whole project in a good studio, at least try to do your mix in one. When I did synthesized music, I used to lay the tracks down in a small room with MIDI (in layman's terms, this means that what you program in one studio can be transferred to the equipment in another). Before the mix we'd dump the tracks onto a twenty-four track tape. We'd record the vocals in that room, and then do the mix. It saved money, and yet the quality was still there.

Make sure you're happy with your mix. It's easier to sell something you believe in completely. You can get very psyched during the mix. When the music is pumping very loud and everyone is into it, everything can sound wonderful. A common problem when you get home is finding that the mix doesn't sound like you remembered it sounding in the studio. Some of the music levels may not be where you would have wanted them. I know the feeling. After a major high in the studio the night before, you can be on a major low when the music doesn't sound right the next day. What a terrible thing to have to either do another mix, if you can get the money, or settle for one that's not what you want.

Here's a suggested insurance policy for getting the mix right the first time. When you do your mix, bring as much playback equipment (Walkman, boom box, car with stereo, etc.) as you can to the studio. After the mix is completed, leave the board as is in case you want to re-do something. Your ears need to cool down. They can get almost numb after a long session of listening to music that's usually loud. Make a copy of your tape made during the mix and make a copy of the copy so you're not listening to a first generation copy (one right off the mix). After ten or fifteen minutes of cool-down time, play the tape in the different systems you brought. See if it sounds the way it should to them. If the bass line isn't up enough, you can go back in and do another pass with the board still up. This way you're not wasting the time and money to remix the levels at a later date.

An engineer can EQ your music when you play it back in the studio. This means they can adjust the levels of the tracks to make it sound better than it will on your stereo equipment. For example, they can enhance the bass, bring down the high hats, etc., while you're listening on their system. Sometimes, when they're in a hurry to get you out, the engineer might make your song sound better than it is. A studio system is probably much better than your own stereo system. Playing it on your own system gives you a more real picture of whether the mix is what it should be. And the few dollars more to stay the extra time is a lot less than the cost of doing another mix from scratch after hearing yours wasn't working. Getting it right the first time is the best!

Another common problem found after a mix is that the vocals are not up high enough. This may be because you already know the lyrics, and therefore you hear them even if they can't be heard clearly. Anyone familiar with the lyrics, including the writer, artist, producer, engineer, etc., will silently sing along. None of these people will be a good judge of the vocal levels. They'll hear them in their heads, whether they can be heard or not. Play the song for someone who's never heard it before. Bring your tape in your boombox to the studio secretary, to someone in the pizzeria downstairs, to anyone you can find who has never heard it. Ask if they understand the lyrics. If it's "no," do another pass with the levels higher on the vocal tracks until that person understands them. When everything sounds good on your Walkman, it's time to take that mix and go home.

It can't hurt to master your demo before presenting it. Mastering fine tunes the sound and makes a good mix cleaner. Although some say it's not necessary, if you can afford it it puts an even better foot forward. Though Steve Ward doesn't feel mastering is essential for a demo, he does say that "Mastering can take a mediocre product and make it go. It can take a good product and make it sublime . . . A mastering engineer can listen objectively. A good one knows the current sounds." Whether you choose to master or not, the better the quality of your demo, the more you may be taken seriously as an artist.

## GIVING YOUR DEMO ALL YOU'VE GOT

Although there are no concrete rules about what should be on a demo tape, the industry standard seems to be three songs. It's always best to start with your strongest cut because it may be the only thing an A & R person listens to. One rule of thumb: It's said that a ballad can be the kiss of death in this industry. For some reason, most artists break on a more uptempo song and then release their ballad. Therefore, you should never put a ballad first on a demo tape, no matter how good it is. It can be second or third. Make sure all three cuts are strong. If you have a whole album done and feel they should have it all, put the rest on the "B-side" of the tape. Label both sides. Kirk Burrowes recommends,

> For a rapper, [a demo tape] should be two to three songs, with the last one being a free-style rap done over a familiar or classic rap beat. That always shows that you can do more than what it is you have written, and that you can rap off the top of your head. For a singer, just make sure that what you're bringing to the song is distinctly you, what you're trying to get across. If you're already singing someone else's song, you don't want to leave a taste in anyone else's mouth that you're similar to whoever's song you are singing. You want your distinct sound vocals to come across. So concentrate on the vocals and who you are so you can be sincere to it, and it comes across on the demo.

Kathy Baylor suggests that you "Send in a demo that really showcases what you're trying to be . . . if you're a singer, the demo should really showcase your ability as a singer . . . if you're a jazz saxophonist, the demo should showcase that. You want to show people you can really do what you're trying to get them to help you to do." You may have just one shot at getting a deal. Make your presentation as good as possible. Don't trust an A & R person's vision when presenting your material. They may not have enough!

## PACKAGING YOUR DEMO

You don't have to do anything fancy in packaging your demo. However, a neat, attractive, professional looking package has a better chance of catching someone's eye. Remember that the competition is stiff. Anything that makes you stand out can be advantageous. I've gotten tapes with the information scrawled in pencil, or that was just plain illegible. Assumptions are made about you based on the way you present your material. No matter what their rules of thumb, most A & R people prefer to work with artists who take themselves seriously. I've actually gotten tapes without a phone number on it. What kind of message does that give? If you had a choice of working with one of two equally talented artists, would you pick the one with the neatly labeled package or the one that looked thrown together? Having sloppy labels is not worth the risk of being passed over. Some A&R people may not care, but more do.

I'm not saying you should spend a fortune, but at least be aware of your presentation. In most cases, it's the first impression anyone has of you. Put your best foot forward, or the best one you can afford at any rate. It doesn't take a lot of money to have a typed label. If you have a computer or have access to someone with one, print your labels instead of hand writing them. If you have the money, you can have the information printed right on the cassette shell. This makes the demo look even more professional and it can also be sold at gigs.

Attractive inserts for the cassette box can be made with a little creativity. Trace a J-card (cassette insert) onto a piece of paper. With a computer, typewriter, pen, or by cut and paste method design your card. Put several on a page. Using a heavier weight of paper, in white or in color, make copies at a copyshop. Cut them out, fold, and insert them into the cassette box. You can get a velox of your photo (made to be reprinted) for as little as $10 so the label can actually have your picture on the box, if you choose.

I've gotten cassettes with actual photos folded like a J-card, which looked very nice. Someone in one of my classes had the names of the songs and the group superimposed on their photo. Clear computer labels can also be used on photo inserts. A nice photo insert catches the eye and gives an A & R person a glimpse of what you look like. I mentioned earlier how many tapes they get. Attractive packaging can catch their eye and you may get listened to faster. Your presentation gives the A & R person a message about what kind of person you are. A professional looking tape may can lead to it getting listened to faster. If it has a professional sounding recording inside, it can lead to getting a deal.

# CHAPTER 8

# MEASURING THE MARKETABILITY OF YOUR MUSIC

MYTH:
*As long as my music is good, I can create
my material in the style I choose.*

In any business, you would have to be concerned with knowing the market in order to make a profit. Trends come and go in all businesses. Certain foods are considered trendy one week and the next week those restaurants are empty. Bell bottoms used to sell like crazy. Then you couldn't give them away. This is a world of fickle people who love and dislike in one breath. It's the people who understand the marketability of products who end their day with a bank full of dollars when they figure out the right ones to market.

The music business works the same way. People follow trends. They follow what MTV is pushing. The radio tells them what's good to buy. In this business it's better to worry less about what's good music and more about what's good to buy if you want to make money doing it. Whether you like it or not, your music must have a niche. It needs to be rock or rap or R & B, etc. for a label to know what to do with it. It has to be made to sell in today's market. Having music that's highly marketable will get you the deal in this business. Having great music without showing concern for its marketability will keep you in your day job.

## KEEPING CURRENT WITH THE MUSIC MARKET

To have the best chance of getting signed to a record label, you've got to keep up with trends in music. Know what's selling! Know what's popular! There's a distinctive sound that's currently popular in each style of music, and you want to be familiar with it. This doesn't mean you should copy music that's hot. Imitation is a bad idea. Trends change quickly and it's better to stay ahead of them. Be aware of what's working today and see if your music can follow it tomorrow.

Lots of demo tapes are submitted to me. Too much of the music I'm sent is outdated. Too many musicians are creating music without a clue as to what's selling, what's being played on the radio, or what's gathering a following on the college market. This doesn't mean you shouldn't write from the heart. But if you're also writing for your wallet, you've got to understand that music is a business like any other. You've got to understand that, despite their quality, some things sell and some don't. You've got to be flexible about your music. Otherwise, call it a hobby and play it your own way. Share it with your friends and relatives, but forget about making money from it. It's your choice.

## FINDING YOUR STYLE

When working on your demo tape, you've got to target your audience. Many artists jump from one style to another. It's nice to be versatile but it makes you harder to market. A label wants to know where to slot you when they hear your music. The audience for your album should be obvious to them after they hear three songs. It's important to choose which genre is your strongest and stick with it, saving other styles for another time. If you like doing R & B the best, just do R & B and save the reggae and rock for your personal pleasure. Your demo tape should be consistent in a style. Don't confuse the label. The songs don't have to be similar. But whatever the variations in your music, they should appeal to a specific group of music lovers. Then the record label will know how to market it.

I've heard many tapes that have jumped from blues to hip hop to classic rock to country and more. The artists usually tell me they can do it all and want to show it. I explain that someone may not listen further than the blues tune which turns them off. Most people who hear one genre of music assume the whole tape will be like that. Why risk losing people who might love the rest of the tape? The artists hear me out and then argue, "But you don't understand. I do great rock but also have some killer country tunes, and even blues. I know the labels will be impressed." "Everyone loves my versatility." That's not how the industry works. Everything is classified. So if you want a record deal, choose your genre and do the others for fun.

Sometimes deciding what specific music to record can be the hardest task for an artist. Ask professionals which one you do best. Or choose the genre you love doing the most. Concentrating on one direction may go against your creative instincts but you have to do it. You've got to focus on the best avenue to your success. Later, when you're famous, you can experiment.

## UNDERSTANDING WHAT RECORD LABELS ARE LOOKING FOR

Essentially, record labels are looking for hit songs. It's the combination of vocals and strong commercial material that makes a hit. Hearing a great voice singing a mediocre song won't capture a label's attention nearly as much as hearing a great song by an average vocalist. A great singer without great material won't be as appealing to a label. But a mediocre singer with great songs can be made to sound great in the studio. When people at labels listen to tapes, if at least one song doesn't grab them, chances are they'll go on to the next tape.

Hooky melodies, dynamite beats, and memorable choruses are all factors that set certain songs above the rest. These are what the labels listen for in your demo. Finding songwriters who can write hit songs for a specific singer isn't as easy as finding a singer who already has songs that work. Having to acquire songs for an artist is more effort and more costly for a label. Why go through the trouble of finding hit songs that work with an artist's style when there are artists who have strong material of their own?

Because it's more convenient for a label if great songwriting and vocals come in the same package, artists that write their own material are a treasured commodity. Labels want it all when they can get it. If you're not a good songwriter, try to find a good songwriter who's hungry for a break to write songs with you. If possible, contribute to the writing and be on the copyright as a co-writer. An artist who has a great songwriter providing his or her material has a much better chance than someone approaching a label without commercial material.

## LEARNING WHAT MUSIC IS MARKETABLE

Understanding what record labels are looking for isn't enough. Nor is watching MTV a few times going to give you a feel for what's popular and marketable. You've got to live, breathe, and eat music. When I was doing house music, I listened to as many dance radio shows as I could. I watched all the video shows. I went to the clubs. It's imperative to know what's popular. Pay attention to the direction in which music is going. Listening to the radio can't be a once in a while thing. You've got to know what's getting the most airplay. You've got to know what videos are played the most. Talk to DJs to find out why certain records are so popular on radio or in clubs. Talk to record store employees to find out why certain records are selling more than others. Talk to people who listen to the kind of music you're doing. Learn what qualities they like in a record. Absorb as much as you can. Then find your own way.

People come to me regularly with their demos for a consultation. They always want to know what I think. I tell them I'm not an expert on music with which I'm not personally working. They've got to know themselves whether the music will click by doing the legwork. A woman recently came to me for a consultation with an R & B dance track. I asked her if it had the same flavor and format of others in the clubs. She kept telling me she just knew it was a great song. She finally admitted that she rarely went to clubs and didn't feel it was necessary if the song was good. I wanted to shake her. She was clueless and refused to accept her song might not be right for today's market.

When I go to clubs today I listen to the music strictly for pleasure. When I was writing and marketing dance tracks, I studied the music. I paid attention to bass lines and samples and many other details. It took many moons before I could listen to a dance track without looking at my watch to count the BPMs (Beats Per Minute). The above-mentioned woman didn't know what BPMs were, yet this is crucial with dance tracks. When DJs mix from one song to another, the beats should be at the right speed so the flow is smooth. Since BPMs change, I followed them like a weatherman follows high and low pressure systems. For four years, when I heard a dance track I didn't know, my watch would automatically go up and I would count beats.

You've got to be aware of the critical factors for your genre of music. What good is a dance song if the BPMs are too fast for a DJ to mix in? You've got to have enough vision to take what you learn and go beyond the limits, while staying within certain parameters. Manager Peter Leeds says musicians should "Watch MTV and listen to the radio. Don't imitate but try to figure out where are the trends and what is being done. You'll probably not get signed if you're a clone of anybody, but you also don't want to do something that's so alien that it doesn't fit into the form."

You've also got to get out to the clubs where your style of music is playing live. There's an energy in the clubs that you cannot duplicate anywhere else. Sitting home won't give it to you. Being in the studio isn't comparable. Musicians and fans getting together to enjoy music is a sensation unto itself. Hearing other artists get an enthusiastic response from the audience can motivate you to do your own music. You've got to plug into that energy whenever possible. If you don't love the music enough to want to be around it, reconsider whether it's right for you. The artists who make it are often the ones with the talent who love it the most. Enthusiasm and devotion can't be faked.

In addition, going to places with live music can give you the best flavor of what's working because you can see how people respond to different acts. Learn from them. What turns a crowd on? What turns them off? If you go often enough, you'll get the hang of studying the music scene. At a dance club see what gets the crowd into dancing. Talk to people. Network. Get to know other artists. Find out where they're playing. Other artists are a great resource. Invite them to your gigs and go to theirs. And most of all, absorb everything you can so you can grow as a musician. Living outside of the music scene makes it harder to succeed. From hip hop to dance to jazz to rock to reggae to country and back, there's a culture in live music clubs. You've got to be part of it to have the best shot at success. There are a ton of contacts to be made while hanging out. And you'll get the best education possible about your music.

## MARKETS AWAY FROM HOME

You may want to learn whether your music will work in various markets around the country or around the world as well. How do you know what's selling in England, Texas, or California? How can you find out what's being played on the radio in New York or Germany? Read the trades. There are tons of trade magazines on the music industry. Look at the charts for different parts of the country if you want to see whether your genre of music is selling in specific places. Again, you have to be well-educated. If you don't know the songs on the charts, how can you tell if the ones similar to your material are working in different regions?

To find out if there's a market for your music overseas, go to stores that sell foreign periodicals. Check out music magazines for whatever countries you choose. I don't buy all these magazines. I just read through them in the stores and buy only those I want to read thoroughly. Otherwise it can get expensive! If there are no charts, read record reviews. This can actually be a better way of gaining insight into what works in different regions. You can see what a reviewer liked or didn't like in a song. A review may be very specific about what's working and what isn't in that part of the country or the world. The specifics of a review can give you an even better picture of what sells in particular locations. Reading reviews can be especially useful when checking out the foreign markets. You can see more exactly what's working or not working and why.

## GOOD SELLER VS. GOOD MUSIC

Even if your material may not be commercial enough to get signed to a record label deal, this doesn't mean it isn't great. And it doesn't mean your friends are BS-ing you when they say they love it. Your great material just may not be right for today's market. There's a big difference between great music and marketable music. The trick is creating great music that's also marketable. No matter what the style, a great song will always stand out. Unfortunately, if a song doesn't hold up to what's selling today, it may not get recorded. There's a ton of talent trying to break into the music industry. If your great material doesn't hit a person at a record label as commercial off the top, that individual will probably go on to the next act.

Last year a friend had me listen to a tape of an act he was working with. I absolutely loved it. The singer was amazing. My friend got all excited watching my reaction until I told him I loved what I heard but felt the material, which I also loved, didn't sound current. It would have worked very well in the eighties. He argued with me, saying the usual, "but everybody loves the tape." I believed him. There are loads of people still listening to eighties music, but not enough to make the act a worthwhile investment for a record label. When I brought the tape to an industry person, he told me the same thing. He loved listening to the album for his personal pleasure, but a record label would consider it dated. We agreed the singer had more talent than most. But he told me that without "hit single" material, her voice wasn't worth that much.

It was hard getting the band to accept the fact that the material wasn't cutting it. Why wasn't I surprised when the main songwriter told me he didn't listen to much radio or get out to the clubs? His musical influences were groups who'd been around for twenty years. He kept insisting his material was good. I agreed with him. It was better than good. It just wasn't current enough for a record label. A & R people are looking for music with a wider appeal. They want to hear an understanding of today's market reflected in the music.

It took asking for opinions about this band's music from outside sources for this songwriter to get it. The songs were consistently labeled as *too eighties.* So he took a day off from work and watched MTV. Then he thought he knew the market. His songs got a little better, but they never really worked. It was a shame. He was a talented songwriter. But he resisted learning enough about current trends to write songs for today's market. So his great songs were almost worthless on a commercial level. He was stubborn. And as of this writing, he's still writing great songs and he still doesn't have a deal. And he probably still doesn't understand why.

**CHAPTER 9**

# CREATING A WINNING IMAGE

MYTH:
*If my music is good enough I don't have to worry about my image, being commercial, etc.*

I t's nice to think that good music will triumph against all obstacles, but that's not always the case. You've often got to work to make it happen. You've got to learn how to hustle and grab at any and every opportunity. You've got to be outgoing to sell yourself. And very often, selling yourself is what this business is all about. Most businesses marketing a product put time and money into packaging to make it as appealing as possible. In the music industry, you are the product and your image is a form of packaging, whether you like it or not.

## IMAGE COUNTS

It would be great if your image wasn't important in relation to selling records, but it usually is. Good looking/cool looking/interesting looking/outrageous looking artists often sell more records in genres that appeal to a younger, hipper audience. Like it or not, younger record buyers are often concerned with what an artist looks like. That's why MTV helps sell so many records. You don't have to be gorgeous, but if your band looks interesting or has personality to spare it can attract a lot of attention. More people will want to see you in concert if they like the way you look. In addition, labels want to see that you're not boring on stage. That's why I especially like using photos to show my acts having fun.

Image is particularly important for female artists. Men can get over by just looking different. Handsome isn't essential in a man. Beauty is more of a requisite for women. Fat is out. It's a terrible but true double standard that female vocalists are expected to look good and be slim. It's not fair but this is a glamour-oriented business, and that's not going to change because we don't like it. It's what the record buyers want. It's what MTV helped to create.

The image of women is changing, however. Drop dead gorgeous is no longer essential. Traditionally pretty women are now being replaced by women who have *a look*. Independent, off-beat, sometimes angry, sometimes aggressive women are starting to gain much power on the music scene. Some call this the movement of *angry women*. These women are expressing what they feel. Female record buyers relate strongly to the lyrics while men just listen in fascination to the explicit messages. The increasing female presence at the 1996 Grammys reflected the beginning of more acceptance for this *new woman.*

While many women have broken the previous image pattern, they haven't eliminated the need to have a look. They just created a new one. I doubt there will ever be a time when there isn't a standard that artists have to adhere to, even if beauty is not the most important factor. The current look is not as rigid as in previous years. More artists can probably fit into it. But the new wave of female singers are still attractive, slim, and young. And they're still considered sexy.

Men may not have to adhere to the same rigid standards as women, but they still must appeal to the eyes in some way. Sometimes a rebellious look may be enough. Great looks or a terrific body can certainly enhance whatever look someone chooses, male or female. Although artists are freer to develop their images than in the past, being unattractive or overweight will probably still decrease chances of getting a good deal. Labels will still try to find artists with the whole package.

Let's face it. There's nothing wrong with having an image that attracts attention, as long as it doesn't feel demeaning. If you think you look good, your confidence can rise and you may perform better. It's just human nature for people to want to be around attractive people. When music lovers go to watch a performer, it can be as much visual as audio. We have to accept that this is just the way it is. People want something to follow with their eyes when listening to the music. So the visual can be as important as the singing and playing in providing enjoyment for the viewer.

I once had a rock band approach me to develop them for a nice price. Their look sucked! I found three of the members pretty repulsive to look at and told them they'd have to make some serious changes in their image if they wanted my services. They became defensive, telling me their great music should be enough. They refused to camouflage some of what made their look so awful (i.e. the heavy-set guitarist didn't have to wear a tight T-shirt that enhanced the rolls around his middle. A looser shirt would have made a big difference). A year later I took a friend who was very much into music to one of their gigs. Halfway through she whispered to me, "They're great musicians but I'd enjoy the show much more if someone could put paper bags over three of them." An artist who also looks good is just more pleasant to watch. You've got to decide what you want to do for yourself. It's much easier when you look good. It can happen without the looks but the chances are slimmer (no pun intended!).

## PLAYING THE GAME

Sometimes you have to be a bit more commercial than you'd like in order to get a deal and establish yourself. While there are plenty of artists who've made it by just being themselves, it can be easier to get a deal if you give the labels what they want, at least at first.

I managed an alternative rock band for two years. They were extremely talented. However, two members of the group were also very stubborn and wouldn't listen to suggestions that went against their creative beliefs. Their music was terrific, though a bit off the mainstream market. They refused to do anything to target a more commercial audience. Fair enough; new trends can have their day. But their image was the pits. Two of them were word processors in their day jobs and looked it at gigs. They were thirty and looking like word processors on stage didn't work. Maybe at twenty their look would have seemed interesting, but not at their age. I asked them to just wear jeans and tee shirts to gigs. They didn't because "all that should matter is our music." I suggested they not do too many slow songs in a row at gigs or on their tape. Their repertoire needed more variety of tempo, even though the ballads were strong. They said I was interfering with their creative flow. They wanted to be accepted "as is." And so they held their ground, refused to change at all, and eventually broke up. Their standards were maintained but now they don't do music at all. That to me is a bigger waste.

It's a shame that talent isn't always the only thing record labels look for. But that's the way it is. If you don't care about a deal, hold fast to your ideals. Perform for fun. Write songs for fun. Enjoy your music for the sake of doing music. But if you want to make money, you may have to bend a little, if only temporarily.

## DEVELOPING A MARKETABLE IMAGE

Now that you've decided to do whatever it takes to get that deal, how do you actually develop a marketable image? Some of you may already have one that's working. But if you're not sure what's right for you or your band, go out and see acts in your genre of music. Study what works for them. I'm not suggesting you become a clone. But there's enough latitude where you can see the range of looks from act to act. Watch MTV. Go to clubs that feature live music. Get a feel for what's successful. Book yourself into clubs to see what about your performance works. Try different styles. Ask people in the business for suggestions. You don't have to do what they say but you might find a common denominator that would be worth trying.

The looks that work today are those that appear most natural, as if the artist isn't trying at all, even if they're spending hours at it. Live and breath your music and you'll develop your image as you go. Jane Blumenfeld, the president of In Media Publicity, believes that "Looks don't matter—style matters." Often, image is more about developing a sense of style. Dressing attractively, taking pride in your appearance, and having a great personality can go a long way toward creating an attractive image, especially for live performances.

## CHAPTER 10

# DEVELOPING YOUR PRESENTATION PACKAGE

MYTH:
*It's not important to do any more than
make a demo tape to get signed.*

n order to let an A & R person or someone in the media know your marketability, all the information about your act should be presented in a nice package. A press kit is an effective way to accomplish this. Having a professional looking press kit shows an A & R person that you're taking yourself seriously, and that you have a sense of the importance of marketing yourself. A & R people like to work with artists who work as hard as possible to advance their career. A press kit shows that you're trying to develop your marketability.

## THE IMPORTANCE OF A GOOD PRESS KIT

When presenting yourself to a label or to the media, it's essential to provide as much *quality* information as you can. I emphasize quality because you want to offer selling points for your band, including ways in which you've already succeeded or the level at which you've developed a following. This means gathering the most impressive materials—such as places you've performed, radio play you've received, interviews, etc.—and packaging them as concisely as possible.

A press kit gives the person you want to reach a better picture of who you are. It can be an important vehicle for effectively presenting your image, credentials, and marketability, all in a small package. People are more likely to read through your material than listen to a long shpiel from you or your manager about what you've done. Press kits can be used to get label interest, media coverage, gigs, and more. What's in them may vary depending on your target audience and your purpose.

## THE ELEMENTS OF A GOOD PRESS KIT

Press kits can be put together in a variety of ways. The most common components of a basic press kit are a cover letter, a biography (referred to as a bio), and a photograph. Press clippings can also be included if you have them, as well as a listing of where the band has been doing shows and some positive quotes from people in the music business. A good press kit should contain as little as it takes to make a positive impression while getting the information across. Don't overload it with unnecessary words or too many sheets of paper.

Good writing skills are essential when developing your presentation package. A poorly prepared press kit will turn most people off. A professional appearance is important. All your written material should be typed. Handwritten letters are out! In addition, everything should be put together as attractively and logically as possible. Your letterhead (or simply name, address, and phone number) should be at the top of everything because things can get separated. Someone might only get to see one of the sheets you've sent and if they find it interesting, they may need to contact you. If there's no info at the top of the page, forget it!

A press kit is a formal presentation of how you want your act perceived. It's a means of presenting a concise picture of who the artist is to A & R people for the purpose of attracting a deal, and to people in the media for the purpose of getting public exposure. A good press kit can open doors. It can be the difference between publicity and anonymity.

## COVER LETTERS

A cover letter is a brief letter introducing yourself and the kit. It's also known as a pitch letter because you're using it to give a sales pitch to the A & R person or journalist. It should describe why they should consider signing you or doing a write-up. You should be very specific about your selling points in as few words as necessary. A cover letter tells the recipient what you're interested in, such as a record deal, a review, a write-up, etc.

Your cover letter should be well written since it's the first piece of material that will be read. It's usually written in the style of a regular letter. If you've already spoken to the A & R person or the journalist, the cover letter should have a personal touch. You might remind them about when you spoke, and that they requested the material.

When you're writing to promote yourself, less can definitely mean more. Short and to the point is the way to go if you want to maximize chances of having your material read. A & R people, journalists, etc. get so much information to check out each day that they relish something that's a quick read. The shorter your cover letter, the better the chance they'll read it all. The more concise your press kit, the more it'll appeal.

Always double space your material as well. Make it easy to read. Make the recipient of your press materials happy to look at your presentation package. The less time it takes to get through it, the less chance of that individual's losing interest! Be conscious of this when putting your material together. Don't make it too busy. Remember, the less there is to look at, the more chance it'll get read.

## PHOTOS

Sending good photos can be a big plus. A photo is usually the first thing seen when opening a press kit, creating the initial impression of the band. It can attract major interest or turn someone off. Be selective in your choices.

Different images work best in different situations. When sending a press kit to a record label, a posed shot showing an attractive looking band may suffice. I don't personally like photos depicting a band posing like a family group. They're boring and you need a better than average looking act to carry those kinds of photos. For the media, I always prefer a more interesting shot. The lack of gorgeous looks, a perfect body, etc. can be camouflaged in a good photo. An interesting photo can grab someone's attention, making them want to learn more about its subject. A smart A & R person or journalist recognizes that if the photo caught their eye quickly, the band may be more marketable.

Press photos are more commonly shot in black and white. It's also more effective to have them shot vertically. This way you can have the artist's name, manager (if there is one), address, and phone number at the bottom. While not all of this is essential, photos sometimes get separated from the rest of the press kit and need to have some identifying information. A professional company that reproduces press photos can usually have this information presented properly. Otherwise, stickers with the appropriate information can be added at the bottom, or pertinent information can be stamped or written on the back. The most common size photo is 8"x10". A 5"x 7" can also be used but it's not much cheaper to reproduce than the larger one. Nonetheless, it is acceptable. Color photos aren't usually sent first. They're expensive. If you have them, you can add a note to the recipient of your press kit that color photos are available on request.

While some photographers disagree on what reproduces best in print, glossy pictures are still the most popular. They look nicer than matte photos. Glossy photos are definitely the choice for a record label package. For publications, it's your decision. Some photographers have told me that matte works better in print. But whether they're the best for reproducing or not, glossy photos are still found in a majority of press kits. Many publicists believe they look nicer in a kit, and reproduce well enough for a publication. Once you're signed to a label, those decisions will be made for you.

## THE BIO

A bio contains pertinent information about you or your band. It presents the image you want to project. It can entice a label into signing you to a recording contract or a newspaper or magazine into writing an article about you. A bio should be an interesting presentation of facts. While it's important to have a bio that's well-written, it's even better to have it written with flair, spicing the facts with description about the artists. Hiring someone to write your bio can be a worthwhile investment.

An effective bio attracts interest. It can be a good vehicle for getting an editor's attention for a story or for attracting A & R people looking for an artist with a story behind them. Media people often look for a story in a bio. If you as an artist haven't done anything particularly special, try to find something unique or interesting that might perk up what you've done and give a writer an idea for a story. Focus on a hobby or charitable activity, for instance. Being an artist who can attract media attention makes you more desirable. Play up anything you can think of, even if it's just a wee bit exaggerated. Also, keep in mind that a bio shouldn't sound like a resume. Graduating from a good college or being an excellent musician will not necessarily set you apart from others, even though they're admirable qualities. Putting in more fun facts can give an editor more concepts to pick up on. Descriptive words can bring you and your accomplishments to life and can make an A & R person aware of the potential you have for being marketed.

In addition, a bio must be current. If things about you change, redo the bio to reflect those changes. Every new thing doesn't have to be added, but every few months your bio should be checked to see if it's up-to-date.

Finally, a good bio should be limited to one or two pages in length. Remember, the shorter the better.

## PRESS CLIPS

When you get a good press write-up, you may want to include it in your press kit. Neatly cut out the article or review. Also cut out the publication's name or logo (or a small version of the name). If the logo is too large, it can be shrunk at a copy shop. Paste the publication's name or logo at the top of the page or down the side, whichever way it looks better. Then mount the article or review neatly in the center below and paste it down. If it's a long article and the columns are uneven, you can cut and place them so they look neater. Once you have a collection of clippings, you can mount several on a page if they're short. If the name or logo is too large, either shrink it or type in the information above the piece. Don't put too many on a page. You don't want it to look cluttered. Now take them to a copy shop and you're all set!

It's not a good idea to send too many press clippings at one time. There's a limit to how many pieces of paper an editor will read. Remember, too, that less can be more. Grouping several smaller clippings together on the same page can also be very effective. However, send a specific clipping to each media person only once. If you have several current clippings, put one or two in your initial press kit and include one in each subsequent release. This adds some enhancement to each release. You can have them all in your kit, within reason, when sending it to an A & R person. They may be more interested in greater detail than the media.

## FACT SHEETS

A fact sheet can be included in your press kit as well, though it's optional. This is more of a resume type of presentation of the specific facts about your act. Full sentences are not required. A fact sheet usually lists the name of each member of the band, what he or she plays, where each of you are from, whether you have a CD released, and other pertinent information, in a concise format. The name and number of your manager or a contact person should be included at the bottom. A fact sheet may be used as a reference by the media or by an A & R person.

## GIG SHEETS

If you have no clippings but have been doing a lot of live performances, a presentation of your gigs on a sheet can be helpful. As

I've already said, labels want to know that you have a following. Presenting a listing of all the gigs you've been doing is a good way for them to see that you're getting exposure. If you play out a lot, and come back the same clubs regularly, gig sheets can tell an A & R person that people are coming to see you, or that the clubs like you enough to have you back. When you get to the point of touring regularly, a gig sheet should indicate your upcoming venues, with dates and times.

One way to present your gigs is to simply list the clubs you've played in during the last year or so. Put all the dates next to each club so it can be shown if you played in some many times. Add the gig sheets to your press kit. This won't get you the best mileage, but it's better than nothing. It can make an empty kit look a bit more interesting. At least those you're trying to reach will know the act is playing out on a regular basis. It can't hurt!

## QUOTE SHEETS

Sending a list of quotes from reputable industry people about yourself and/or your material can only be effective when you've gotten some exposure and come into contact with people whose opinions would be respected. Once you've received positive attention from industry people or the press, you might want to make a quote sheet. Consolidate some great comments or information published about you onto one sheet. Take a sentence or two from various publications, put quotation marks around each, and write the name of the source directly underneath. Space whatever number of quotes you use evenly down the page so it looks attractive. Your quotes can be presented as bullets, with a star or dot in front of the beginning of each quote.

Quote sheets can be used as a quick summary of your press material, or to consolidate clippings that otherwise wouldn't be used for lack of space. If laid out nicely, they can be a nice enhancement for your press kit. I've also seen bands who had no clippings get quotes from industry people such as DJs, club managers, talent agents, and notable industry professionals to add to their quote sheet. Just make sure you have their permission to use their quotes. Quotes from the media don't need permission.

## PUTTING IT ALL TOGETHER

Press kits look especially impressive in a folder. Remember that when an A & R or media person takes your press kit out of the envelope, the folder will be the first thing they see. It should make them want to look further. With more large stationary stores opening, a package of a dozen folders can be reasonably priced. Though you can do a press kit without them, I highly recommend using a folder for your material when trying to reach the most important people and especially when presenting a tape to a label.

Most publicists recommend pretty, glossy ones. Folders keep all the components of your press kit together, so they do more than just look good. It's preferable to have the name of the artist printed on the cover of the folder or labeled with a sticker. The folders can be decorated with your logo, stickers, and anything else you can think of. It's also a good idea to have a place for, or make a place for, a business card on the inside of your press kit. Tapes and CDs can go right into the folder as well.

When organizing your material in a folder, the photo can be put on the left side, usually by itself. Whatever papers you decide to include can go on the right side. The cover letter should be on top or clipped to the outside of the kit. Next comes the bio and then any press clipping or other sheets you might want to include. If you have a number of sheets, the less important ones can go behind the photo to balance your kit. Just don't overload your folder.

If you choose not to use a folder, the order of your material is a matter of personal preference. The cover letter is always first, however. Since the photo is usually most eye-catching, it works well being right under the letter. The written material should be behind it in the same order as in the folder. You can then put a big clip at the top and insert your business card underneath. It all goes into a large envelope for mailing.

# PART FOUR

# GETTING SEEN AND HEARD BY THE RIGHT PEOPLE

## CHAPTER 11

# HUSTLING FOR MEDIA EXPOSURE

MYTH:
*You can't get media exposure
until you have a label deal.*

ow that you've found the right people to help you advance your career, and you've prepared an effective presentation package, you need to begin work on getting seen and heard by the right people. This can be accomplished by getting some media exposure. If you can get yourself out there and make a lot of noise, you've got a chance of attracting some attention. The hardest part can be convincing yourself that anyone would be interested in reading about you or seeing you on TV. You have to look beyond your shortcomings to focus on your strong points. You've got to dig within yourself until you find something worthy of receiving attention.

Getting media exposure can be a lot of work, but it's worth the effort when it happens. Receiving reviews of your demos or your gigs, or having an article written about something you're involved in, can enhance your chances of getting signed to a record label. Showing that you're worth writing about before you're signed can indicate to an A & R person that there's an even greater potential for getting media coverage once your album is released.

## USING A PRESS RELEASE TO ATTRACT ATTENTION

A press release attracts attention. Although it can accompany your press kit, it's usually sent out alone. A press release is primarily used to alert the media to something very specific that's happening. To be effective, it should be brief and to the point, providing concise, concrete details about a particular event or current news. A press release ought to contain enough information to let an editor or producer know what's going on without going into great detail.

The specifications on a press release are simple. Plain $8\,1/2$" x 11" paper can be used. Some publicists recommend prettier paper to get more attention. The margins ought to be about one to one-and-a-half inches all around. Your typing should be double or triple spaced. The ideal length is a single page, with each sentence and paragraph kept short. A press release should be printed up in an attractive manner, using bold faced and larger types to emphasize key information. Space your paragraphs evenly.

Your business name, address, and telephone number needs to be in the letterhead with a contact person specified at the top of the page as well. In addition, the top of your press release should indicate whether it is for immediate release or to be held for a later date. At the upper left side of the page (under your letterhead), you can print either <u>FOR IMMEDIATE RELEASE</u> or something that indicates a later date. Contact names may be listed underneath, or in the upper right corner. Headlines can be used to emphasize your main announcement.

Finally, be sure to read your work backwards and forwards to make sure everything is accurate. There should be no errors, typos, smudges, or other negatives. Use spell check if you have it. You don't want to turn anyone off because of a careless goof. Check everything before sending it out. If necessary, get a friend to proofread all your written material. The receiver's first impression of you should be a positive one.

## TARGETING YOUR MARKET FOR MEDIA EXPOSURE

Once you've prepared for going after media exposure, you've got to decide where to send your press release or press kit as well as what you want it to do for you. First, visit as many magazine shops and music stores as you can that sell magazines relating to your musical genre. I used to stand in stores and read them. Check out local free papers, many of which are given out in music stores. You've got to do plenty of legwork but it's worth it— there are a lot of publications all over the country that write about music. An excellent listing for local publications by region can be found in *The Musician's Guide to Touring and Promotion,* put out by *Musician* magazine (see the resource list in the back of this book).

Make sure each magazine you target is appropriate. For example, if you're trying to get a review for an R & B record, don't send your press to a country magazine. If a feature story is your goal, don't send it to a more technically oriented publication. You don't want to alienate a magazine by sending something that shows you're unfamiliar with their format. If you're not sure about a magazine, call them. Ask all your questions. You don't have to identify yourself, so you have nothing to lose!

Keep a record of which magazines are appropriate for different kinds of write-ups. Some specialize in reviews, while others go for feature stories. Some have sections that focus on new artists, some review gigs. Be aware of what you're after before you send out your material. It makes targeting publications a lot easier. Newspapers cover a wider realm. If you're trying to get written up in one, decide where you think your story would fit best. Is it a human interest angle, a review, or promotion for an upcoming show? There are so many directions to go with a newspaper that sometimes the hardest part can be deciding where to try. Free newspapers are often more accomodating about doing a story or review. Newspapers might be more likely to give you a write-up of a show or event than a magazine. It's often simply a matter of luck.

## NEWSPAPER AND MAGAZINE REVIEWS

There are many publications that will publish reviews of demo tapes, especially the local free papers. If you entice writers enough, they might even come down to your gig and write it up. You have to let people know you're out there, loud and clear. When you're doing a gig, target writers for your announcements. If you keep sending press releases or postcards announcing your event, someone may eventually show up.

A nicely packaged tape sent to a newspaper or magazine can pass as a finished product. One of my students called me up very excited when her demo tape had been reviewed in *Billboard*. All of the info about it (name of act, name of songs, phone number, etc.) was printed right on the shell of the cassette, and it looked very professional. She'd sent her tape in on a whim, never expecting someone to review it. Nonetheless, I wouldn't push too hard for the real big publications at first. It's a shame to waste that kind of publicity if you don't have a product for sale. Of course, there's no harm in selling a nicely packaged cassette.

When sending material in for review, it's not necessary to send a full press kit as accompaniment. You can send a clipping or two, if you have them, though a copy of the tape with a cover letter is sufficient. You might make the letter in the form of a press release. Announce the tape and perhaps mention a gig or something interesting the act will be doing. Try to find out the name of the appropriate reviewer (just call the publication and ask) so you can send it addressed directly to that person. Also, when someone has given me a review, I either call or write a very brief note to say "thank you." This is a common courtesy that may make it easier to get a review the next time.

## NEWSPAPER AND MAGAZINE WRITE-UPS

When trying to get a write-up or feature story about the act itself in a publication, you should send more than what's needed for getting a review. Your press kit will be helpful here.

Whenever you send a press kit to a publication, call first and find out the name of an editor or writer you can address it to. Get the correct spelling of all names or risk alienating an editor. Your cover letter or press release should announce a gig, the release of a CD you pressed up yourself, a fund raising event your act is participating in, or anything else that might make an interesting story. You can't just announce that your act exists, or that you're putting out good music because that doesn't make a good read. An interesting angle will always give you an advantage.

Sometimes you can even try to capitalize on a hobby that may be interesting. Perhaps you're a volunteer in an animal shelter. Maybe your band is singing at your grandmother's second wedding. Whatever you can think of that someone might find interesting should be added to your bio or press release. You never know when a writer is having a dead week and may decide to do a story on you. If you can get friendly with people at local publications, they might come down to see your gig and write a piece on it.

As mentioned earlier, action or fun photos in a press kit can be advantageous. I've had a photo with a blurb underneath printed several times in a magazine because they needed a filler and liked the photo. Some exposure is better than none. Sometimes you can get away with sending small snapshots, especially those of your act in an interesting situation or with a celebrity, to certain publications that often print small shots. If you're not sure what size to send, you can always send one size and make a note that you've got photos available in other sizes which can be sent on request. I recommend starting with an 8" x 10". I rarely send more than one photo unless an editor expresses an interest in a story, although some people will tell you to send two or three. I find that just too expensive.

## TELEVISION EXPOSURE

Television exposure is harder to get. But, like newspapers, they always need stories. If you're lucky enough to send in your material when they're looking for something to fill a time slot, something can happen.

Producers need a good reason to bring you or your artist on a show for an interview. Few beginners can provide that reason. However, there's no harm in trying. Sometimes a local news show may be interested in an event you're involved with, especially on a slow news day.

Television talk shows, such as Oprah and Ricki Lake, aren't just looking for interesting people to interview. I know, because I've been a guest on them. They're looking for a story, topic, or concept to explore that includes other people who can come on the show with you. They prefer you to have those other people lined up. They also prefer something with at least a bit of sensationalism. If you're able to come up with something in that vein, you can send the producer of a talk show a press kit. But you need to have an angle first. Cable T.V. shows can provide the initial exposure that's hard to get on a commercial station. The producers on some of these shows are much easier to approach, and may be less reluctant to try a newcomer on their show. I'll repeat myself again. It takes lot of research to find the shows on the smaller cable networks. But it can be worth it to get on the air.

If you can get your act on T.V., no matter how insignificant the show, view it as an opportunity to get a performance video. If you're going to do at least one full song on the show, give everyone you know who gets the show a blank VCR tape so they can make a copy of it. This way you don't have to pay to make copies. You can then offer a videotaped performance when approaching the larger stations. Producers want to see how a potential guest comes across in an interview. If nothing else, consider it practice and use it as a learning experience. You can learn a lot from watching the tape, perhaps helping to make your next interview or performance better. You can use a performance video to book gigs as well. When you're shopping your tape, it's always nice to be able to say you have a video of the band performing, available on request. Taping yourself off a T.V. show is an inexpensive way to get a visual.

Cable T.V. shows can be small, but who knows—someone important may be watching the show that day. You never know who might be channel surfing and stop to watch your act. My first rap record, "Girls Can Do," came to the attention of N.O.W. (National Organization for Women) when I performed it on a T.V. show that my friends almost laughed me out of New York for appearing on. I've been on enough shows to have learned that you never know who watches them. Never knock any kind of exposure. It can only help your career.

# CHAPTER 12

# GRASPING THE IMPORTANCE OF PERFORMING LIVE

## MYTH:
*Playing out in local venues won't do me any good.*

One way to get that needed buzz on your act is to get out and perform live in a variety of venues. I've had bands argue with me that it isn't worth the effort. Most of the time when your act is unknown you won't make money for doing a show. In fact, you might even lose money if you have to do a mailing to get people to attend. Doing gigs as an unknown act can be frustrating. People may not show up. The management for the club may not give you the respect you feel you deserve. When I did management we played clubs where the band wasn't even given a free drink. They had to pay full price for them! So why do it?

### THE IMPORTANCE OF LIVE EXPOSURE
You play out because you have that option. Anything you do in this business is a gamble. It's like spinning a roulette wheel. You keep placing bets that something will happen from one of your efforts. And when you do a live performance, you don't know who might see you. Many A & R people often do go to clubs. They want to

keep current on music trends and are always looking for new talent. Erica Ruben, producer of Central Park SummerStage, told me that she frequently goes to clubs to check out talent for her very popular venue. Managers, agents, producers, etc. go to hear live acts when they need someone to work with or book.

I know a band that got the attention of a top music publisher because the publisher's daughter went to a club and liked the band. She went home and raved to her father that this band was talented and had great material. Daddy came to their next gig. Every time you perform live, you have a chance that someone who can get you a deal will be there. It's a gamble. The chances of having your number come up on the roulette wheel aren't in your favor either. But the more times you play roulette, the better the odds of your number coming up. The more gigs you perform, the greater the odds of having someone in the audience who can help you. Some do beat the odds.

Karen Yee, Senior Director of Artistic Development for Island Records, focuses primarily on developing the *baby bands,* the new up and coming ones. She told me, "Touring is absolutely essential, because it's another avenue for people to notice you. It does depend on what style of music an artist does. It's especially important in rock and alternative before getting signed. A rap artist, though, may find touring more important after being signed." Yee cited Guns & Roses as an example of a band that toured constantly for about a year before their record and video hit. She went on to say "We have a band called Tripping Daisy. They built a reputation of being a good live act. Promoters love them because they bring in lots of people when they play. It makes them more marketable."

Bob Grossweiner, New York Bureau Chief of *Performance* Magazine, says

> The more experience you have on stage, the better you
> are. In my experience, I've seen groups that have had no
> stage experience think that just because they make a tape
> they will get signed, and it really doesn't work that way.

The longer you perform and the longer you perform together, the more the cohesion of the musicians, which is the key to getting signed, along with the material. You have to feel comfortable live. Many artists don't play enough.

A good example of a band doing well due to playing out is October Project. They started out in a New Jersey garage. The group worked its way through local clubs, charming listeners and developing a fan base of people of all ages who enjoyed their melodic harmonies. Once people heard them, they were hooked. According to co-founder and lyricist Julie Flanders, "We sold 200,000 copies of our last album on Epic, yet so many have never heard of October Project. Who is buying our CDs? All the fans we've cultivated over the years . . . We continue to keep in touch with our fans by doing mailings."

Flanders says that October Project started off playing in small clubs in New York. Their very unique sound made it hard at first to fit in. But their music attracted many fans who kept coming back to see them. They were careful about not playing out too often, though, to avoid overexposure and to give themselves a better chance of attracting a good crowd each time. As their fan base grew, so did the excitement about the band. Within a year of playing out, October Project got the attention of Epic Records. According to Flanders, "We found the people who mattered at first were the sec-retaries, interns, etc. at the labels. They were the ones we invited to hear us. They go back and talk about a band they like. The music business is really about relationships."

PERFORMANCE MARKETABILITY

Playing out provides an opportunity for someone interested in your act to see you live. It's great to be able to say to an A & R person who's showing interest in your act that he or she can come down and see you at a gig. A & R people want to know that you're able to please an audience. Most of us know what technology can do in the recording studio to enhance our sound. Some acts don't sound good out of the studio. I've heard famous performers sing live and turn everyone off! An act that has a good on-stage personality, that can work an audience, and that can sound as good if not better than their recording is a marketable one.

Once you're signed to a recording contract, you'll have to do live appearances and you have to be able to cut it. Concerts and various live performances benefit the label as well as the artist. Fees paid for touring can be high. They can be a money maker for the artist. They can keep you content, especially when the royalties aren't coming in yet. For the record label, it's a great form of promotion. Every time you do a great concert appearance your records will sell. If you're good, it enhances your chances of opening for a top act when your album is released. And the capability of doing lots of paid gigs lets the label know there's a better chance of having a happy artist. If you're earning a lot of money through gigs, you'll be less likely to rock the boat when you're not earning royalties.

From a record label's point of view, Karen Yee believes that "Enthusiasm for someone who plays live will transfer to sales for CDs. There is a very direct relationship between touring and selling CDs. That's why labels like to see a band that can tour. The fans that come to see a band are a more loyal audience than those gotten from radio or video." According to Yee, "A band has to build up performances as part of the building of the success."

## DEVELOPING A FELLOWING

Part of being marketable is having a following. This means there are people who regularly come to see you play. It's essential to develop a following if you're serious about being successful. A large following will impress club owners, who will be happy to have you play for them again. In addition, A & R people look to see if a band has a following. This can be a big factor in determining whether you get signed. The Spin Doctors played in all the local clubs in New York for what seemed like forever. I used to watch their progress. More and more people kept coming to see them. As their following grew, so did interest from record labels. I can't say for sure this is the main reason they got signed, but there are many who feel it was a major factor.

Viceroy Records' Arnie Goodman believes a band should

> build up a following and an interest. Then the interest will come from labels. The key is getting a following. I get brilliant tapes, but we can't get them from ground zero. We signed Sunset Heights because huge crowds came to their gigs. It has nothing to do with being great. People have to know who the band is.

People will get to know your band when you play out regularly. And a strong following will insure the steady gigs. Getting disgusted with not getting signed soon after doing gigs is not the way to get signed. Goodman says that "Bands may sit home and complain that nothing is happening instead of going out and playing. If the band is out gigging, there's a chance that someone will see them and like them." A chance is a chance.

How do you develop a following? By persisting in going out to play clubs. If you make sure you have good material and a well-rehearsed set, people who hear you play will want to hear you play again. You can't count on your friends all the time, but friends are the start of a following. When you have a gig and need people to attend it, send or hand a card to EVERYONE you know. When I managed a rock band we did some key venues where it was very important to have a large crowd. We put the word out to friends and family. The band's parents came. People of all ages came from their day jobs. It might not have been a typical rock and roll crowd, but in the dark it was a large crowd. They bought drinks. The club was happy.

Being in a band can be an imposition on your friends, but hopefully they'll like your music enough to want to support it, literally by paying to see you over and over. Even the girlfriends of our band members paid to get in. The only ones on our guest list were industry professionals and the media. Tell your friends to invite friends. Invite everyone from work, your neighbors, and anyone you may have met in your lifetime. Ask them to bring friends.

Make sure you have a mailing list for people to sign at the gig. I prefer to take index cards or 3 x 5" pieces of paper and print on them:

---

NAME _____

ADDRESS _____

PHONE # _____

COMMENTS _____

---

Pass them out at the gigs or leave a few on tables. If you can get some miniature golf type of pencils, have them handy too. Have someone (a friend/your manager) hold on to whatever you choose for people to sign. Announce the opportunity to get on your mailing list several times during your gig. Followers of other bands playing that night might sign up. The friends your friends brought down might now be on your list. Now they can bring friends. As your mailing list grows, so does your following.

If you have a place for comments on whatever they sign, read them, let the praise spur you on, and learn from the negatives. I always like to get feedback from those who sign my mailing lists. In addition, make sure to thank your fans for coming down. Let them know how important it is to you that they attend. Julie Flanders says that "October Project has always had really close relationships with our listeners. We have always been friendly to fans after our gigs. Don't ever take your fans for granted. You'll have a higher return if you think of the names on your mailing list as people."

It will help if you can create a support system. Try to network with other bands to share information and help each other. As Flanders told me,

> Getting friendly with and supporting other bands will
> help you in the long run. We shared our mailing lists and
> contacts. We went to other bands' gigs and they came to

ours. This is how a support network is formed. One of those bands may remember you when they get bigger and have you open for them.

Don't think of other bands as competition. There's room for many good musicians.

## SHOWCASING YOURSELF

If you have industry people interested in your band, you can do a showcase. The intent of a showcase is what the name implies—providing an opportunity for people who may be interested in your band to come and see you. It's the gig you work hard to develop. It's the one you invite as many industry and media people as possible to come to. Clubs like having a band come in for one because it usually brings in a lot of people.

When you call a gig a showcase and invite a lot of industry and media people, you've got to work hard to have the gig go as well as possible. This starts with choosing a good venue, with a good sound system. You need to get your following down. Do a mailing to everyone who signed your mailing list, and again call everyone you know. Tell them this is an important gig and you need a massive turnout. Hopefully your friends will come through for you. Industry people like to see a lot of enthusiastic attendees.

You can also apply to perform at a music seminar showcase. Many seminars have live entertainment going on in a variety of clubs for all the days that it runs. Some seminars are easier to break into than others. Don't expect miracles, but it can be good exposure. It also can help add to your following. There are many bands who have played at a seminar showcase and went on to become very big.

There are seminars that are more general and some that focus on one genre of music. Choose one that would be right for you. For example, if you have a band that would work well on the college circuit, the CMJ Music Conference (see Chapter 13) in New York City, usually in September, would be a good venue. A majority of people there are involved with college radio stations, so appearing there could lead to airplay or a gig. If you do black music, Jack the

Rapper in Atlanta, Georgia in August might be the choice. There's a list of seminars in the resource section. Follow the *Billboard* calendar section for more.

Pounding the pavement to get gigs and hounding people to come to them isn't always fun. It can get expensive, tiring, frustrating, and seem like it's going nowhere. But each time you play, there's another chance that someone might be there who can help you get to the next level. When you're feeling discouraged because nothing further is coming from your gigs, just think of them as rehearsal time. You're getting the experience needed for when you get signed.

## BOOKING GIGS

At the beginning, you most likely will have to book yourself. Much depends on your genre of music. Rock and blues have the most opportunity to book into a club. In certain areas, there are a lot of venues for country. For other music, you have to find out what's available. Be prepared to perform for free at first.

Once you've discovered what clubs are appropriate for a live performance of your style of music, call and ask who does the booking, and when they're available to speak with you. Many times you'll be told to mail a tape. Send your tape in with a cover letter. A press kit and a photo can't hurt either. Sometimes you can deliver this material in person. Rarely will they listen to it on the spot, or even after you've called a few times to remind them. It's a frustrating chore, but never let them feel your annoyance.

You've got to do the leg work. Nobody will come to you in the beginning. There's so much competition, good competition, that you've got to hustle for your spots. There are clubs that offer promotional appearances for dance music and hip hop. They're harder to get when you're not on a label or if you have no one representing you. Send in the most professional looking tape that you can to impress the person who books for the club. Get friendly with people who work in the clubs. Sometimes the bartender may do the booking. DJs may also have a lot of influence, so get to know those who play in the clubs where you want to perform. Give your tapes to these people and see the response. If they like it, ask them to do you a favor and put in a word with the right person at the club.

## TRADITIONAL VENUES

For music other than rock, dance, or hip hop find the venues where your music is performed live and be prepared to hustle. These are the hardest gigs to get. According to Kathy Baylor, exposure for R & B and hip hop needs to be worked.

> Use any opportunity for exposure. Artists can go and sing for jingles, commercials. You just have to get out there. A good way to do that is by registering your songs with a performing rights society, either ASCAP or BMI. They have quite a few showcases every year where a lot of people that perform are unsigned. Opportunities like that are important. You have to get out there and hit the pavement . . . really talk to people . . . spend time in clubs. Find out if they have unsigned acts open for signed ones that may be performing. Even if you do it for no money, you still have that club full of people who will get to see you.

In addition, Kirk Burrowes believes that "Someone doing hip hop can get exposure by doing open mics and doing free-styles at clubs . . . by getting on the DJ mix tapes and doing little promos for radio programs that cater to rap . . . by being a part in the circle of other rappers that are doing something, because usually they put their crews down." It can take some resourcefulness, hard work, and knowledge of the people involved in your music.

Rock and blues has its own routine. When you speak to the booking person, they'll want to know where the band has played and how many people you can get to come to the gig. If you think you'll want to play there more than once, I don't recommend lying about the number of people. I'd rather say I'm not sure how many people will come than alienate them by not having a good turnout after I'd promised one. According to Julie Flanders, "We have always been very honest with the clubs about the numbers we could bring in. It helped us develop better relationships and be taken more seriously."

Clubs that offer venues for unknown rock or blues playing original music don't usually pay much, if anything. Most commonly you'll get a percentage of the door, which averages from $1 to a few dollars per person, depending on what's being charged. Some clubs will pay a flat fee of $50 to $100. Sometimes people play for tips. This is part of paying your dues to break into the industry. The financial arrangement is something you have to work out with each. Policies and payments vary from city to city. Established clubs with a built-in following will pay more, but they're harder to get into.

No matter how little you're earning for your efforts, the club will expect to see a turnout generated by your promotions. When you book into a club, you're supposed to do a mailing to everyone you know, giving them the details of your gig so they can attend. Most bands make up postcards. Sometimes the club provides them. Usually you have to print them up yourself. Make sure you send out a card to the press and to A & R people, announcing all your gigs.

## ALTERNATE VENUES

Besides the obvious clubs, there are other opportunities for performing. Again, there's a lot of leg work involved. You might have to perform for free but remember that any exposure is another opportunity to be exposed to someone who can open a door. Sometimes public schools bring in performers. In larger cities there are street fairs and festivals at certain times of the year. They often have a stage set up and lots of folks watching. There are publications that list the big ones that book live entertainment (see the resource section in the back of this book). Various charities sponsor events where they use live entertainment. I told a producer I know about a Dance-a-thon for drug abuse that needed acts to entertain the participants. He brought his act down. The event was co-sponsored by a big radio station and the DJs attending loved the act. Now this producer has friends in higher places.

Keep your eyes and ears open for any events where you live. It can never hurt to ask if they need live entertainment. You probably won't get paid, but it's what you have to do to get that buzz going. The Roots, now signed to Geffen Records, created their own live exposure when they were trying to break into hip hop in Philadelphia. According to group member, ?uestlove,

> We thought that since America's never seen a group like us before and we're talented, that we'd make it. That was not the case at all . . . There was a lack of outlets and venues for us to exercise our skills, so to speak. What we did was we started playing on the street corners. We figured we'd be our own PR machine, by any means necessary. That took a lot of sacrifice. We would play the corners every week to generate enough spending cash . . . In our case, doing these shows every Saturday on South Street enabled us to get other gigs. People would approach us and say "do my barbecue." . . . We did that diligently until the right person saw us, Jamaladeen Tacuma. He's a jazz bassist from Philly. He took us to Germany with him because he was doing jazz festivals and he wanted to take some rappers. We were representing American hip hop over there without a record!

The Roots looked for every way they could milk the opportunity they'd attracted from giving themselves exposure busking on a street corner. Since they had four months before they left on tour, they saved up and recorded an independent release, which they called *Organix*. Assuming that labels would be impressed that an American group got many encores, they sent some of their CDs out to record labels. When interest in The Roots began to generate, ?uestlove says "We got a good lawyer. That's for starters. What he did was set up some showcases for us to perform." They had offers from many labels and eventually signed with Geffen Records.

The Roots have continued to capitalize on their ability to tour. ?uestlove told me they're not getting rich from it, but they can at least live reasonably well from touring. He says "We're doing well because we paid our dues. We're one of the few groups that don't even sell that much that can make a comfortable five figure salary a show, or high four figure. Usually for a group like us, touring isn't even an option. It's such a rare thing." But it can happen. Doing gigs can be a thankless venture at first. It's not always fun. But you have to accept what comes with the territory of trying to break a band. Getting discouraged, angry, and frustrated won't get you anywhere but discouraged, angry, and frustrated. If you're not willing to go the distance and pay your dues, get a job outside of the music industry.

## CHAPTER 13

# TARGETING THE COLLEGE MARKET

MYTH:

*The college market isn't lucrative enough to target.*

hen I started my record label in the mid-1980's, marketing a band through the colleges was a tool used most often by smaller independent labels and unsigned bands. However, the majors have woken to the fact that the college market has tremendous buying power behind it. These labels now have promotions people who focus on nothing but college radio. At music seminars I've met several Music Directors from larger college radio stations who told me off the record that they'd been flown in, all expenses paid, by a major label. So while colleges used to be easy to get support from, today there's more competition from larger record labels.

While things aren't quite as open in the college market as they used to be, a majority of the college radio people I've spoken to, even those getting perks, are still idealistic enough to ultimately try to be true to the music. These are students who don't get paid, so ratings and money are not their main issue. College students are probably more interested in and excited by new bands, new sounds, and new trends, than most other consumers. Although younger people are also fervent about their music, they don't always have the money to buy CDs and go to concerts that college students have. College students are young enough to follow trends and to support what's new in music, and old enough to have sources of income to support the bands they love. The attention to the college market by the majors is a definite indication of how lucrative this market can be.

## THE POWER OF THE COLLEGE MARKET

The college market offers an artist the opportunity to reach out to a large number of people within a relatively small area. Enthusiasm can spread quickly through a dorm. The concentration found in most colleges of music-loving young adults who are open to the cutting edge is unequalled anywhere else. Students working at college radio stations, newspapers, and in the Student Activities departments are easier to reach than their counterparts in the commercial world. Yet they've got the power to reach an incredible number of people who might join your following if they knew about you.

There are several avenues at colleges that can be tapped to get a buzz going on your act: radio, gigs, and college publications. Depending on the genre of music you play, at least one of these outlets can be used to get your group recognized in the college scene. Even if there aren't a lot of reggae radio shows, for example, students may still want you to come and perform. Or they may check out your material if they read about it in their school newspaper. It's up to you to tap the resources. Most colleges with a diversified population have students who listen to all genres of music. But depending on the region, some music will be more readily marketed on the college level.

For instance, I got a call last year from Lawrence, who had taken one of my classes. He was working with several rap groups who had pressed up their material themselves. Lawrence tried to work the college market in New York but got nowhere. Rather than quit, he took a trip to the Southeast. There he had considerable success getting his acts into the colleges. He found a different student population than in New York and a different attitude toward hip hop on the college level. Lawrence called to tell me he and his groups were permanently relocating to the South. They were so thrilled about the possibilities of marketing their music through the colleges that they decided to make it their home.

Marketing music on the college level can be hit or miss. Since most of the people you deal with are students, it can also be extremely frustrating to work with their schedules. When you call long distance to a Music Director or Student Activities Director who is scheduled to be in during certain hours and are told they're out studying for mid-terms, exasperation can set in. Volunteers aren't as fastidious about their hours as paid staff in a more commercial environment. Once you do reach them, though, the results may be rewarding. Patience can be the utmost of importance when dealing with students who hold the key to your opportunity for success on the college level.

## WAYS OF REACHING THE COLLEGE MARKET

Working the college market can be a lot of hard work. It involves locating the schools and then finding the people at the radio stations, venues, and other locations to call. Libraries have listings of colleges. If you get friendly with the people at one college, they might recommend you to other schools. ASK! DJs in one college often know DJs in another. If you spend time in the live music scene, other bands may give you leads. An excellent source of information regarding the college market is CMJ.

### CMJ

CMJ, which stands for College Music Journal, is an excellent resource located in Great Neck, New York (see resource section). CMJ offers many services for those wanting to break into the college market. For example, they put out CD samplers and special publications, and they have a conference called *CMJ Music Marathon & Musicfest* in New York City every fall.

The conference is a good place to begin your education about the college music market. People show up from college radio stations all over the country. Because it's a good conference to attend if you're trying to break into this market, industry people and musicians on all levels flock to CMJ as well. The panels focus on topics relevant to breaking music on the college level. I've found this conference to have a special emphasis on a grass roots approach to the various topics discussed. This enables a less experienced musician or industry person to get practical tools for the advancement of their career. Last year for instance, I went to several panels devoted to different levels of touring and booking tours. The panelists seemed to understand that many of the attendees were just starting out and thus addressed issues relevant to beginners. After all, it's a college seminar.

At night attendees get to see the many showcases presented in a wide variety of New York City clubs, most of them free. Getting your act into one of these showcases can give you great exposure in front of a college-oriented audience. Attending the *CMJ Music Marathon* is an opportunity to be a part of one of the largest concentrations of college radio personnel assembled in one location. I recommend bringing a portable tape or disc player with a recording of your act. You'll then be able to play it for each person you meet from a radio station who expresses an interest in your genre of music. If you sense enthusiasm, offer a copy for them to take back to play on their station. Some college radio stations will play home-made tapes. If the vibe you get isn't enthusiastic or they say they don't know if your material would get airplay, say "thanks anyway" and you've saved yourself from wasting a copy. Only give your recording to those who seem most likely to play it.

In addition to its annual conference, CMJ is well-known for its music publications. *CMJ New Music Report,* for instance, is a weekly tip sheet—available only by subscription—published for the alternative marketplace. It focuses primarily on non-commercial radio-related information and contains airplay charts based on reports from college, non-commercial, and commercial radio stations as well as from retail outlets all over the country. It also carries reviews of new album releases, so you can try sending in your new material for a possible write-up. The tip sheet is a great source for all sorts of information concerning breaking into college radio. Musicians reading this publication are able to see which regions of the country have music most similar to their own being played. They are also able to keep up with the latest trends in college radio, thus becoming more aware of the most influential college radio stations.

With a bit of luck, musicians can eventually watch their own records chart in the *CMJ New Music Report*. And while they are watching, so too will the Music and Programming Directors of other college radio stations. A large number of stations subscribe to *CMJ New Music Report* to follow what's new and good that they don't have yet. If DJs see a record charting at several schools, they may be more inclined to play it on their own station. Knowing that others like the band can make it more appealing to check out. DJs (or anyone else, for that matter) listen with a different ear when they expect a record to be good.

CMJ also puts out a consumer magazine called *CMJ New Music Monthly*. It contains information similar to that contained in the industry tipsheet, but is slanted towards the person buying the music rather than for those playing or marketing it. The magazine also carries reviews, charts, in-depth editorials, and feature stories. One very special feature is its exclusive monthly compilation CD included in each issue. By including the CD, the publication not only brings information the latest music to its readers, it lets them hear it, too. Getting included on one of these compilations is a great way to reach a wider audience.

CMJ puts out an industry compilation as well called *Certain Damage*. It contains music from both established artists and talented newcomers. This CD is put out in conjunction with *CMJ New Music Report* and goes directly to its subscribers, who include all the radio stations, retail and video outlets, record companies, press, and more. All submissions for *Certain Damage* must be pre-approved by the CMJ editorial staff. CMJ also publishes an annual industry directory, listing radio stations, retail and video outlets, management, record companies, booking agencies, and music publishers. Many of the names and numbers in this directory would be hard to find elsewhere. Call them directly to learn about these and other services they offer.

## COLLEGE RADIO

One of the best avenues of reaching the college music market is by getting on their radio stations. Most college radio stations like to pride themselves for being on the more cutting edge of music. Very commercial Top 40 music usually doesn't get much, if any, play. College DJs like to air what the commercial stations aren't playing. They like to be ground-breakers for new music. Radio listeners know they'll hear new music first on the college stations. Often, when a record broken on college radio starts getting commercial play, the college station may stop playing it. There's always a new band coming up that they can jump on. Since most college radio stations are funded by the school rather than through advertisers, they are able to concentrate more on playing what's new and fresh, rather than on what sponsors would like them to play.

No matter what anyone says, alternative rock and heavy metal do much better by far than most other genres of music on college radio. Things have changed a bit since I started my record label in 1987. Alternative rock has become more mainstream. But less commercial rock is still played the most on the college level. A lot depends on the make-up of the student population. Different ethnic groups may encourage their stations to play different varieties of music. Some stations will even play demo tapes, which can increase the variety played. Sometimes the station's Music Director may just decide to give a certain genre extra exposure because it's something he or she likes, and the listeners may catch this enthusiasm.

When you try to get something played on commercial radio, you have to go through the Programming Director. Most DJs can't play anything they want. A record must be on the stations *play list* for them to use it. On college radio, DJs have the freedom to choose what's played on their shows. Many bring their own CDs to put on the air. Depending on the region, various genres of music may get a lot of airplay as well. Lawrence, whom I mentioned earlier in the chapter, found a great niche for his hip hop artists on college radio in the South. When I worked with hip hop artists, we got our demo tapes and then our records played on many college radio shows. It wasn't enough to break them in New York, though, as Lawrence found out. But in the South it was a different story. Reading the charts in CMJ can give you a clue about what type of music gets more air play in different parts of the country. You can also call a college radio station to ask for a copy of their show schedule to see how many hours a week your type of music is on the air.

Almost all genres of music are heard on at least some college radio stations. But in order to break an act, a song has to be played a lot. Airplay for a record in regular rotation on a commercial station is an average of seven times a day, every day. Hearing a song over and over is what gets someone interested in a band's music. While hearing it once or twice a week probably won't do much, it nonetheless may be all your genre of music is being played. And remember, it's still some exposure, which is better than nothing. Just the same, keep your expectations down.

How much a college radio station can help you may depend on a number of factors besides what it plays. Some stations have more power, prestige, and audience than others for a variety of reasons. There may be less competition from local commercial stations in smaller cities. College radio stations can range from being very powerful, covering a reasonably large area of listeners, to being heard only on campus. In New York City, for example, New York University's radio station has a pretty wide range of people it reaches. It has a large following that goes way beyond its student population. Then there are colleges whose radio stations can be heard only inside the school itself. They may be played in the cafeteria and other places on campus, so many do listen whether they like it or not.

Sometimes you might not be aware of the influence of a radio station by simply speaking to its Music Director or seeing its charts in CMJ. I saw an example of this when I visited my friend Leslie, who had a show on what was then considered a prestigious college radio station in the Midwest. Leslie told me there were probably very few listeners because many of the school's power lines had been down for over a year and, despite the pressure, hadn't been fixed. At that point, only a few dorms had access to the station. Yet this school was sending its charts regularly into publications, and was targeted as a powerful influence. Leslie laughed when she told me what a joke it was that people actually coveted her play list. When she went on-air the night I visited she actually asked anyone listening to please call in. Nobody did. Scary.

## THE CLUB AND CONCERT CIRCUIT

Whether or not you have something that can be played on college radio, the college arena can still be lucrative, again depending on your genre of music and the region of the colleges. College students go out to hear live music more frequently than many other groups. They often have more money to spend on music than do high school teens, and they'll come back to see bands they liked.

There are many levels of venues on the college circuit. Probably the easiest to break into are the local bars. Most of these cater to audiences that like rock, blues, and folk music, although this still differs in various regions. Some of these bars have large stages and others just offer a small space for a band to play. But the crowds, especially on weekends, can be large and enthusiastic. Bands can earn a living playing out in the college circuit.

Private colleges, especially the ones not located in major cities, regularly bring in talent to perform. They usually pay very well, too. Many of these schools are open to a large variety of music. The further in the sticks a college is located, the more likely they may be to bring in live music to entertain their student body. Their concern is that if students get bored without a large city nearby, they may consider transferring to an institution with more social activities.

Therefore many schools import music, usually through a Student Activities Department that decides what acts to bring in. Getting in touch with the students in this department can be as exasperating as trying to reach the students at the radio station, since most of them don't get paid either.

If you're getting radio play on a college station, you might ask the DJ to hook you up with the Student Activities Department. Sometimes they know them. Even if they don't, you can still use the name of someone at the radio station when you speak to the person in charge. "Hello, my name is _____ and I just spoke to _____ at your radio station. He said my record is doing very well so I thought you might want to consider having the band play for your students. What is the procedure for submitting material?" You can use any variety of this pitch depending on your situation. Be aware that most schools book way in advance, however. David Cohen of Dancing Bear says that bands trying to break into doing college gigs need to have a performance video available. He won't represent an act without one.

College gigs can pay serious money. When I was in Boston I met Brad, a manager who regularly booked his bands at colleges in the New England area. He concentrated on those in smaller towns, booking several shows in towns not too far apart over a weekend. At first Brad worked his butt off finding schools that would bring in his bands. He learned about cheap motels where the whole group shared a room to save money. He sometimes made a zillion calls to get one booking. But once Brad developed that all-important *relationship* with the people involved in student activities, he was able to book his bands in the same schools every year. He and his bands developed a regular circuit doing college gigs.

Brad told me that a band wanting to break on the college circuit has to be prepared to work very hard, give up many comforts, and be available to travel a lot. He had a van that they traveled in together with their equipment. It was cramped. Sometimes they'd sleep in it. No matter how many people, they always shared one cheap motel room, bringing their own sleeping bags and blankets.

Whenever possible, they'd try to crash with someone they knew. Sometimes a school would provide dorm rooms, but you can't count on that. By keeping expenses to a minimum, however, the band had money in their pockets when they returned home. Brad's 20% share of the gigs made it worthwhile for him to keep booking bands. Colleges themselves pay well.

Many groups try to work the smaller bars to get started. These don't usually pay much, but they can be good exposure. Many rock bands have done well by developing a large following at bars in college towns. It can help you get the attention of the Student Activities people and the radio stations. It can be a good opportunity to invite people with whom you're trying to develop relationships. If you sell CDs and tapes when you play, it can put some change in your pocket. Getting into the college venues can create a nice buzz.

Some pre-planning can get you the maximum mileage out of the college circuit. When you book gigs in college venues, try to milk them for everything you can. Once you get the date, contact local publications to let them know about your act and to learn to whose attention a press release should be sent. College publications are often more informal than commercial ones, so you might be able to get someone interested by just calling. If you can get someone willing to write a story about your act before the gig, it can help to get more people to come see you perform. If you have a tape (even home-made) or CD to sell, it helps to have it mentioned in the article. Afterwards, a review of the gig is good, too.

Getting the band an interview on the college radio station will also help bring people to your show, especially if your group has some personality. Depending on your music, you can sometimes perform a song live on the air, always reminding people there's a tape or CD for sale. You can also try to hook up with a local record store to sell your material. Promise to announce on radio or at your gig that your CD is on sale at that store. The store may like the publicity. If you have time, talk to a store about making a personal appearance after a radio interview or gig. If you have nice 8" x 10" glossy photos and see photos of other bands, ask whether the store, club, or radio station would like an autographed picture of yours. I always like to ask the bartender, sales clerk, etc. and keep lots of photos of the band already signed "Thanks for your support" with a black marker. Then I ask whose name should go on it. I usually write that in myself. When the person wants his or her own name, they'll probably want to hang it so people will see they know the band.

Finally, let NACA assist you in reaching the college market. NACA stands for the National Association of Campus Activities (see resource section). About 1,200 colleges belong to NACA. People interested in taking advantage of the college market can join as associate members. Membership is on either a national or regional basis. As a member you get a directory—updated each year—of all the member colleges in the region you joined, or the national directory. Associate members are also listed so that colleges have your information, too. The directory includes the names, addresses, and phone numbers of the different contact people involved in student activities, as well as information concerning what sorts of music they book. Using the directory saves you the time and hassle of trying to find the specific people you'd have to speak with to book your act.

NACA also provides its members with the resources for booking college tours. Members get a subscription to their magazine with articles of interest to Associate members and information about new releases. NACA also publishes a tabloid. This newspaper-like publication averages about 20 pages, with each issue having one or two articles with a how-to emphasis for campus programmers. Associate members can list their tours in the tabloid. This enables other colleges to see where your band is playing, and to possibly hook themselves into your tour if it's within their region. In addition, schools submit reports on the artists who perform for their students, including highlights of performances.

NACA sponsors regional and national conferences as well. These conferences, most of which are in the fall, offer opportunities for artists to showcase their acts for a large number of people who book for their colleges. There are opportunities to bring video or audio tapes and exhibit artists. While there are fees for all these services, it can still be cheaper than sending a lot of cassettes to schools cold. This way you may be able to *develop a relationship* with some of the college personnel, and get your questions answered in person.

CHAPTER 14

# CHAPTER 14

# PRESSING YOUR OWN RECORDING

## MYTH:
*Pressing up my own CD won't do me any good.*

Pressing up your own recording is another avenue to getting a record deal. More and more artists are taking the route of putting out their own product. It's another way to generate that all-important buzz. If the record sells, A & R people may pay more attention. They do pay attention to CDs that are put out independently. Radio stations are also more likely to play a CD than a demo tape, as are clubs. Reviews may come easier with a finished product. Agents and clubs will take you more seriously when you try to get gigs, and a self-pressed CD can be an effective tool for attracting a label deal.

## USING A RECORDING AS A MARKETING TOOL

Pressing up your own recording is a nice way of presenting your material to an A & R person. It will obviously say more than a homemade demo tape. Manager Mark Pitts, who's also Vice President of A & R for Universal Records, told me, "A lot of guys are putting themselves on wax. They get it to mix tapes or they get it to DJs and when they're being played, they're being heard. That's what's putting buzzes on them."

According to Wendy Goldstein, Director of A & R at Geffen Records,

> For alternative bands it's been really highly successful of late . . . if you can't seem to rattle A & R departments, get the means together to put the record out yourself. If it's really happening, people will find it. You can mail it to CMJ or college newspapers to write reviews. That's how a lot of bands have gone on to get signed in the alternative world. A lot of bands don't knock on the door of A & R departments immediately anymore.

Since 1991, my "How to Start & Run Your Own Record Label" classes have been filling up as people creating every genre of music are choosing to put their music on the market themselves. While there's a strong upside, there's also a more expensive risk and I don't recommend doing it without plenty of forethought. Pressing up your own record can be a good tool, but it can cost several thousand dollars depending on your format. Think carefully about where your potential sales might come from, and how far you're prepared to work it. Don't expect to automatically enhance your career, or get signed, because you've released your own CD. I know loads of excellent singers who complain about how many CDs they have laying around their apartment. It can get discouraging.

Never press up your own material without first devising a plan. You need to determine what your purpose is, who's going to receive your recording, whether you intend to sell it yourself, and where your best outlets can be found. Even if you can get your recording into record stores, people won't buy it unless there's a reason. Putting out your own product is an option, but it's definitely not a sure-fire investment.

## DETERMINING THE RIGHT FORMAT FOR YOUR MUSIC

The format you press up depends partly on your genre of music, and partly on where you live. If you're pressing what I call *listening music* (not played in dance clubs), from rock, to blues, to jazz, to classical, to reggae, to pop, and back, a CD album is probably the way to go. Unless you get major radio play on a commercial station, people don't usually buy singles of unknown *listening music*. Pressing up a CD single is considered a promotional endeavor. It's an expensive form of promotion, especially since there are no guarantees that anyone would play it.

For certain styles of rock music, 7-inch singles have been popular. Some people put out EPs, which contain less songs than an album, but neither an EP nor a single is considered cost effective on a CD. CDs are expensive to begin with, and they cost the same whether you put an album's worth of songs or just a single. But the less songs there are, the less you can charge. If you don't care about selling them and want to use the CDs strictly for promotion, then it doesn't matter. Most people who put out a CD want to sell it, however. When people buy a recording, they play it for others and a buzz can begin that way. Word of mouth can get sales started.

If you're pressing up what I call *danceable music*, referring to any type of music that could be played in a club by a live DJ, a single may suffice. And that single can be on vinyl, which is a lot cheaper to produce. When I began my record label, everyone was saying that vinyl would be dead shortly. Well, that was another example of everyone not knowing everything. I didn't give up on records and neither did DJs, who still like them best for mixing in clubs. But DJs in clubs are probably the only ones buying vinyl these days, so keep that in mind before pressing.

Deciding whether to go with a CD or a record can depend on where you plan to market it. Recently I had an offer from Mr. B., a graduate of my "How to Start & Run Your Own Record Label" course, who wanted me to get his act started in the New York City area. His single would have worked in the clubs, but it was on CD only. I went to several of the top stores selling dance music in New

York, and none had a CD player accessible. They all had a turntable for records, though, and recommended that the recording be pressed up on vinyl. Yet this CD single was doing very well in the Southeast, where Mr. B. was marketing it. And a DJ in one store who was in from a small town in Pennsylvania told me CDs did well in his area.

The bottom line is that you have to know the region where you plan to market your product. Before you press up a 12-inch single, do some research. Talk to people in record stores and see what format they recommend for your music. Go to the clubs where you feel your record would work and ask the DJs what they think. Do they prefer records or CDs? And while you're talking to these folks, let them hear your tape. Ask if they think it's worth pressing up to begin with. You may save yourself some time, money, and effort if there's not much enthusiasm from those you wish to reach. However, just because something may not work well in your region doesn't mean it won't work elsewhere. But if you don't have the means to market it elsewhere, you may want to wait before pressing it.

From the manufacturers I've spoken with, the format that seems to be on the fastest decline is cassettes. That's because the quality of cassettes is so much lower than a CD. DJs in clubs won't play them. Radio DJs don't want them. As a result, their value as a promotional tool is low. Cassettes can be duplicated more easily to be sold at gigs, and sometimes in stores. But most people prefer buying CDs because of the difference in quality. People like cassettes to play in the car or in a Walkman, but often they would rather have the CD for home listening. Retail prices on CDs have dropped considerably and people would rather spend the extra few dollars for the better sound.

## GETTING YOUR RECORDING MANUFACTURED

Most manufacturers will handle practically everything for you, depending on what you want. A few companies, such as Disc Makers in New Jersey, have in-house printing. They'll help you design the labels and other inserts for your product. Most pressing plants will farm out what they don't do themselves. The cost difference between doing each part of the process yourself and letting the plant do it for you is usually minimal. The choice may depend on your time and your resources. Do you have time to check out various services elsewhere? Do you have someone who could do the artwork for you?

It's always more cost effective if you can provide the manufacturer with camera ready art for your material. However, you've got to know what you want: two colors or four? How many pages do you want for your CD insert? Would you like a black or white cutout jacket with a nice label for your 12-inch single, or would you like a picture jacket? Certain colors are considered standard, and if you choose one of them it may not cost extra for a two-color insert. I've always handled artwork myself for my record label. Luck was on my side because the turquoise blue chosen for my labels was considered a standard color, so using it didn't cost extra.

Access to a computer and the knowledge of how to use it can help you to design your own labels, jackets, and inserts for CDs and cassettes. The printer can do it for you, but may not have the fonts (the style of type) you want. I've had the print for my inserts typeset at the printer who makes them and they worked fine. Again, it depends on what you want. I brought in a photo of one of my acts for the front panel and the printer superimposed it. The cover looked professional. But it all depends on your vision, and your ability to work with the printer to choose fonts, sizes, and designs that work. Otherwise, get a graphic artist to do the design.

What you put, or don't put, on the outside of your CD, record, or cassette can make or break its sales. Therefore, the package should be attractive or interesting enough to grab attention. When Ice T's record came out with a picture of his wife in a bikini on the cover, it caught people's eyes and sold. I don't recommend going that far, but having an image that attracts attention may provoke people to want to hear your recording. Ultimately the music will prevail, though. If the album sucks, people won't buy it just for the artwork.

But in the beginning, the visual may help to get someone interested enough to want to hear it.

When designing your labels, jackets, inserts, etc. use other artist's work as a guide as to what should be included. There's no right or wrong, but certain information is standard on most products. The presentation on the outside of the package is especially important for attracting people's attention once you've gotten your product into stores. The presentation can be simple, but it must look extremely professional. Having a picture or other graphics is optional. However, it must have a contact address or a telephone or fax number so that if someone hears your product and wants to get in touch with you, they can. Don't include your home address, though, unless you like unannounced visitors! Use a PO box or simply include a phone or fax number. You just want someone who may be interested in selling your product or signing your act to be able to find you.

Once you've put your package together, how many do you press up? It's probably best to press up no more than 1,000 units at first. You can always press up more if you need them. Develop a relationship with your manufacturer and see how fast the turn-around time is for when you need to reorder. For records and CDs, it's usually more cost effective to do a run of 1,000 at a time. The biggest expense is for the set-up. Once the machine is set and a run is being made, the difference between 500 and 1,000 copies is often minimal. Bigger numbers won't change the price that much. If you were thinking of just doing 500, it might be worth it to reconsider and do the larger amount for just a few dollars more. When ordering your printed material, it's also cost effective to order larger quantities. I always order extra labels, jackets, inserts, etc. because it's much more economical in the long run.

Cassettes are duplicated from a bin loop. The set-up is less so smaller quantities are not as painful. Make sure you shop around, though, because there's a price difference between manufacturers. Also, be sure to get a test pressing for all formats before your copies are pressed up. This way you can see if the quality is up to par.

Once you give your approval, the liability is with you. Before you order anything, ask for a sample of something manufactured at the company you're considering so you can see if the quality lives up to your standards before you invest.

## UTILIZING THE FINISHED PRODUCT

You're sitting the middle of your living room surrounded by a pile of CDs. You don't know whether to feel exhilarated or to scream "Oh my goodness, what am I doing!" To avoid the second response, create your plan before the product arrives. Have your research done. Have gigs set up. Have a list of stores to approach. Prepare a mailing announcing the release. In working with your manufacturer, make sure you order enough product so that you can give away some to people who may help you.

It's always better to have your promotional copies without the plastic wrap. Having it off makes playing the product more convenient. People hate the inevitable struggle to remove it and will be more likely to pop your recording in their player if it's ready to go. It's called lazy. When people give me CDs, I usually listen to the ones with no wrap sooner. This "No Shrink Wrap" policy applies to copies for reviewers, stores, and DJs. Either order your packages without the shrink wrap or remove the wrap from any pieces you intend to give away. Depending on where you get your product manufactured, you can often ask for a certain number without the plastic, which may save you a few dollars as well.

When going to stores or distributors, prepare some promotional pieces. Unless you have special labels marked "promotional copy," this means doing something to the packaging to indicate that it was given for free. Unfortunately, rubber stamps don't usually work because most surfaces are glossy and the ink smears. Most people punch a hole in the insert, or cut the corner of the insert or record jacket. Manufacturers now have CD jewel boxes available with a hole already added to signal that the product is a promotional copy. Use whatever way works best for you to indicate that it is a promo and not for sale. This is to protect you from the stores or distributors who might later try to sell you back the copy you gave them for free.

## LETTING THE PUBLIC KNOW ABOUT YOUR RECORDING

Once you have your product out, you want to let people know it's available. Different genres of music require different strategies. One way that can work for almost all music is to get media coverage. Start by sending a copy of your recording with a press release providing pertinent information. It might at least get you a mention of the release. Sending it to the person who reviews your style of music is also the way to go. It can be accompanied by a press release, or by a short cover letter asking for consideration for a review. Get a copy to as many appropriate reviewers at pertinent publications as possible.

When people read about your product, they may be curious enough to at least go to a store and ask to hear it. Reviews in *CMJ* will encourage interest from college radio. Reviews in national or international magazines may spark the curiosity of people in places you ordinarily can't reach. For example, *Billboard* is distributed all over the world. Labels looking to license records from the U.S. may request a copy as well if they read a positive review that indicates the record may meet their needs.

If you live in a city where there are clubs, *danceable music* can be taken into the clubs and given directly to the DJs to get a buzz going. If there's a specific club where you want to get your record played, call and find out who the DJ is on a night you're able to go down and what time they start. Give them about an hour to get set up and then approach them before it gets busy. I always ask DJs to please listen to my record and see if it could work for them. If you're friendly and confident, most will at least listen. If they really like it, they may mix it in while you wait.

I've had many pleasant surprises, especially when DJs tell me upfront they can't play my record that night, and then they play it. They warn you not to expect them to play it because they have to cover themselves. DJs also don't want to tell you they won't play it if they don't like it, so they'll say they may play it another time. Hopefully you'll learn to distinguish between being polite and being sincerely enthusiastic. When a DJ truly loves your record, there's a reasonable chance it'll be mixed in. DJs love good music, and good music speaks for itself. The bottom line is always the quality of your product.

## SELLING YOUR RECORDING

Ask almost any artist who has produced a record, tape, or CD as a marketing tool. They will probably tell you that finding a place for the product is the hardest part. Be prepared to store a lot of what you press up, at least at first. But have the game plan ready before the products arrive. If you do mailings to your following, an announcement of the release can be included in your next postcard or flyer. Include an address where fans can send money to order it. Make sure to state the fee for postage and handling. Figure out the cost of the mailing bag and postage and round it off. Wait until the check clears before you send the package out.

If you're doing gigs, that's obviously the place to begin marketing your music. When you do a song that goes over especially well, announce it's from your CD. Don't feel funny about announcing that it's for sale. It's expected. When people like a band, they're often happy to be able to buy the group's recording. Most rock and blues clubs don't care if you sell your product during your gig. If it's a venue you're not sure about, ask the manager if it's okay. It's usually good, though, to have your manager or a friend holding onto the product at gigs. It's also good to have some change for people who don't have the exact amount of money. Try to price your product at less than it would sell for in a store. If a store took some copies they'd pay you a lot less anyway.

Getting out and playing live can definitely help you sell your product. If you're as good as you think, people will want to buy a copy. If you don't sell it at the venue, you can announce what stores have it for sale or where they can get it by mail order. The more people hear you do a good live performance, the more demand there will be. If your music will fit in, try to do outdoor events in the summer. In addition, try to do free showcases and get on the mike whenever you can. Always announce that you've got something for sale.

Getting into stores with your recording is easier with some styles of music than with others. You've got to give stores a reason why your product will sell. Just being a good record isn't usually enough. You can have the greatest piece of music ever, but if the public doesn't hear about it, how will anyone know to buy it? The stores don't want your CD taking up precious space if it's not going to sell. Be prepared to tell stores what gigs you have, and where the act is getting exposure. Have a list of clubs where the record is being played. Is it getting radio play? Bring along copies of any reviews or other media attention you've received.

Unless there's a major buzz on your record, most stores will take it on consignment, a few at a time. However, you don't need to leave too many anywhere. The more copies that get left in stores, the more that can potentially be returned in six months or a year. Don't give out so many on consignment that you've got to re-order because the first batch may never sell. When stores sell out, they can order more. When leaving records on consignment, it's always good to have some sort of invoice the store can sign to show they were received. Handle the sales as professionally as possible if you want businesses to take you seriously.

Some styles of music do well with *in-store play*, which means the records are played in the store. Getting friendly with the people who work behind the counter (or the store DJ, if there is one) helps to get your music played for customers. They then have the opportunity to buy it on the spot. This is particularly effective with danceable music. DJs buy many records at once. At stores that sell a lot of danceable music, the store DJ can play a record and then pass copies out to all the enthusiasts whose hands go up. DJs want good new music and will buy whatever they like. You don't need artist development to sell to DJs. As long as the music is great, they'll buy it. Stores will be much more likely to take in your product, or buy copies outright, if they are danceable. They know these pieces will move when the DJs hear them.

Except when dealing with chain stores, never offer to leave your product on consignment, especially if your music is danceable or has a buzz that can help it sell. You can always change your mind, but leave the option open because many stores will buy them for cash on the spot, especially the smaller, specialty ones. With rock or other kinds of music that need to be heard on the radio, consignment is more likely. When you do leave your material on consignment, find out what their payment policy is before you leave anything. Have something for someone at the store to sign to show your product was received. It can be a real invoice or something you made up in a computer. Most stores will pay you when you come in after the product is sold. You always have the right to ask for your product back when it's been in the store for a while and isn't moving. At the same time, be sure to get paid for any copies that were sold. I've found most stores to be pretty good about this.

Finally, keep in touch with the stores to see if your product is selling. Always remember to thank anyone who helps you, even if it doesn't seem like much. Kind words will pay off later. If the people working in the stores get a good vibe from you this week, they may push your record harder the next. Then you'll really have something to say "thanks" about. Showing appreciation will never hurt you. But it can mean the difference between your record being pushed over someone else's.

## PART FIVE

# REACHING THE RECORD LABELS

## CHAPTER 15

# DIFFERENTIATING THE ADVANTAGES OF MAJOR AND INDIE LABELS

## MYTH:
*It's always better to sign with major labels because they have more money & power behind them.*

In my classes, most people are looking to get a deal with a major label. Major labels have a higher profile and spend more money, making them seem more appealing to sign with. But despite their lower profile and smaller budgets, independent labels have been responsible for breaking some of the biggest acts on the music scene today. Considering signing to an indie gives you more possibilities when it come to getting a deal for your music. Don't limit your possibilities when shopping a deal. Look to all labels as a possible home for your music.

### WEIGHING THE PROS AND CONS
Both major and independent labels have their advantages and disadvantages. If you're in the enviable position of having a choice of which label to sign with, there are many factors to take into account. The biggest is probably what style of music you're looking

to get a deal for. Certain genres, especially more commercial ones such as pop, which need a lot of radio and video promotion, might favor the majors. Music that's more specialized, that's a little off of the mainstream, or that's still too new to be widely accepted might find more potential on an independent.

I usually recommend signing with a strong independent label over a major, if you have a choice. The people working at indies seem to have more creativity, vision, and courage in terms of trying to break music that's innovative. Major labels have been picking up indie labels like crazy because they see these labels having tremendous success at recognizing and breaking new talent. Karin Berg, Senior Vice President of A & R at Warner Bros. Records, says, "If I were starting in the music business today, I would probably work at an independent label because I feel that everyone at independent labels is dedicated to breaking new music."

Independents work very differently from the major labels, often to your advantage. I saw an example of this when I released my third single. When the record took off, I got a lot of calls from major labels about picking it up. Because it was doing well, I wanted the deal to be quick. However, three or four months was the shortest period of time any of the majors could offer me for taking care of the paper work and pressing up product. Everyone felt badly knowing that although the single was doing well, it would probably die in the red tape. As a result, I accepted a deal with a strong indie and the single was out in the streets in two weeks. This is a good example of the difference between the majors and the independent labels.

Most strong independent labels are tied in with a major label for distribution anyway, or they have a good network of independent distribution. Indies usually specialize in a specific genre of music, and consequently know more about the nuances of marketing it. You won't get quite as lost at an independent label. Of course, being signed with a major can give you more prestige, as well as more exposure in promoting your music. Booking agents may take you more seriously as well. The choice may or may not be yours. I've put together a table to help you understand some of the differences. I admit I'm biased. But I know a lot of others who would agree with me. If you're lucky enough to have a choice of labels, think about the following:

| Major Labels | Independent Labels |
|---|---|
| Major labels are larger. They have bigger staffs working the projects. They can be less personal. | Indies are smaller but can be more personal. You can get to know the staff easier. |
| Majors have more money behind them. They can spend the most on promotion. They have higher budgets for more videos. | Indies don't always have as much money, but there's usually less waste. They may spend it more wisely and more creatively. |
| Majors are distributed by major distributors, which they own. | A large number of strong indies are distributed by the same major distributors. |
| Majors don't specialize in a particular genre of music, so their marketing focus is not in one particular direction. This is especially true of new styles of music. They do have specific divisions for some genres. | Indies usually specialize in specific genres of music, so they become extremely knowledgeable about marketing and focus their connections in one direction. They can get a reputation for doing certain genres. |
| Majors have a *sink or swim* policy with most new releases. When they release artists' recordings they wait to see which ones head for the top without much help. They let the others sink. | Many indies work each act as if it were their last. With fewer acts to market, they can give each more attention. They can't afford losses like the majors so they promote more of what they release. |

| | |
|---|---|
| Many of the people on top at the majors have been there for many years and may not know quite as much about current trends in music. They may rely more on staff to make musical judgments. | Indies tend to have younger people working for them who are more into current trends in music. These labels are usually founded by people who love the music they put out. The staff may go out to the clubs more. |
| There's more turnover in the middle level staff (promoters, sales reps, etc.) at major labels so it's harder to develop a rapport. There are more acts vying for attention. | The people who founded the label may be its staff. Often they bring in friends who are more loyal to the company. The staffs are small and tend to stick around longer. |
| Major labels have more clout in getting radio and video play and other sorts of promotion. | Indies don't always have it as easy as the majors to promote their product, but they do work hard. |

## DECIDING ON WHICH PATH TO CHOOSE

One consideration in deciding whether to pursue a major or an indie label for your record is your style of music. Artists with a more commercial appeal may need the big money and contacts of a major label. This is especially true of music such as pop and commercial rock. High budget videos and promotion may be more important, as well as heavy radio promotion. On the other hand, certain alternative styles of music may be more attractive to a very specific audience. Such an audience may look to the indies for their recordings. According to Wendy Goldstein at Geffen Records, "A lot of bands don't want to be signed with major labels because they've heard such nightmares from their friends about what happens. A lot want to go to smaller labels."

Independent labels who focus on marketing only what they do best are appealing. Kirk Burrowes says his label looks for specific types of artists: "Because we're Bad Boy Entertainment, not Elektra Records, who might have . . . a boutique set-up as far as their artists go . . . Anita Baker on Bad Boy would not probably work as on Elektra or Sony, etc., etc. Bad Boy itself is a movement, and we want the artist to fit into the flow of the movement and to further enhance it." Find a major label with that philosophy!

On the surface, the big budgets of the major labels may seem enticing. But ultimately, much of the money spent may come out of your royalties (see Chapter 22). And if your record sales don't make the money spent back pretty fast, you may be history just as quickly. Therefore, an A & R person at a major has to be concerned about being able to break an artist on their first or second album, before the artist goes into too much debt. Indie labels don't spend nearly as much money, so they have more leeway in terms of giving the artist an opportunity to develop. Karin Berg says

> I also believe that it's easier in terms of doing A & R to sign new, fresh bands to an independent label than it is to do that at a major. At a major, very often the bands need to have established their base already. You can make cheaper records at an independent label. When I started out, there were hardly any independent labels. The majors signed new bands, and broke bands, and it was all right to do that over a period of three, sometimes four albums. I don't know that we have the luxury of doing that.

Those inviting major label budgets can turn out to be what ends an artist's career on a major label. As Karin Berg explained,

> Very seldom is an artist dropped because the company doesn't believe that the artist is a good artist. Very often artists are dropped because their sales are not increasing and the record company cannot afford to keep increasing its debt. With each record release, as the debt becomes huger, the artist must sell more, to the point that they

must be platinum to recoup . . . It's very difficult for a major to offer an inexpensively produced record to radio and expect it to get played. That's not to say that we don't want to do it. But there's different expectations once you're on a major, not just from the major but from radio and from the "marketplace" . . . I still think it's possible for majors to break acts, but in order to do that there has to be a big campaign, and almost total financial commitment on every level. Which is not to say that majors are unwilling to do that, but if you do that with every release, somebody's not going to make some money. That can only last for so long. Right now there are a number of start-up labels and they are generally given about five years to recoup. A major that is already in the business, and has been in the business for a long time doesn't have that luxury.

How do you decide whether to go for a major or independent label deal? You may not even have a choice. But if you target labels to go after, focus on both indies and majors that seem like they would do well with your music. Since there are advantages and disadvantages in going with either choice, my recommendation is to make decisions based on the individual label. Be open-minded about major and indie labels, giving yourself the most possibilities for your music.

## CHAPTER 16

# GETTING
# THE RIGHT
# ATTITUDE

MYTH:
*Everyone in the music business
has an attitude so I need one, too.*

When I first got involved in the music industry, I had a hard time understanding the attitudes of so many of the people I encountered. I noticed a discernible lack of respect for punctuality. "Everybody in the music industry is late," I was told. My artists and producers were late for the studio. I'd wait over an hour for someone I had an appointment with. Instead of apologies I got "you know how it is." But I honestly didn't.

At first I was considered a nobody, so certain people with more credits under their belts seemed to expect their asses to be kissed. Now that I've paid my dues, people who want something from me try to kiss mine, which is annoying and unnecessary. This business can change a person. I see industry people get a new title or a hit record and they forget where they came from. In what can sometimes be a plastic world, the kissing up is phoney. I've seen nice people turn into jerks I don't want to know anymore. When I call them on it, they say "That's the way this business is. If you can't beat 'em, join 'em." What creates this counter-productive attitude?

## DON'T JOIN 'EM. BEAT 'EM!

There are a lot of creeps in the music industry. This is a glamour oriented business, so a lot of people are anxious to work in it. Competition is stiff and salaries, particularly at the lower level positions, can be low compared to other industries. Because there are so many people willing to work for a lower salary in exchange for the perks and prestige of working for a record label, there are a lot of folks who aren't really happy in their chosen profession. They may have the job they wanted, but they aren't making the sort of money necessary to support the lifestyle they'd like to live. Prestige can't feed the family. As a result, many of them try to let the prestige at least feed their egos and we're expected to buy into it.

I've seen the industry change some very nice people. Many feel it's the only way to survive. They believe if they don't become cutthroats, their own throats may be cut. So they forget about respect and manners. They play on other people's needs. And they do as they please, often just as an affirmation of their perceived power. I've had people promise me the sun, the moon, and the stars, and then never return my phone calls. I know of people who've had their songs ripped off, their contracts broken, and their artists stolen. Then they adopt a dog-eat-dog attitude themselves. If you want to sell your soul for this business, go for it. But decency and respect can go a longer way. It might take a bit more time, but the rewards of feeling good about yourself as a person might be worth it in the long run. Booking agent Jeannie Stahlman says "You always outlast the assholes. They always self destruct because they're so busy pissing people off that they make mistakes."

Public Relations specialist Terrie Williams is president of The Terrie Williams Agency, the largest African-American owned communications firm in the country. She's also author of the book, *The Personal Touch: What You **Really** Need to Succeed in a Fast-Paced Business*. In her book Williams emphasizes her refreshingly simple approach to dealing with people: *By treating people with respect, being there for them, and showing integrity & compassion, it will come back to you multiplied.* When I first met Terrie Williams, I was impressed with her warmth and easy-going manner. She told me that

> The fact of the matter is, everything that goes around, comes around . . . it is the law of nature and you do not put your foot on anyone's back. . .you can't get away with doing wrong or evil . . . eventually there's no place for it. Nothing lasts forever. The way you treat people when you are on top is the way you'll be treated when the lights go down. It is imperative to treat everybody the same and never forget where you came from . . . you can lose all this tomorrow and then where would you be? How could I even think . . . because I've achieved a little bit of success . . . of not taking time to talk to someone who's on their way up?

This attitude has brought Williams great success, and even more respect from everyone she works with. Her wonderful positive attitude attracted Eddie Murphy as her first client. You don't have to screw people to advance in the music industry. Doing a good job and having the right product or talent wins out in the long run. When you have what it takes to succeed, you can get the respect you deserve, without having to lose your values. And you sleep better at night.

## WHAT GOES AROUND COMES AROUND

There are a lot of terrific people in the industry. I never sunk to the level of not being straight, friendly, and respectful with everyone, and that was a large factor in my getting as far as I did. People liked me and wanted to help a decent person. I stood out among the not-so-nice people. Nice people attract other nice people. If you keep your standards high, you'll find each other. Over the years I've gotten amazing support from people who said they were helping me because they wanted to see a nice person win!

One incident in particular gave me heart. When I was getting ready to mix my fourth record, I asked Chris Gehringer, a top engineer who's now at DMS, the mastering lab at the Hit Factory, if he would listen to my demo and give me suggestions for the mix. I only knew him because he'd mastered a few records for my label. Chris asked me when and where the mix would take place, as well as whether I'd like him to come down and help. Although he gets a lot of money for his services, Chris ended up coming down to the studio and assisting in the mix, doing the edits himself, all as a favor to me. When I asked him why, he told me he'd like to see a nice person like me succeed. He appreciated the consideration I'd always shown him, and that I always thanked him for doing a good job. We still keep in touch.

I teach classes called "Nice Girls On Top" and "Nice Guys On Top." People who take them say they're tired of being nice, which is sad. We absolutely can be nice, as long as we selectively choose who to go out of our way for. Being nice doesn't mean groveling or getting taken advantage of. It does mean treating people with respect, no matter what you get back. It does mean not stabbing people in the back or taking advantage of someone. It does mean not doing to others what you don't want done to you. We have to maintain these standards. If the nice people in the music industry get so fed up that they go in the other direction, this will be a pretty sad place. There are many decent people out there. We just have to be patient.

## TO THINE OWN SELF BE TRUE

If you want people to treat you with respect, make sure you're treating yourself with lots of it, too. If you want to get taken seriously, take yourself seriously first! The way you treat yourself reflects on the way others see and treat you. People treat you as you allow them to. If you act apologetic, like you're not sure you have a right to go for a deal, people won't take you seriously. A confident, yet courteous approach will help people to take notice of you in a positive way. Respecting yourself and expecting to be treated as a professional will reflect in your attitude. Believe in yourself and others will follow your lead! Don't sink to the level of the disrespectful. You won't like yourself. As Terrie Williams told me, "This is not brain surgery! It's not revolutionary. It's treating people the way you want to be treated. It's that simple."

There are many simple actions that you can do to help you be remembered as a decent person. Be aware of these things when you create your music business persona. People in my music business classes always laugh when I tell them not to forget their manners. *Please* and *thank you* can go a long way in this business. It makes people remember you. It's amazing how many people get so jaded that they lose their basic sense of courtesy. In comparison, people like and respect me more because I try to be polite and gracious to everyone in my dealings. This allows people to remember me in a positive light. I always thank anyone who helps me, no matter how small the favor. Assume everyone will be nice to you. If they're not, it's their problem, not yours. Nonetheless, always keep your guard up. People say things they don't intend to follow through with all the time. That's just the way it is. Don't take anyone's promises seriously until their actions own up to their words. Keep your expectations realistic. This avoids setting yourself up for disappointment and resentment towards the person making the promise. If you don't take things seriously, you won't have to feel angry later on if they don't follow through. If their word is good, it can also be a pleasant surprise when they do as they say.

People say a lot a things they don't mean to please you in the short run. At the time you're speaking, you'll feel good about them. Sometimes making promises makes insecure people feel more powerful. Sometimes people mean what they're saying at the moment, but just forget about it later. Don't have any expectations. If someone promises to take your tape to an A & R person, don't put all your hopes on it. You can't fragment yourself by running after people making promises. It's too exhausting. Keep networking until you find the people who do follow through. And make sure you keep your own word. It'll give you a good reputation in the long run.

Don't be unsolicitous to those you think won't be able to help you. If you meet others in the same position as you, be friendly and helpful. Don't be afraid to share information. No one is your competition if you have what it takes. Build a support system among peers instead of blowing them off for those in higher places. The struggling musician sitting next to you at a seminar may get signed tomorrow. And that individual *will* remember if you snubbed them today. They *may* also remember to help you if you were friendly. Make friends with everyone. It increases your chances of contacts.

## DO THE RIGHT THING

My own personal music industry etiquette goes like this: Don't worry about others who may not be so nice. Just be concerned about taking care of yourself and keep going in the direction you've set for yourself. Laugh off the obnoxious club manager, the A & R guy who doesn't return your calls, and the promoter who doesn't remember you after souping you up last week. It's just the way it can be in this business. They'll get theirs in the end.

Rather than getting angry and frustrated when people don't return your calls promptly, understand that there's sometimes a warped sense of etiquette in this business. It's very common for industry people, even decent ones, not to return calls promptly, or not return them at all. This is a personal business and phone calls can reach high volume. There are days I can get no work done because the phone doesn't stop ringing, and I don't even work for a label. People can get legitimately backed up, put your message aside with the intention of calling later, and never get to it. It's not uncommon to have the call returned when you've long since given up. The message may surface weeks later. Just accept it.

I've learned that "Can I call you right back?" can mean "I can't talk now and am in a hurry. I mean well and will try but just want to get off the phone now." I just accept it. Don't bombard people with calls. If they want to talk to you they will. Wait at least a few days the first time and a week or two after that before trying again. If they're backed up they don't need to be pressured. Not long ago

I left messages for five people at labels, all of whom know me. It was a busy time of year. Over two weeks later I got the first return call, with an apology. Four of them eventually got back to me. The last was almost a month later. She didn't apologize for the delay and just said she was returning my call. I had to stifle myself from asking "Do you feel no shame about calling after a month and acting like it was yesterday?" Of course I just thanked her for returning the call. That's the way this business is. People are very busy. And until you are a big success, you're not a priority.

Of course you should return calls promptly. Some will notice. Punctuality is another thing I highly recommend to make you stand out. Music people tend to live by a different clock. People at record labels and other corporations may keep you waiting for hours for the appointment you made weeks before. Things come up. Gigs are known for starting late. When my seminars begin, there may be three people there. I always warn them not to spread out because the room will fill up. It does, with students arriving as much as an hour late. It seems to be a music thing to disrespect punctuality. That's a crock. I always remember those three people who arrived on time.

Be cheerful. Don't forget to keep smiling. It makes you more pleasant to talk to. Many people are always happy to see me because of my upbeat, friendly personality. In London I can get in to people at most labels, and I've been told people like seeing me because my personality makes me like "a breath of fresh air." Don't tell industry people your problems. Let everyone but your closest friends think you're doing well. When you meet people along the way who ask how your career is going, always give them an enthusiastic "great!" No one will check you out. People are usually more attracted to those who they think are doing well, and who have positive things to say. Be one of them and you'll attract even more positive contacts and deals. The only attitude you should be showing is a confident belief in your talent.

# CHAPTER 17

# FINDING THE ALL-IMPORTANT A & R PERSON

MYTH:
*An A & R person is not that important
in getting a record deal.*

t's amazing how many people come up to me before a music business seminar and whisper that they feel stupid asking because they know they should know, but "what exactly does A & R mean?" Most people know that an A & R person is who they want to get their material to at a label, but many don't know why. Even more have no idea what A & R stands for. And because it seems so obvious, they're too embarrassed to ask.

## UNDERSTANDING WHY A&R PEOPLE ARE SO IMPORTANT

A & R stands for *Artists and Repertoire.* The A & R person at the record label is the one who you as an unsigned artist want to reach. This is the individual who listens for new talent and makes decisions or recommendations as to whether to sign an artist to the label. Once you get signed, the A & R person oversees your development. An A & R person finds the *Artists* and develops their

*Repertoire* of material. Kirk Burrowes of Bad Boy Entertainment explains that "[An A & R person's] primary role and function should be, once an artist is signed, to know what that person is all about and how they can make that artist become fully realized in their potential as an artist, and select the repertoire that's going to aid them in becoming the artist they want to be."

An effective A & R person finds the right songs and producers to work with the artist, if needed. In general, an A & R person supervises the development of the artist from inception of ideas to a completed product. Kathy Baylor of Universal Records says that "In the beginning [an A & R person is] the most important person because they are the point person for your project."

And according to Jeff Fenster, Senior Vice President of A & R at Jive Records, the A & R person "is hopefully closest to the artist's vision, and will help motivate the entire company to get behind the artist." Fenster also says that an A & R person will deal with the artist's manager, especially in getting the artist out touring, and keep in contact with the label's publicity, marketing, promotion, art, and video departments.

A & R people may also determine the amount of your recording budget. But they aren't necessarily the ones who handle how the budget is allotted or the actual production in the studio. A & R people used to have more responsibilities when it came to production of an album. But with the growing use of independent producers, the days of an A & R person handling all production matters are in the past. The A & R person may exercise the right to tell you to use certain people for specific areas of your production, however, and will have the final say on the finished product.

## BUILDING RELATIONSHIPS WITH A&R PEOPLE

You want to stay on good terms with A & R people because they're responsible for guiding the production and development of the artist. A good relationship is important to help the process go smoothly and get the job done properly. According to Wendy Goldstein, the Director of A & R at Geffen Records, "A & R is all about relationships. I've been doing A & R for fourteen years, and I've been more effective on certain projects over others because of my relationship with that particular artist. The role of an A & R person is sort of like the role of an agent to an actor. It's a personal relationship, built on trust . . . mutual respect."

Most A & R people I've spoken to emphasized the importance of developing a good relationship when working with an A & R person. It can help get a better project done. It can get you more label support. Although an artist usually doesn't have a choice, it's good to get signed by an A & R person whose ear and judgement you do respect. When the A & R person and the artist don't respect each other's judgment, it can put a damper on the project. It can create a tugging of wills, leading to disharmony, which is obviously not good for the project.

## CREATING THE ALL-IMPORTANT BUZZ

Although it's possible to record a good demo, send it to an A & R person, and get signed on that alone, this doesn't happen very often. So how do you get an A & R person's attention? How do you get one to take notice? One way to call attention to yourself as an act is to create that *buzz* I talked about in Chapter One. Kathy Baylor explains that "A buzz is a really, really, really good tool in getting a record deal. If there's a buzz out there about you, the same way the people on the street are going to hear it, we're going to hear it."

Many A & R people say they are impressed if there's a *story* about your act, such as knowing that you have large numbers coming to your shows. According to Jeff Fenster, "The first step is to develop the artist. You've got to bring it out of the basement to some degree, to get someone to know about you. We want to know that artists have the drive to get their stuff out." Many A & R people have scouts who go to clubs, while some go themselves. Fenster emphasizes that he likes to see an artist who's willing to work and push to get his or her music out there. Having drive will impress an A & R person, as long as you have the talent and material to back it up. Karin Berg at Warner Bros. says "I don't like to listen to tapes of bands that aren't playing live." Once a band is touring and playing live, they can send a tape. As to what else she wants in a band, "First I look for originality, depth in the material . . . some depth, not all of it has to be deep . . . and intelligence."

A & R people have contacts all over the place. I've gotten deals because someone working in a store called an A & R person to recommend a record I'd released. A good A & R person always has their ear, or someone else's, to the street. Wendy Goldstein says that A & R people looking to sign alternative bands will often buy independently released records to see what's being put out. Many bands, especially alternative, get signed based on putting out their own CD. She says that in hip hop or R & B she gets recommendations from producers whose work she respects and from lawyers she knows to have a good ear. Goldstein also has scouts on the streets.

Rose Noone, the Director of A & R for Island Records, is always on the look-out for good bands. She says

> We look down the CMJ charts . . . we read local papers from all over the country looking for bands. We make phone calls to people we know in different cities and ask "what's happening? What's going on? What bands should I look into?" If you create a buzz and create some action about you or your band in your area . . . in your town or territory, you're bound to be heard of. If the music stands up, people will come and see you. It's word of mouth. You have to give someone a reason to talk about your band. Some times it doesn't necessarily take creating a whole buzz, but I think it's healthy for a band to build a foundation, even before you get into the process of shopping to a label . . . Tripping Daisy created a huge buzz. They did a lot on their own . . . and people came to them. I found out about them and went down and looked into it.

Kathy Baylor also looks for something special. "It's a very subjective thing. I know it when I hear it or see it . . . I look for the makings of somebody who is trying to set a precedent in music, who's not necessarily rehashing what everyone else has done. If it makes the hair stand up on the back of my neck, then I would sign." Arnie Goodman puts out mainly rock and blues at Viceroy Records. He says he's looking for "bands that are ready get deals. I not only want to hear their tape, but I want to see what they look like. Then I'll go see them play."

Rose Noone was involved in signing singer Tracy Bonham. She says "We heard about her through a publicist friend in Boston who called us up and said 'I saw this artist last night who's phenomenal.' She sent a tape down and it was great, fantastic. We went up to see her . . . and she was great. We wanted to sign her right there and then." This was a case of Tracy being discovered by someone in her city.

## FINDING THE RIGHT A & R PERSON

Ideally we should be concerned with finding the right A & R person to work with because not all are good at what they do. Some have been around a long time and aren't as up as they should be on current trends of music. Realistically, we'd probably be content with anyone as long as we got a deal with a decent record label. Kathy Baylor advises

> Don't be discouraged when somebody passes on your material because the A & R process is not a diplomatic one necessarily. One or two people are listening to your material and deciding whether or not it's viable. You have all of their little quirks . . . their likes and dislikes . . . their musical history going into that decision. Just because one person, or even five people decide that they don't particularly care for it doesn't mean it's not viable.

Baylor emphasizes that an artist has to persist after being rejected because the next A & R person could love their material.

Most large labels have A & R people who specialize in different types of music, so it's good to try to find out who focuses on your genre. If you're not sure, call the A & R department at the label and ask. Independent labels tend to focus on more specific genres, so their A & R people may sign everything.

A & R people can be the key to your successful music career. They are instrumental in getting you signed to that deal you want. They also have the power to lead you in the direction that will help you get the most out of your record deal. Since each A & R person is different, you've got to try every way possible to get their attention. There's no one way, however, or as Rose Noone says, "There are no rules."

CHAPTER 18

# NETWORKING FOR SUCCESS

## MYTH:
*It doesn't matter how good my music is—
it's who I know that counts.*

t's who you *can* know that counts, and you *can* get to know the right people. Everyone can make the contacts necessary to get signed to a record label. If you learn to consistently be where industry people are (seminars, organizations, industry parties, clubs, etc.), to set specific goals and learn how to ask for what you need, eventually you'll get to know the right people. Having said this, I'll also tell you that no matter who you know, a record deal is still contingent on your having enough talent *and* strong material to merit a deal. Make sure that end is in place before you work your contacts.

## SENDING UNSOLICITED MATERIAL

To get anyone to even listen to your material, you need to know people who'll get you the right introductions. Most A & R people don't want what's known as *unsolicited tapes*. Unsolicited means the label didn't ask for it. It also means they probably don't know you, the tape is being sent in cold, and it may very well go directly into a box to be discarded. According to Wendy Goldstein at Geffen Records, "For the most part, the general stock statement when you call up any major label is 'we do not accept any unsolicited material.'"

One reason A & R people are reluctant to listen to unsolicited tapes is the threat of lawsuits. They don't want to run the risk of later being accused of stealing a piece from the song of an artist who sent in unsolicited material. It has happened that a singer/songwriter submits a tape of original material, doesn't get signed, hears a similarity between their song and one released on the label, and sues the label for copyright infringement. Not listening to tapes that weren't requested is a label's way of avoiding this problem.

If you do get lucky and an A & R person agrees to hear your material, ask how it should be addressed so it won't be thrown in what's known as the "slush pile." You may have to write something special on the envelope or send it to someone else's attention. So how do you make your tape a solicited one? How do you get to the contacts needed to reach the A & R people?

## LEARNING TO ASK

If you don't have contacts, you still have your mouth. Learn how to use it. Your mouth is your best resource. Networking is important because you need to get to know people in order to make contacts. Networking entails communicating what you need. More often than you might think we don't get what we want because we don't clearly articulate what we need. We assume people won't accept us or will say "no," so we don't bother asking. We cut ourselves off before we begin, possibly passing up our biggest opportunity by second guessing others.

It's amazing how much more comes your way when you get over the fear of asking. I'd never be where I am if I hadn't accepted the fact that the worst thing that can happen is a *"no"* response, which I can handle. When I started my record label, I kept asking for introductions and resources. If I didn't know how to do something, I'd ask for help. Sometimes I'd get turned down, but I kept asking. Eventually someone gave me an answer or a name. You've got to ask for more and expect more. A confident attitude gets taken more seriously. Ask as if you expect to get what you need without sounding apologetic. Raise your expectations. Only asking for a little rarely gets you a lot.

## SIX DEGREES OF SEPARATION

When I first entered the music industry I knew no one. I was a school teacher, a white female rapper, who no one took seriously. But I took myself seriously. I went out and talked to everyone I could, letting them know what I needed. Lots of people think I talk too much. But it helped me to get my needs out there and find people who could help me. As I kept asking for contacts and resources, my rolodex got fuller. My world kept expanding. The more you ask for, the more you'll get.

It's very important to learn networking skills. I emphatically believe that we're all six degrees of separation from the people who can get us what we need. The theory behind six degrees of separation is that even though the world is big, you would not need to go through more than six people to get to someone you need to reach. We're all connected to each other by someone.

Everyone knows someone. My own networking has proven this. I didn't get where I am today by luck. My contacts weren't handed to me on a silver platter. I didn't know a soul in the music industry at first. But I talked to everyone. My first contact came from the mother of one of my students whose father turned out to be a successful songwriter. I asked to meet him and he gave me the number of someone else. This next person hooked me up with a music attorney who loved the concept for my rap. She introduced me to someone else. And so on and so on. The bottom line is that I worked every contact! Everyone became a potential foot in the door of someone who could help me.

There's always someone you know or can meet who knows someone who can get you further ahead. Your dentist may have a cousin who works at PolyGram. The man sitting next to you at a seminar could be the lawyer for a famous artist. The woman from whom you buy coffee every morning may have a sister who's married to a big manager. You'll never know if you don't speak up. If you keep talking to everyone you can about what you're doing, you'll make the necessary contacts. But you've got to be sure to mention to everyone you meet what it is you're looking for. The more people that you put your needs out to, the more chance you have of finding the one person who can help get you in the door.

Use each contact as a stepping stone. You've got to find that first someone who can send you to someone else and so on and so on. If you're shy, get over it or get someone to represent you. Hone your people skills. The more that people like you, the more they'll go out of their way for you. Continue with a courteous, friendly attitude as you work the people you meet. Networking is the best tool we've to get ahead and it doesn't have to cost a dime. So how do we get the most out of networking?

Public Relations specialist Jane Blumenfeld believes that in the music industry we are only three degrees of separation from anyone. "I don't know a lot about the actual theory on it but I remember that when I saw [the play *Six Degrees of Separation*] it stuck in my mind. It's three degrees of separation in the music industry. Where is the six coming from? I keep bumping into people I know. Interns that I've had working for me are now doing press for The Rolling Stones." The music industry is actually a very small community compared to the rest of the world. It actually has never taken me more than two or three people to make a contact. The key is putting yourself in the thick of the music industry, which may eventually mean being in a large city.

## THE ART OF NETWORKING

Networking is an art. Learning this art will enable you to start developing those all-important relationships. Knowing what your needs are is the key to networking successfully. By evaluating the overall picture of what you're trying to accomplish, you can focus your efforts more effectively.

Develop both short and long term goals. Target specific things you're looking for when you network. Make either a list or an outline of what you need. Don't be too general, such as just saying that you want to get a record deal. Figure out the first piece of information or contact you need to get that deal. Create specific goals for your networking, letting each goal reached take you a step closer to getting a record deal.

For example, you might first want to figure out which would be the best labels to approach. Once you've made your list of potential labels, ask around to find the best contact person at that label. You can even call the label itself to learn the name of the A & R person who specializes in your genre of music. Next, your goal is to find someone who knows him to give you an introduction. It doesn't have to be formal.

Again, don't be afraid to ask. If you meet someone who vaguely knows a person at a record label you're interested in, ask if you can use their name when you make the call. Often just dropping a name (i.e., "Richard Brooks suggested I call you") can get you through. Sounding professional can also help you to pull it off. If you go to a label person who says they liked your tape but can't use it, ask for a recommendation to other labels. They might know a label where it might work well. Labels do send material to one another. If you get signed on a label recommended by another A & R person and do very well, chances are that both you and the label will remember this connection. That person will now be hooked up for a favor. Ask to use their name, or if you want to be ballsy ask whether they'd make a phone call on your behalf. ASK!!! It can't hurt. The worst anyone can do is say "no." And all you need is one person to say "yes."

When I first went to London with my rap material I met one person, Martin. He was a rock promoter who introduced me to one friend at Phonogram, Jeff, who was in A & R. When I met with Jeff, who turned me down for his label, I picked his brain. I asked him to recommend anyone he could think of to call. I also asked permission to drop his name. In addition, whenever I met anyone through that initial contact, I'd ask for the names of more people to call. I'd also ask to use their name. I always phoned afterwards to thank them. From my one rock promoter I networked my way into almost every label in London. I learned to ask everyone if they could get me on guest lists for clubs and concerts. I never paid to get in anywhere in London and I have no doubt I could still do it! All you need is one person and then you have to work your way to a large number of contacts.

## FINDING YOUR INITIAL CONTACTS

One way to meet industry people is to join industry organizations. Find the group or groups that are right for you. Sometimes there are free events sponsored by the performing rights organizations. You don't always have to be a member to attend. There are also many songwriters' organizations, as well as workshops in which to participate. I've been to events at the National Academy of Popular Music and the Songwriter's Guild and met wonderful people at both. The Songwriter's Hall of Fame has free showcases featuring the material of their songwriters. Loads of industry people attend. Rap Coalition has regular free seminars for people trying to break into hip hop. NARAS (National Academy of Recording Arts & Sciences—The Grammy people) has free panels periodically, as well as showcases. They've been great!

Many of these organizations have chapters in a number of cities, although it's harder to find them in smaller cities. Call the number in my resource section to find out about their activities and locations. If you're really serious about pursuing a music career, you may have to move to a city that offers opportunities. Or, be prepared to travel to other cities to take part in activities.

When you join an organization, get involved. Try to volunteer some of your time for the organization. It's a great way to meet others in the industry. While doing volunteer work you never know whose brain you may get to pick for contacts. Joining and not participating can be almost worthless. You'll get the most for your money by working with other members and learning from them.

For example, I've interacted with some very informative people as an active member of Women In Music, Inc. and NARAS. You've to find the organization best suited to your talents.

Go to industry functions, seminars, etc. and meet people there. Keep track of the *Billboard* calendar section for the dates. Many seminars are listed in the resource section of this book. When you go to any industry event, talk to everyone you meet. Be friendly, have business cards handy, and see how many you can collect from others. Seminars that specialize in your style of music can be better than very large, general ones. It's more productive when you know that almost everyone you meet is involved in the kind of music you are. I've made some of my best contacts in dance music and rap sitting around the pool at the Winter Music Conference held in Miami every March.

Most seminars have showcases where you can apply to appear. But you still have to take care of your own expenses, even if you perform. It can be more economical to find seminars more convenient to where you live or where you have people with whom you can stay. My parents live in Miami, which was why I went to the Winter Music Conference every year.

Being at a music seminar offers numerous opportunities for meeting people. Participants wear badges with their names and often their company or position, so you can always check out who's around you. Talk to all the people you can. Don't be selective about finding someone "important." You can learn from everyone. Talk to people at the exhibitions, at the showcases, and in the bathroom. If you want to attract even more people, during a panel think of a good question or statement and get up on the mike. Make sure you give your name and occupation. If possible, mention what it is you're looking for. If you sound good, people will come over to you afterwards. I've met some great people that way.

Usually after a panel concludes at a seminar, a majority of the audience gang-rushes the speakers. Most speakers hate that. I do. When everyone comes at you at once, it's hard to absorb anything. Often people I meet right after a seminar become a blur to me.

Under these circumstances, I wouldn't recommend throwing a tape at a panelist even if it's someone you very much want to reach. That's still unsolicited. While everyone is straining for their attention, you can be patient. When the crowd clears, in a very professional manner introduce yourself and ask for a business card. Say you'll get in touch after the seminar. If you make a good impression, they might remember you when you call. Ask if it's okay to send a tape next week. Or take a chance that they're not leaving immediately and try to find them later on in a more congenial setting. It's better to send your tape later, though, rather than risking it getting buried under all the tapes dumped on the person.

I like to put out my hand when introducing myself. It creates a more professional connection. Always shake hands with a firm grip. It makes a good impression and shows confidence. They don't have to know you might be squeezing hard because of nerves! A wet noodle limp handshake depicts a lack of confidence. A solid grip makes a nice impression. Be as professional in your approach as possible. It can make a difference. You might stand out from the many being pushy for their attention. The comparison may help you get taken more seriously. It may also help you be remembered in a positive way when the individual receives your tape.

## GET DOWN WITH THE MUSIC PEOPLE

I've always said in my classes that my best friends in the music business have been the DJs and the people who work in record shops. As mentioned in Chapter 16, people at labels often take their jobs in order to get the glamour, the perks, etc., and aren't always as kind as we'd like them to be. On the other hand, those working in the stores are usually there because they love music. These folks are often DJs, producers, and engineers, and they can be the best people to have on your side. They're usually the most up-to-date on everything current in the music industry.

People who work in record shops know what's selling. They know what label is putting out what type of music. They know who's good with females, R & B, alternative, etc. If you're able to get friendly with them, they can be a great source of information. They can recommend producers, recording studios, and almost every other resource you may need. Many know the names of A & R people and some know them personally. If they believe in your act, they may want to help you. They can then brag to everyone about how they discovered you. I've gotten two record deals through the recommendation of someone in a record store. He's now an A & R person at a major label. Things change quickly in this business.

Pick a quiet time and go into the stores that sell your kind of music. Bring a demo tape and a friendly smile. Introduce yourself to the DJ or the salesperson who handles your genre. Say that you're about to start shopping the tape and would appreciate some suggestions, if they have time to listen. Many will, especially if you pick a time when there are few customers in the store. If you get turned down, say "thanks anyway" and move on. Someone will talk to you. The people in stores are usually friendly and many of them are trying to get their own careers off the ground. I don't know if I would have succeeded without the help of my friends in stores. They gave me contacts; they offered encouragement; they taught me about the industry and its standards and traditions; and they gave me an opportunity to network with people I sincerely liked. I'm still grateful to them.

Club DJs can also be very helpful. Talk to the ones that work with your style of music. They'll be your toughest critics, but they know music. Many of them are producers, and do work for the labels. ASK for help!! If they bring you to a label and you get signed and do well, it reflects well on them. Hang out in the DJ booth. It can get annoying when they ignore you while they're spinning records, but you can meet good contacts there. Other people hanging out may be able to help you. Go to the clubs that play your music a lot. Often A & R people are there as well. Keep asking for help until someone gives you a name or a recommendation.

## NETWORKING TO THE MAX

Networking is selling or marketing yourself. You need to get people's interest in your talent or material. The music business is a business. If you want to earn a living doing music, keep a business perspective as you work towards getting a record deal. Read books on successful marketing and apply the skills to your music. It'll help you seem more serious about what you're doing. Business people like working with creative people who have a business sense.

Public Relations specialist Terrie Williams recommends dropping a note to anyone who helped you, such as an A & R person who met with you, a journalist who came to your gig, a promoter who gave you a contact that worked, etc. Williams has sent me friendly notes when I've done something for her and they always make me feel even better about wanting to do something another time. Courteous notes can work. Make sure you follow through on your endeavors. Make the follow-up phone calls.

Joy Pedersen, a networking consultant, is president of New Jersey-based Express Success, and says that "networking is an effective method of accessing the knowledge and contacts of others to achieve goals." She suggests asking people you're dealing with who they know that you can also talk with. Making sure to thank everyone who helps you even a little is essential, according to Pedersen. It's up to you to decide whether a verbal thank you is sufficient, or whether a note or gift would be more appropriate to the favor. Pedersen encourages people to ask lots of questions when meeting someone who might be a good contact. People love to talk about themselves. Ask questions about their position that will allow you to find what they can do for you.

Public Relations specialist Jane Blumenfeld advises bands to have their own business cards to give the act a more professional front. I always recommend having a nice business card no matter what end of the business you're on. People can be superficial and a card that stands out will impress and send a message of success. It's amazing how many people have said to me "Nice card. You're doing well, right?" Right! Doing well at putting up a successful front.

A large function such as a seminar or party can be a great place to make contacts. I recommend wearing a jacket with pockets so you can keep *your* cards in one pocket, and keep a pen in the other. Put *other people's* cards in the pocket with the pen. When you've finished talking to someone and have their card, make a note about who they were on the back after you walk away. If it's a good contact, make a note of personal stuff, such as their kids, a favorite ball team, their allergies, etc. This allows you to bring something personal up when you speak with them again. If this individual had a cold, ask how they're feeling. If they love the Yankees, wait until the team wins to call and comment on something they've done. It makes people feel good that you paid attention to them personally. It creates a sense that you know each other on at least a small personal level.

Networking is the beginning of building those all-important relationships. If you want to get to almost anyone, it can be achieved through working everyone you encounter. By using a combination of confidence, professionalism, perseverance, friendliness, and patience, you can find your way. We are all six degrees of separation from everyone, and in the music industry, you may very well get your contact in three.

## CHAPTER 19

# DETERMINING WHO CAN SHOP A DEAL FOR YOU

MYTH:
*It doesn't matter who shops my deal,
as long as they have contacts.*

Labels don't like to deal with an artist directly. They prefer to speak with your formal representative. It's considered more professional. An A & R person can speak more candidly about your material to someone else, so no matter how much you think you can speak for yourself, as the artist it's always better to have someone else representing you. The person shopping your tape should have good contacts, know what they're talking about, and have your best interests at heart. The question then becomes, who should shop your deal?

## CHOOSING BETWEEN A MANAGER AND AN ATTORNEY

Ideally, you should have a manager shop your deal. Since managers get a percentage of what you earn over a period of time, they'll work the hardest to get you the best deal possible. A manager is most likely to look out for your long term interests. But sometimes you may not have as good a manager as you'd prefer, so other options need to be explored.

Some artists use an attorney as their manager. However, I find it preferable to have someone who specializes in only one responsibility to represent an artist. Remember, managers are managers and attorneys are attorneys. If you consider using a attorney as your manager, find out where their priorities lie. It's amazing how many attorneys are trying to get into the more creative end of the business. Straight legal work can get pretty tedious. I used to have an attorney who never took care of the simple paperwork I needed done, admitting he put it off because it was boring. He kept putting my business aside as he went into the studio with the acts he managed. It got pretty stupid after a while and I finally had to switch to someone else.

Gail Boyd, Esq., an attorney who opened her own management company, Gail Boyd Artist Management, feels an attorney should either represent you as a manager or represent you legally. She believes it can be a conflict of interest to do both. Boyd keeps the two professions separate and doesn't legally represent her management clients. If you do get involved in a situation like this, know that you can always get another attorney to handle your legal matters, or at least check contracts for you.

## USING AN ATTORNEY TO SHOP A DEAL

While an attorney is looking to get you a good contract, some may be thinking more short term. If your representative is getting a percentage of your advance, their priorities may be skewed in that direction. Although most attorneys are ethical, there are some who put their own needs first. As a result, it's up to you to be careful. Since a manager is concerned about your career over the long haul, they'll be more focused on getting you signed to the right label, with the appropriate promotional and video budgets. And if you use a manager to shop your deal, you'll still have the benefit of an attorney negotiating your contract, hence two people watching out for you.

There are attorneys who will offer to shop your demo tape for a fee. Beware of them. They may promise to get your tapes to a number of labels for a fee of many thousands of dollars in advance. I've been told that sometimes these attorneys simultaneously shop material from other artists who are also paying a fee. This doesn't offer you much of a chance of getting signed. It's a business for these attorneys and they get their money no matter what. They have little incentive to push for a deal when they get their money up front.

Record labels are well aware of some of the attorneys who make shopping deals a business. Arnie Goodman at Viceroy Records says, "When I see a package from certain attorneys, I won't even open it because I know they'll shop garbage if you pay them. There are a lot of attorneys that are like ambulance chasers. They'll shop anything for money. You want to find an attorney that really likes your music." Attorney Wallace Collins told me that an A & R person recently asked him if he knew a certain attorney. When Collins asked why, the A & R person said he was getting a tape a week from this attorney and assumed he was taking fees for sending these demos. He told Collins that he can't take an attorney like that seriously because it's unlikely that anyone would have one act a week that was so good it was worth shopping on speculation.

If you do use an attorney who shops for a fee, find out where they're sending your tape. Make sure it's going to an A & R person who signs your genre of music. Get names. Request feedback as to why a label passed on your material. Ask for follow-up suggestions. Try and get your money's worth. You have a right to know the specifics of what was said about your tape. If the attorney can't give you an answer, they may not have shopped it effectively. Establish your requirements up front. If you pay a fee, let the attorney know you expect to get specific feedback. Put it in writing! Don't just hand over the money on their terms. Let them know what you want for it.

## SHOPPING ON CONSIGNMENT

I always recommend that if you use an attorney or anyone else in the industry to shop your tape, get someone who believes in your music enough to be paid only if they get you a deal. It's harder for someone to get you a deal if they don't feel good about your music. Part of the pitch to an A & R person is enthusiasm, which is hard to fake. If an attorney believes in your music enough to shop it on a contingency basis, obviously they'll work harder.

Attorney Larry Rudolph believes that using an attorney is "an excellent way to shop and get deals. However, there are many lawyers who try to take advantage of young, aspiring artists." He recommends avoiding attorneys who charge fees and believes if they ask for money up front, you shouldn't do it. Rudolph shops a very limited number of acts a year. "If I shop a deal it means I believe in them." Getting someone who believes in your material to represent you is the best way to go.

Wallace Collins agrees. He rarely, if ever, shops for a deal, believing an artist needs a lawyer who can negotiate contracts and advise them in legal matters. "An artist is better off having a manager shop his tape or doing it himself." Collins says he didn't go to law school for three years and practice law for over ten years to act as an agent. "You should choose a lawyer based on his ability to be a good legal advisor."

Micheline Levine, Esq., an attorney in private practice in New York City, says that "Sometimes it's difficult to find an experienced manager with contacts, or who has faith in the group . . . A lawyer should have good contacts and with such contacts can shop a deal effectively." Levine feels that if an attorney is charging you a fee for shopping a tape for you, it's not appropriate. Instead, she recommends using a music attorney in shopping a deal who either bills by the hour or who does what's called *value billing*, which means "Every time they do legal work, a project or an agreement, a lawyer will bill based on the value of that particular deal. Generally the fees for such projects tend to equal somewhere between five to ten percent. Anywhere in between is average."

If you give up a percentage of your advance for shopping the deal, be careful that the attorney doesn't settle for less in another area of the deal in lieu of a larger advance. If in doubt, have a second attorney look over the agreement.

Some attorneys will charge a smaller fee up front and still ask for a percentage. You need to be careful what you give away. According to those attorneys I've interviewed, the most typical arrangement is to give the attorney a percentage of your first album. Sometimes it's only taken from the advance and sometimes it's from royalties as well. Some attorneys will want their percentage to apply to all future albums. This is too much! You need to have something left over for yourself. There are some attorneys who will try to take a piece of everything you earn, including money earned from songwriting. Stan Soocher, Esq., the editor of *Entertainment Law & Finance,* says that "The real issue is what financial compensation the attorney should receive rather than whether the attorney should have a copyright ownership interest in the musician's songs or sound recordings. Musicians should be wary of the latter."

In most cases, an attorney will ask you to sign a written agreement if he or she will be getting a percentage of your deal. You need to read this over carefully because signing an agreement with the attorney who's supposed to represent you is a conflict of interest. Don't just assume you're being offered a fair deal. Most will but there are always a few . . . . It's best to have another attorney look the agreement over, although that can get costly. Soocher says that you should be aware that "An attorney who is giving a musician a contract to sign has an obligation to tell that musician to seek independent counsel to review the agreement. What many attorneys will do is to place a clause in the agreement with the musician stating that the musician has been advised to seek legal counsel." If they do not advise you, it can be a way to get out of the contract later.

The method of tape shopping that I prefer, if you can get it, is working out a flat rate finder's fee. The person gets paid only *if* you get a deal through them. This is not an easy arrangement to find, but there are people who will shop this way if they have a strong enough belief in your music. I've been told that finder's fees can average from $2,000 to $5,000, but can go a lot higher depending on the size of the deal.

If your music attorney doesn't shop deals at all, an alternative approach is to write a letter to the specific A & R person you want your tape to reach. List your attorney as the contact person (establish this before you use their name) or ask if they would send the letter on their stationary. If there's interest, your attorney can then negotiate the deal at their hourly rate. There's a difference between representing you and shopping a deal for you. Representation is ideally what an attorney should do. But since the music business isn't ideal, we sometimes have to do things in whatever way gets us to the deal we want. Wallace Collins says that this is the method he prefers to use. "But check with your attorney before using his name."

## CHOOSING A TAPE SHOPPING COMPANY

It's become increasingly more common for recording artists to be solicited by companies offering to shop their tapes for a flat fee. The people who do the shopping aren't necessarily attorneys. They tend to be individuals who have industry contacts. Their fees are usually a lot lower than what attorneys charge. The trouble with dealing with anyone shopping for a flat fee is that A & R people are aware that these shoppers are doing it for the money and not necessarily because they think the product is good. So the A & R person's frame of mind may be not as positive as when listening to an enthusiastic manager or lawyer who doesn't shop many tapes.

When someone shops an artist because they believe the artist has what it takes, an A & R person is more likely to develop interest in the act. But if you have nobody to shop your tape and feel more comfortable with having it done for you, using a service is a viable option. Every tape shopping service is different, and some are selective about who they represent. Many do have good connections. If your music knocks them out, I'm sure they'd shop it very enthusiastically. When someone from a service hears your music, see if they seem to really like it. Although most will say they do, it's not that hard to discern real sincerity from pumping you up. Put your ego aside and listen to their reaction objectively.

It's not that the people at these services won't try to get you a deal. After all, they need a track record to stay in business. Selling your tape helps them, too. But before you go with a tape shopping service, shop around. Request references. Ask a lot of questions. What clients have they placed? How do they determine what labels to pitch? How many will they approach? Will you get feedback afterwards? How far will they go for their fee? Choosing a good shopping service requires the same selectivity as choosing a good attorney or manager. Don't lose your patience and be in such a hurry that you get sucked into promises that deep down you know probably won't pan out.

## GETTING A PRODUCTION DEAL

Sometimes artists don't have enough resources to go into the studio and make a good quality demo. Consequently, they may hook up with a production company who believes in them enough to get their material recorded and out to record labels. If you sign with a production company, they usually get a percentage of your deal-often as much as 50%. A production deal might be limited to your first album, or for the length of your recording contract.

According to Wallace Collins, a lot of people go around calling themselves production companies even when they don't produce. These companies may be acting more as management in order to go to a label and shop a deal. But they often take a lot more than a manager. In many deals, the production company signs an agreement with the artist similar to a deal with a small record label, splitting everything 50/50. The monies paid by the record label commonly go to the production company. They're supposed to take their half of the money, paying the artist their share.

Collins warns that "More problems in this business arise based on production type contracts because all the money goes to the production company as a middle man, and it's human nature that people will calculate the money in the most favorable way to themselves." There are many ways to interpret the way the money is recouped and dispersed. Sometimes a production company will take all expenses out of the artist's share. By the time everything is paid for, the artist is left with little money while the production company has made a nice profit.

Collins recommends that if you sign with a production company, you have the record label pay you directly, giving the production company only their share. Many labels prefer this because an artist is happier when they have money coming in. Collins says that there are many whacky ways that people can play with the money and it may not be in your best interest to have just any production company running your business. That doesn't mean production companies always rip people off. The producer may be a good person but have no business sense. You shouldn't suffer for that ignorance, though.

Micheline Levine says that when representing an artist she'd prefer a direct deal with a record company because the artist gets more. But if an artist has no other way of getting directly to a label and finds a producer/production company with talent and good contacts, it's an option. If you sign a production agreement, Levine recommends that you

> Try to get as much as possible a value of the deal as you would have received had you gone directly to a label . . . try to get the major deal points as close to a direct deal as you possibly can . . . try as much as you can not to give up any portion of publishing and certainly avoid sharing merchandising whatsoever, which are two points that production companies frequently attempt to secure . . . educate yourself . . . find out what a new artist deal looks like when dealing directly with a record company (in terms of major deal points), so you can see how far off

you are. Frequently [a production company] does a 50/50 deal ... They make a production agreement saying whatever they get, you'll get half. When I make a production deal. I say [the artist] will get half but not less than____.

Both Levine and Collins assured me there are many legitimate production companies that do quite well for their artists. But you have to be careful to choose a reputable one. Make sure it's a company that has a track record, lots of label contacts, and a good sense of how to do business if they'll be handling your money. Be sure you have an attorney review the agreement. Collins finds problems with production companies to be a universal concern. A lot of artists wind up taking their production companies to court.

Many production companies are capable of getting you a good deal. Whether to take a production deal or not depends on what you need and the quality of what's being offered. No matter how much you need access to a studio, it's also important that you have lots of faith in the producer's ability, both musically and business-wise. There are producers and there are producers. Just because someone has a studio doesn't mean you should sign a production deal with them.

In Chapter 5 I spelled out the role of a producer and the importance of finding a good one. For a production deal, working with a person who knows how to produce well and has a good feel for your music is even more critical. When you hire a producer, you can eventually work something out to replace them if you're not satisfied. In a production deal, you're tied to the producer. They usually own your recordings, and possibly a piece of your career. So the person you sign with had better be good.

Some independent producers that you hire for a project will use their contacts to shop a deal for you without signing a production agreement. If they're getting producer's points on your album, they'll make money if you get signed. So you may hire a producer to work on your album who offers to take it to the labels, either for an extra point on the album or a finder's fee. Some producers will give it to people they know at labels because they believe in the project and want to help get it out. They may just pass it to people and not charge you any fee. It depends on the producer.

## REPRESENTING YOURSELF

Since it's considered unprofessional to represent yourself, a last resort for someone with no representation has been to create the facade of a manager. Artists have told me they do something similar to what I did when starting my label: Use fictitious names to sign letters when your own tag just won't do. When my label first opened, I was also the artist and didn't want people to think they were calling me to talk about myself. To create the aura of a real business, I signed letters with different names for PR person, president, promoter, etc. Nobody knew the difference.

I'm told that when some artists contact A & R persons, they do it as their manager. It makes label people more comfortable to think they're dealing with the artist's representative. Once there's a deal on the horizon, the label can talk with a lawyer and the manager can disappear. The label can be told that individual was temporary. This isn't a recommended route, but it's an option that has worked for some. Manager Mark Pitts says that when he first started out, "I would call people up and say I was somebody else just to get them on the phone. Once I had them on the phone I had their attention." Many industry people have told me that an artist has to do what an artist has to do to get signed. Wallace Collins agrees. "You gotta do what you gotta do. If you cannot get in through the front door, try the back door. If that fails, look for an open window. You must use every trick in the book to get your music heard."

## CHAPTER 20

# APPROACHING A RECORD LABEL YOURSELF

MYTH:
*You can't go to a record label if you don't know anyone.*

You're ready to rock and roll. Your demo is done. You have a nice package to present to an interested party. Your image is in place. Your music is right for today's market and you've got songs that'll grab people. You've been able to create a buzz on your act by developing a following, getting write-ups, selling your own CD, etc. You've also networked your butt off and have names of A & R people that might be good choices for your music. Perhaps you've got names of industry people you can use to get in the door. Perhaps you don't. Nobody has offered to call the A & R people, so you've got to do it yourself. Whether you're the artist, manager, or producer needing to make that first pitch, how do you give yourself the maximum opportunity to get your material into the right hands?

### PREPARING TO SHOP YOUR OWN DEAL

It's not easy to get in the door at record labels, but it is possible. This isn't something you should rush into, though. Trying to shop your deal directly takes preparation. Consider it the pre-production of tape shopping. Patience can play a major role in determining whether you're thoroughly prepared to take the first step.

Naturally you first need to have an appropriate package ready to present before you make your move. It would be absurd to get someone interested and then have to rush to pull your material together. Patience is essential in keeping yourself from running to labels before your demo is done to your total satisfaction, before your bio is written in a professional manner, and before you have effective photos. In other words, it helps you to wait until you can put your best foot forward.

As you're preparing to shop your material, you need to take on the persona of an industry person. Whether you're a manager, producer, friend of the artist, or the artist, a professional facade can help you get in the door. Earlier I recommended immersing yourself in your musical genre as you develop your music. By the same principle, you'll be more effective at opening doors if you immerse yourself in the culture of the music industry when approaching labels. Besides learning the business end of music to get a good deal, it's also helpful to learn about the people who run this crazy industry. Remember, the music business is basically a very small world. You want to understand that world, its protocol, language, relationships, etc. if you want the best chance of becoming part of it.

## GETTING EDUCATED ABOUT THE PEOPLE IN THE MUSIC INDUSTRY

Before you begin to try rubbing elbows with people at record labels, you need to educate yourself about the people who work within the industry. While it's not crucial to know who works where, it can help. Getting to know the names of people who work in the industry can be a useful asset when you're networking. For instance, if you're involved in a conversation with people in the music business you may at least be able to sound as though you know who they're talking about when they mention friends or colleagues you've read about. If they think you know these people, too, you'll be more likely to bond. I'm not suggesting you should lie, but if you know of a person you can talk about them in more familiar terms.

If you're familiar with the names of key players at labels you'd like to reach, you'll be more likely to hook up with someone who can get you inside. You'll recognize their names if they come up in a conversation. For example, if you're in a record store and two promoters you're chatting with mention someone you know as to the assistant of the A & R person you want to reach, you can ask them for an introduction. Had you not known this name, it would have been an opportunity gone right over your head.

If you're at a club or a party and someone mentions a person you've read about, you can act as though you know them and say something like, "I know her. Do you have her phone number? I need to reach her." In addition, if you happen to meet someone from a label unexpectedly, it helps to be able to recognize their name. "Are you the Lauren Daniels doing artist relations at Atlantic? I've been meaning to get in touch with you." Again, if the name doesn't ring a bell, the opportunity will be wasted. You just never know who you might bump into at a club, party, or in your dentist's office.

## LEARNING THE INDUSTRY WALK

Learning about people who work in the music industry is taking networking a step further. The more knowledge you have, the more ammunition you'll have. The more knowledge you have, the more you'll sound authoritative. The more knowledge you have, the more you'll come across as a professional. The more knowledge you have, the more confidence you'll feel when speaking with industry people. It's almost the parallel of name-dropping. You can drop names you're familiar with even though you don't know them personally. The music industry is a business of schmoozing. People chat and interact and gossip and observe. In order to do this well enough to fit in, you need to have knowledge of the people, politics, and interactions of those with whom you're mixing. As attorney Larry Rudolph emphasizes,

Get educated. If you're gonna be in this game you have to know how to walk the walk and talk the talk. If you do get to the position where you are finally standing in front of the person who may be your ticket to getting where you want to get, and they start to talk to you about some industry something, if you have no idea what the heck they're talking about they may not take you seriously. Learn what's going on. Read *Billboard*. Find out who's who and what's what.

I'm a die-hard people watcher. Before you can get inside the industry, it's good to make long observations from the sidelines. My first few music seminars gave me a great opportunity to see the interaction between professionals. At smaller conferences where the pros were more visible, I watched everyone. I listened in on conversations. Sometimes, if I was lucky, I'd be seated next to a group in a restaurant where I could get a real earful. I went wherever groups of industry people might be to get a feel for how they talked to each other and how they bonded. Then I'd practice speaking with people I already knew. I found it to be an art.

If you have the time and access to a major music city, a great way to learn about the industry is to get a job as an intern at a label. So many of the industry people I interviewed recommended it as a way to learn about all aspects the music industry. While colleges often have formal internship programs, many individuals won't turn down an informal free helper either if the candidate seems to be good. Getting a job as an intern involves using the networking skills already mentioned. Talk to everyone you can about your desire to work for free. Try music-related businesses, too, such as management companies, large agencies, publicists, etc. You'll make excellent contacts if you're personable. Then you work them.

## FINDING OUT WHO'S WHO

How do you learn about industry people? Read a lot. Study the trade (meaning industry business-related) publications. Chris Schwartz, C.E.O. and Founder of RuffHouse Records, says

You should read any and every trade publication you can get your hands on, i.e., *Billboard*, *R & R*, etc . . . If you can't afford these, then take them from people's lobbies. It is important to know who are the players, labels, artists, producers, etc . . . Also, it helps to have a historical knowledge of the music industry. Until very recently, this information was only available in books about the film industry. However, there are numbers of books about the record . . . business available at the public libraries. Remember: KNOWLEDGE IS POWER!

Obviously *Billboard* is a great place to begin. Read all the articles you can relating to what you're doing, as well as what you're interested in doing. This way you can have knowledgeable conversations with people you meet. You'll also be up on who's doing what and where. You may also learn about who's looking for new artists. You'll even become familiar with the names of CEOs of smaller labels who may have good distribution deals with the majors. Read as many trade publications as possible.

It's helpful to learn everything you can about industry people. All knowledge has the potential of being useful at some point. For example, if you read an article about an A & R person you may someday want to approach, you might learn something you can use to get your foot in the door. If they have an interesting hobby, be on the look out for an article on that topic. You can send a copy of it with your pitch. Keep files on A & R people or others at labels where you might want to shop your deal. I keep track of specific people on index cards and write down any pertinent information.

I know of a blues musician who read about an A & R person who signed rock but was a major blues fan. Based on this hobby, the artist convinced the A & R person to come down to one of her gigs. After sending reviews and numerous invites to blues clubs, the musician got the A & R person to show up for a gig. He loved the artist and gave her an introduction to a friend of his who signed blues.

Be sure to read *Billboard*'s "Executive Turntable" column. It talks about people who just got hired or promoted. Often people new to a company are a little more accessible. Sometimes they're looking for new material right away. If there's someone in particular who might be helpful to your career, drop them a note congratulating them on their new position. Don't pitch anything at that time, though. Later, when you approach them again, they may think they know you!

## GETTING NAMES AND NUMBERS

It's good to have listings of record labels and industry-related people for reference. There are many listings available. Get at least one of them. Study it. Read it often enough to get to know some of the names.

There are several publications I wouldn't want to be without. One is an excellent directory that's good to have when you're ready to go to A & R people—the *A & R Registry* put out by S.R.S. Publishing and compiled by a terrific guy named Ritch Ezra. It lists the A & R staff for all major and independent labels in New York, Los Angeles, Nashville, and London, with their direct dial numbers and the names of their assistants. The best part of the directory is that it's updated every eight weeks. People change jobs so fast in this industry that listings can get stale quickly. Ezra works on this directory full-time to insure that the information is accurate. Many of his subscribers are successful industry people, producers, songwriters, managers, and label and publishing people who are themselves listed. Many have told me they find it a tremendous source of accurate information. Ezra also publishes *Music Publisher Directory* and *Film/TV Music Guide*.

Another source of names I wouldn't be without is published by Pollstar, which, as I mentioned earlier, put out a nice assortment of Contact Directories. Twice a year they publish *Record Company Rosters* with a listing of executive contacts for almost every major and independent label in the business. For each label, there's a listing with the person's title and direct phone number for A & R people, promoters, publicists, artist relations people, etc. Almost everyone in a specific position at the label is listed. This has been the best source I've had for getting acquainted with the personnel at record labels.

There are plenty of other listings, directories, registers, etc. available as well. The two I just mentioned are reasonably priced and have proven accurate. I've listed these and many more in the resource section of this book. *MIX Bookshelf,* a mail order catalogue for books on all aspects of the music industry, has directories and resources available as well. Some are specific to different genres of music. Choose according to your needs.

Paying attention to names can help make Public Relations specialist Jane Blumenfeld's theory of three degrees of separation a reality. For instance, I once wanted to interview a band and looked up their representation in *Performance Guide's Talent/PM.* As I scanned the list of personnel at the band's management company, I saw the name of someone who had once taken my seminar. Of course I called him and asked for an introduction to the person who could help me get the interview. He put in a good word for me. I'd never have known he worked there had I not read through the names of the people at the company. While I don't remember everyone's names, he'd called me twice for information so I was familiar with his. The music industry really is a small world, especially in a specific city.

## GETTING IN THE DOOR TO A&R PEOPLE

I want to do an exercise using imagery so you can better understand the various factors effecting an A & R person each day. If you can get a picture of what they deal with on a regular basis, you might better comprehend why it may be impossible for them to be accessible to people they don't know who approach them with demo tapes. The following isn't necessarily a day in the life of an A & R person, but it's a typical scenario.

*Imagine that you're an A & R person. All day long you deal with tons of phone calls from managers, producers, lawyers, and mothers of signed acts and wannabe signed acts. You have contracts to go through. You're still unsuccessfully looking for three songs for an important album. One of your biggest acts isn't selling and you're getting pressure from upstairs. Then there are a zillion other things going on with some of the acts you've signed. Added to this, you may have been out late the night before checking out an act you might sign so you're tired. Your secretary walks in with the latest mail and puts it next to the mail you haven't had time to review from days before. There's a pile of packages of all sizes containing tapes and press kits. You don't recognize the return addresses on any of the packages. Your phone is ringing off the hook. What mail would you give your attention to if you were an A & R person? Whose phone calls would you take? Be honest!*

A & R people have a lot of pressure on them. If you were one, you too might have little choice as to how to prioritize your time. As much as A & R people might like to spend their days just listening to tapes of potential talent that could be signed, the system doesn't allow for it. The A & R people who would ask their secretary to hold their calls so they could listen to all the tapes or return calls of people they never heard of would be in a very small minority. Chances are the tapes are put in a box and are never listened to.

## FINDING THE RIGHT APPROACH

There is hope. I painted the above picture so you know what you're up against. Perhaps your idealism has been bruised but your approach to the labels may be more realistic. When you try to get in touch with A & R people, show respect for the fact that they're very busy. Your approach should exude a professional exterior. It should also keep you on the lookout for any cracks in the door that you can push your way through.

There's no one way to reach A & R people because each one is different. Some are more fun-loving and so seriously into music they may respond to a creative overture. Some may respond to an extremely business-like approach. Some may not respond no matter what you do. Sometimes you can get a feel for their personalities or attitudes by asking around. Usually it's just trial and error finding one who responds to your approach. Some A & R people do listen to unsolicited demo tapes. It's just that more of them don't.

The easiest A & R people to get the attention of can be those at indie labels. They're more approachable because their ears are often more attuned to the street to begin with. Most indie labels have attained their success by being open to what's new and fresh. They can also be more open to hearing demo tapes, aware of the treasures that may be found. Based on the people I've interviewed, the A & R people doing urban music can be the most open-minded to demo tapes. They know that so much of the music on the charts comes from young people who don't have the money or contacts to get to labels through more traditional routes. These A & R people also seem the most likely to see beyond the poor quality of a demo tape and recognize the talent. In general, a more specialized label usually has a staff of people who are into that form of music. The staff is usually younger and more knowledgeable about their particular genre. They may remember more easily what it was like to try to get heard, so their doors may not be shut as tightly.

### REACHING A & R BY MAIL

It's usually best to make your initial contact with an A & R person by mail. Forget sending a demo tape cold unless you know that the person accepts unsolicited recordings. Public relations specialist Jane Blumenfeld recommends sending mailings to key publications and targeted A & R people as your career develops. Keep these people as regulars on your mailing list. If you're playing a gig, make sure they always get a card. When you're ready to shop your demo, they may be familiar with your name after seeing your mailings. This can help you to get taken more seriously.

Some people have used creative approaches to get an A & R person's attention. I once heard of someone who sent a boombox with his tape in it. The A & R person did listen. People have been known to send tapes in gifts as well as in creative presentations (i.e., in a bouquet of balloons, in the hand of a stripper, etc.) These approaches sometimes get the tape listened to. I've never heard of someone getting signed that way but it's possible. The bottom line is still having a good product.

A well-written letter can get the attention of an A & R person. If possible, develop your own stationary on a computer. Write a professional sounding letter introducing yourself and explaining something about your music. Describe it in a sentence or two so the A & R person will get a feel for your act. Mention where you've performed, any gigs that are coming up, who has written about you, and anything else that is evidence you're a marketable artist. End the letter by saying that you'd be happy to send more information about the act. Keep what you say as brief and professional as possible. If something in the letter catches the A & R person's interest, they may request a demo tape or come down to see you play.

About a week after you think the A & R person would have received your letter, you can make a follow-up call. When asked what your business is, say that you're calling to see if your letter was received. If the A & R person is interested, you'll eventually get through. If there's no response in a reasonable amount of time, there's probably a reason. I don't usually call more than three or four times without getting encouragement.

## GETTING THROUGH ON THE PHONE

When you call an A & R person, you'd better have a very specific agenda in mind. Just in case you actually do get through, be prepared to quickly explain why you're calling. Is it to follow up on a letter you sent? Is it to invite them to a gig? Is it to ask them if they'd be interested in hearing your tape? Is it to ask for a few minutes of their time for you to come up to present your act in person? Whatever your agenda, be prepared to spell it out in thirty words or less. Acknowledge that you appreciate their taking the time to talk with you and promise not to keep them on the phone long. State your case and thank them for their time. If they're interested, they'll let you know.

## THE POWER OF SECRETARIES, RECEPTIONISTS, AND ADMINISTRATIVE ASSISTANTS

You call an A & R person. Someone may have recommended them or you may be doing it cold. Their secretary tells you they're busy and will have to call you back. After waiting a few days, you try again. Same scenario. "She's on the other line." "He's in a meeting." "She just stepped out." "He's in the middle of something." "She'll have to call you back." This can go on for months. Assistants know all the excuses. Is it useless to call? Can you get past the person on the other end of the line?

Instead of simply trying to get past the person who answers the phone, attempt to get friendly with them. The people who answer phones can be the key to opening those tightly locked doors. Remember that they're on the inside. And who better can you talk to about the A & R person's schedule, artist needs, attitude, personal preferences, and other information? The people who answer the phones are the ones who guard the door you need to get through. They're the gatekeepers for A & R people. Developing a friendly relationship with them can get you to their superiors. By the way, a number of A & R people started as a secretary or a receptionist and worked their way up, so the one you get on the phone today may be the one you're trying to reach in a few months! Many have higher ambitions, and calling attention to an act that gets signed can benefit them as well.

I always have a short, friendly chit-chat with whomever answers the phone, no matter who I'm calling. To me, it's basic courtesy to treat everyone as a somebody. Getting on familiar terms can give you license later on to ask them for advice. Does the A & R person have an assistant and what's their name? What's the best time to try and catch them? How do I get them to come to my gig?

Will you come to my gig? Yes. Invite the people who work for an A & R person to your gigs. Put them on the guest list. Treat them like honored guests. These people often love music and will come to see you. Thank them for coming. If your performance blows them away, they'll go back and talk about you inside the doors.

How do you get on familiar terms with the people up front? If you have the *A & R Registry*, look up the name of the person's assistant. Or you can call the label and ask for the name of the assistant you want to reach. Call back later, armed with the name. Use it when you call. After asking for the A & R person you want and being told to leave your phone number, you can say to the person, "Is this Lori?" She might think she knows you, or that you know her on a professional level, and she'll take you more seriously.

Whenever I call anyone, from an A & R person to a plumber, I ask the person who answers the phone for their name. I do this after they tell me why the person can't come to the phone. Then I say "Thanks so much, Michael. I'd appreciate your giving BH my message." Again, it's called courtesy and it's not that common. So many people treat the ones who answer the phones as non-entities. They aren't! Treat them with respect. Be friendly. I have wonderful relationships with the various assistants of business people with whom I deal. When I call back later in the week if my call hasn't been returned, I'll ask if I'm speaking with Michael. If it's Jenny, I talk to her in a familiar manner, saying I'd just spoken to Michael a few days ago. Is Michael there? If not, perhaps Jenny can help me get through to BH. Friendly, friendly, friendly. If Michael answers, I remind him who I am and ask him how he's been. Then I say I didn't get a return call. What would he advise? Sometimes it works, sometimes it doesn't. It's worked for me more than it's bombed.

## GETTING PAST THE GATEKEEPERS

Something that works for me a large percentage of the time is calling with so much confidence, so much professionalism, and such a positive attitude that the person assumes they know me. A colleague and I were recently talking about how few listening skills people have these days. If I call and say my name immediately, they'll still ask for it later on, as if I'd never said it. If you say your name in a crisp, positive manner it may never occur to them that they don't know you. I can't tell you how many times I cold call people and when asked who this is I just say my name in an extremely firm, confident voice, like they should know who I am. I'd say over 25% of the time I get put through to the person without being asked my business. My whole approach tells the person I expect my call to be taken seriously.

The best time to try and reach any industry person directly by phone is after hours. That's when their telephone guards go home and they often answer the phone themselves. This applies to all ends of the industry. When I want to reach someone directly, I often try every evening after 6:00 or 7:00. Industry people tend to work late. I love doing work after 6:00 because I'm not hampered by as many phone calls as come in during the day. I've been told by many people that late in the day may be the only time to get them on the phone. Of course it's like a crapshoot to call every day for a while in hopes of catching the person I want, but it's worth a shot. Even if it works occasionally it's better than nothing. Sometimes I can get a clue as to the best day to call late from their assistant.

## FINDING A MENTOR

People may not always want to help you, but they usually love giving advice. And whether they mean to or not, their advice can help. Asking for advice or opinions is much less threatening than asking someone to get your tape to a record label. People feel put off when you ask for a specific favor. They feel flattered when you ask for their opinion.

It's nice to have friends in the industry. Sometimes being able to just sit down and talk to someone with experience can give you the encouragement and confidence you need to go on. Jane Blumenfeld believes

> Most everybody in the music industry is open for advice. Even though they're not going to sign you or do anything for you, most anyone will be willing to talk with you and give you advice. Call up or send a letter followed by a phone call, asking 'would you mind if I stopped by your office for a few minutes just to meet you, and talk with

you. I'd love to hear your advice.' Most people will give you a few minutes of their time. An entertainment lawyer would be good. Bring them a cup of coffee or something. Make a little extra effort. Establish a rapport with somebody who then might talk to other people about you.

Going to an industry insider for advice can be the beginning of establishing a nice relationship. If they like you, who knows where that advice can lead. How do you approach these possible mentors? Blumenfeld recommends sending them a letter and following it up with a phone call. If you live out of the city where the person is based, she advises faxing them that you're going to be in their area, saying "I wonder if I could just stop by and speak with you for a few minutes of your time. I understand that you probably won't be interested in signing me, but I would love to have your advice."

Blumenfeld says that a great way to find the people most likely to give advice is to see who's teaching. Industry people teach classes or guest lecture at colleges, adult education programs, music seminars, etc. "Because they are already reaching out to help people, you can say to one, 'I know you were teaching at Columbia. I couldn't afford your class but I wondered if I could stop by and speak with you.' A & R people are looking, by the very definition of the job, for new music. They want to meet people." They may not have time for everyone, but they may make a few minutes for a resourceful person who asks politely. It's definitely worth the effort.

Here's another approach. Ask the person who answers the A & R person's phone if you can send them a tape for their opinion as to whether it would work on their label. You won't have to ask them to pass it to their boss if they like it. But asking for their opinion is a lot less forward than asking them to give it to their boss. It also strokes their ego, which most people love. You want their opinion. You ask nothing more at that moment. You treat them as an expert. Trust me, if they like it they won't miss the opportunity to get it into the right hands so they can later brag that they discovered you.

I regularly "adopt" people who I meet and like as mentors. By not making a pig of myself and limiting requests, I get help when I need it. How do you think I got to interview so many people in this book? I got most of the interviews before I even had a book deal. I asked my industry friends to recommend and put me in touch with the appropriate people. And they did. Now I have more friends!

# PART SIX

# GETTING A GOOD DEAL: THE BUSINESS OF MUSIC

## CHAPTER 21

# CONTRACT COMMITMENT: LESS CAN BE MORE

## MYTH:
*The longer I sign my contract for, the better.*

The *term* of a contract is the length of time you're tied to the record label. Most recording contracts require a commitment of exclusivity for a specific period. This means during that time you can only record for them, unless your label gives you permission to record for someone else. Sometimes a label will allow their artist to do a special project with an artist on another label. Usually all members of the band that sign the contract are obliged to record exclusively for that label. Someone that leaves the band can't just go out and record for someone else. A release is needed from the label.

Most often you can still work on other aspects of your music with some freedom. If you're also a producer, you'll probably be able to produce and develop other acts on your own time. The same is true if you write songs. Unless someone owns the rights to every song you create, you can write for other people too. Of course none of this can interfere with your primary obligation to your record label. But as long as what you're doing isn't a conflict of interest, you can usually work on independent projects.

## TERM OF COMMITMENT: FROM NUMBER OF YEARS TO NUMBER OF ALBUMS

When I started my record label, the industry was signing recording artists for a specific number of years. A typical deal started at one year with the option to renew the contract four times, which amounted to a five year commitment. These days the term is established by the number of albums you're committed to record instead of the number of years.

Record labels prefer a commitment of albums instead of years because they then know up front how many albums they'll have the option to record, no matter what the circumstances. The term of a record deal will be for a specific number of albums to be completed. Until an artist records the number of albums called for in their recording agreement, they're still bound to that record label. Therefore, the commitment of a successful recording artist could end up going beyond the old five year limitation.

Specifying one or two albums a year doesn't always pan out. Some bands take a long time recording. I've heard of bands taking two years or more to create an album. Some albums have a multitude of hit singles, so a new album isn't called for as quickly. Some bands go on long tours that keep them out of the studio. If the tour is successful and the current album is still selling well, the label may be content to wait longer for the next album. If the terms were for a limited number of years rather than albums, the label would feel more pressure to record quicker.

## LESS IS ALWAYS MORE WHEN YOU'RE THE ARTIST

For an artist signing a record label deal, the shorter the term of the contract the better. This might not seem right to you at first. I know. Mentally it feels great to have a larger commitment to the label. It can make you feel more secure in the beginning. You might assume the label will do more with you if they've signed you to more albums.

Unfortunately, it doesn't work that way. While it sounds good to get a deal with more albums, the fact is that if you're not doing well the label won't pick up the album options anyway. No matter how many albums are in your contract, they have the right to ignore you if they choose.

Record labels have it sweet. They never have to record any albums if they choose not to, no matter how many are in the terms of your contract. That's right. No matter how many albums are agreed to, the label doesn't ever have to pick up their options to record them. They don't even have to release one album. They can put you in the studio, give you a nice recording budget, get the finished album, and let it collect dust on a shelf no matter how many albums are in your agreement. If they don't choose to exercise their options for your act, you, of course, will eventually try to break your contract. But that can waste a lot of time.

Why wouldn't you want a long term contract? If your agreement is for a lesser number of albums, the label will still want you for more albums when that contract expires, if you're doing well. So a short contract won't hurt you if you're successful. And if the label isn't supporting your act, you're better off out of your contract because they probably would have left you on the shelf anyway. You're better off being free to pursue your career with another label, one which might support you. Sadly, I meet recording artists regularly who are signed to labels that don't even get their records into most stores. What's the point of staying on a label that doesn't market your music? The status of having a deal wears thin when nobody has heard of you.

If you're doing well, you'll want to be out of your contract as soon as possible. A new act doesn't usually get the greatest deal. So if your records are selling well, you won't be able to get out of your contract fast enough to suit you. With some success, you'll have clout to call the shots a bit more. If you're becoming more popular and the label is making money from your recordings, you can probably negotiate to get a much better contract or sign with another label as soon as possible, once you've met your recording commitment. If you do well, the label will usually renegotiate your recording agreement before the terms are over just to keep you happy. But the best arrangements are negotiated when your agreement runs out. That's why you're better off signing the shortest deal as possible. A short term contract is a *win-win* situation for the artist. If the record label is doing nothing with your act, you can get out of your contract quicker and move on. If your act is doing well, the label will want to renew your contract when the term is up. Then the ball may be further in your court for getting a more favorable deal. Or, you may get interest from another record label. Then they can bid on you. Either way you can do well.

## MORE IS ALWAYS MORE WHEN YOU'RE THE RECORD LABEL

The record label, meanwhile, is always trying to get the longest terms possible. WHY NOT? It can't hurt to have all those albums locked up, knowing they never have to be produced if the act isn't working. If you're not doing well, they'll ignore you despite the long agreement. But just in case you become a hot act, the record label has the option on more albums. And they're content knowing that if circumstances keep you out of the studio for a long period of time, you'll still have to produce those stipulated number of albums before getting your freedom from their recording agreement.

So a contract can last way past the five years they used to tie you up for. How reassuring for them to have you until you fulfill the required number of albums. But for you as the artist, a shorter term gives you more freedom to advance financially, or at least not to be stuck too long on a label that may not do right by you. Attorney Micheline Levine says that the average number of albums that record labels want a new artist to sign for are six to eight. She says seven to eight is the most common number of albums. "When [the labels] are putting the investment in, they want more because they want longevity."

You can't rush into signing a recording agreement. When a label wants to put out your music, you need to look beyond the initial excitement of having what may seem like your dream coming true. You need to discuss the terms with a good lawyer. You need to accept that being tied to a record label for a long period of time may not help your career. Be patient and prudent in deciding whether or not to take the deal. If your lawyer says the terms are for too many albums, respect the advice. If a label is serious about developing your career, they'll try to compromise at least a little.

## CHAPTER 22

# RECORD ROYALTIES: WHAT THE ARTIST ACTUALLY GETS

MYTH:
*If my record sells, I'll be rich from the royalties.*

ou'd think that an artist whose record goes gold would be rolling in royalties. Royalties are what artists earn from the sale of their records, CDs, and tapes. While receiving large royalties is a possibility, an artist's receiving practically no royalties is a possibility as well. According to ?uestlove of The Roots, "The biggest misconception is that you can make money through selling records. We definitely milked the other area of our talent. Our live show has kept us on the road, working." Many artists will never see a dime in royalties beyond their advance due to a number of factors that will be discussed in this chapter.

There are some provisions of royalty agreements that you absolutely must understand. While these provisions will be discussed here, under no circumstances should you use this information to negotiate a deal on your own. Let a music/entertainment attorney speak with the record label. This information is being provided only so that you'll have a working knowledge of contract provisions. You should be to be able to discuss your contract with your attorney while having some understanding of its terms. Nevertheless, please don't discuss any part of the contract with the label, even informally. This is why you've hired an attorney.

## THE RECORDING CONTRACT

There's no such animal as a standard recording contract. Although record labels will always try to get as much of an advantage as they can, nothing is set in stone. There are certain provisions of a recording contract that are considered "customary." Many apply to deductions the record label can take from your royalties that exist because of traditions, rather than because they're relevant to the recording industry today. Most were instituted many years ago out of necessity, when technology wasn't as sophisticated as it is today.

Since finding ways to pay you less royalties benefits the record label, they'll continue to try and keep these "customary" provisions of a contract if your lawyer allows them to. But they can be left as is, toned down, or be eliminated. The deciding factor is how badly you want the deal vs. how badly the label wants you. Unfortunately, the ball is usually in the label's court. Unless your act is so hot that people are clamoring for it, you'll probably be the more anxious party. Micheline Levine says

> A lot of points aren't worth fighting tooth and nail over. You've got to learn and hopefully choose an attorney who is able to not only be an good attorney in terms of legal analytical skills, but as well a good negotiator. This entails, seeing the forest behind the trees, which is one of the most difficult tasks for most attorneys I've encountered. Some can't let go of a point, and you have to determine which points are worth fighting for and how to let go of the ones that aren't worth it.

## POINTS ABOUT POINTS

When you sign a recording contract, you agree to accept a certain number of *points* as your royalty for making the record. *Points* mean a percentage of sales. Usually the rate is based on retail prices, although some labels do still base their accounting on a wholesale price. I've been told it doesn't matter most of the time because wholesale rate is considered half of retail. Therefore, wholesale points are usually twice as much as retail points. Thus, the royalty should end up to be the same dollar amount either way.

When you have a ten point deal on a retail agreement, it should technically mean that you're getting 10% of the retail selling price of your recording. If this was all there was to it, things would be easy. But beware. Record labels ain't giving it up so fast! I said that *technically* 10% of the retail selling price should go to you, because the labels have all sorts of deductions that can be legally taken. Your lawyer can attempt to negotiate some of these deductions out of your contract. Many are simply annoying provisions that are just accepted as standard, however. For example, the record company always retains anywhere from 10 to 25% of the retail selling price, depending on the format to cover the cost of packaging. This is usually much more than packaging really costs, so in actuality it's a way for labels to make a larger profit.

Many deductions are based on outdated reasoning. For instance, some companies still only pay on 90% of sales to cover breakage because records used to break easily in the old days. Record labels may also deduct a portion of your royalties as *free goods,* another tradition that works in the label's favor. This means they increase the wholesale price of each recording so that the price of 85 records is now what the price of 100 records was. They bill for 85 records at the inflated price and say they're giving the stores 15 out of 100 pieces for free. The record labels make the same amount of money wholesale. You get no royalties on the 15% of records that are supposedly given for free, even though they're sold. Since they pay you on a retail price, rather than take into account the inflated wholesale price, this means you get less royalties. Although the record labels get more money on their wholesale price, this benefit isn't passed along to you. In a way it's a legal scam, and everyone knows it.

Another provision to watch for is the number of records the label hold as a "reserve." This reserve postpones paying you a percentage of your royalty to cover the label on returns. Record labels have a very liberal return policy. Having run a label myself, I know that it's a difficult situation for the labels. Stores have a lot of time to return products. Because of this, as much as 35 to 50% of what's been shipped may be held like an insurance policy against returns. Your contract should have a limit on how much can be held as well as a time limit on when this money will be released to you.

Issues such as these may be negotiable and it's up to your attorney to work out the best deal possible. Labels will try to pay on as little as they can. It takes a good attorney to make sure you give up only what's necessary to seal the deal. I've heard it said that this is a business of pennies. For a hit record, a few cents can mean a lot of extra money in someone's pocket. For example, if a record sells 300,000 copies, one penny extra means $3,000 extra. A dime gets an extra $30,000. That's why there's so much haggling about pennies between the record label and the artist's attorney. You want that penny in your pocket.

The CD rate is another provision that record labels can alter to their advantage. Although it's gotten better since CDs were first introduced, the CD rate is usually lower than the rate paid on other formats. Micheline Levine suggests being careful about how much the record label is paying you on CDs. "The CD rate is very important . . . more important than anything else because that's what sells the most. You've got to negotiate and everything is dependent on bargaining leverage."

In order to insure that you'll receive at least a reasonable amount of money from your record label, it's important to ask for a decent advance. This way there'll be at least something to show for your recording efforts. You need to enter a recording agreement with a realistic attitude, not expecting the big bucks in a few months. You don't want to set yourself up for disappointment.

## ALL-IN DEALS

It's becoming more common these days for record labels to give an artist an all-in deal whereby they set aside a fund for recording costs. All expenses come out of this fund. The A & R person monitors the spending of the fund, as they do the production of the album. The record company does not hand the fund over to the artist. They pay the bills out of the fund. When the recording is finished to the satisfaction of the record label, the artist gets to keep as an advance whatever money was not spent from this recording fund. Micheline Levine says "In an all-in deal, the average royalty is between twelve and fourteen points, twelve being fair and fourteen just a little on the high end for a beginning artist."

Most smart artists try to budget their spending on a recording so that they have a reasonable amount left over when all bills are paid. I've seen artists who were given large budgets get carried away with fancy studios, top name producers, and other non-essential recording splurges. They end up regretting it when they have nothing left as their advance. Being prudent about spending will assure some cash at the end. You have to remember that every expense comes out of your pocket.

If you used a producer who's entitled to points on your album, the points will come out of your end of the deal. Artists don't always realize this when they agree to give a producer a nice chunk of points. Take into consideration whether the points being offered to you by the label will cover the producer's share and leave you with something fair. I hear less experienced musicians promising points to people such as the mixer or engineer when there might not be that many points to go around. The average rate for producers is two to four points on retail sales. Big name producers may want as much as five or six points because their name on the record can help it sell.

## ROYALTY PAYMENTS

Royalties are usually paid twice a year, with the royalty period ending on June 30th and December 31st. The record label then has from sixty to ninety days to calculate how much royalties you've earned, and they must give you a statement explaining the amount. Sometimes these royalties are paid on what's called only *on paper*. That's because you see the figures you've earned written down on paper, but they go back to the label as reimbursement for what is known as *recoupable expenses,* money the label is entitled to take from your earned royalties to reimburse itself for certain expenses. *Recoupable expenses* include things such as studio expenses, advances, tour support (money spent to support you on a tour that you lose money doing, provided the label believes the tour will help sell records), equipment, at least part if not the whole video, at least part if not all of the cost of hiring an independent promoter, and whatever else the label can justify. There can be other miscellaneous expenses depending on the label. Thank goodness most expenses related to pressing, printing, advertising, publicity, and marketing are *non-recoupable.*

Once the royalties have finally been computed and the aforementioned deductions have been taken out, the record label will then deduct all their recoupable expenses before you ever see a dime. The label can pay itself back by keeping all artist's royalties (from the sales of the record only) until the designated recoupable expenses are paid back. Not until all of those costs have been recouped will the artist be entitled to collect royalties.

Very important: Be aware that when the label is spending money on you that seems generous, such as bringing pizza to the studio, buying new clothing for a TV appearance, or sending a limo for you, they will probably recoup these expenses later. That means you're paying for them yourself. And the price recouped may be much higher than if you bought them on your own. Keep this in mind when you're offered extras. Ask if they're recoupable expenses. If so, buy them yourself.

The way the system works is simple. As the artist, you will get your first royalty statement at the appropriate time. Let's say you've earned $1,000 in royalties. Don't head for the mall because the label will first repay itself for your recoupable expenses. Let's say these expenses are $100,000. So, *on paper* you have earned the $1,000 but it's deducted from the $100,000 you "owe" the label. Now you owe them $99,000 more. Six months later you've earned $10,000 *on paper,* and then you owe the label $89,000. It keeps going on like this until the money is fully recouped. If that doesn't happen, what's left over of your debt (called the deficit) on the first album will be added to the amount to be *recouped* from the second album. This is called *cross-collateralization.* But if you as the artist still "owe" the label money when you've completed your contract, you'll never have to pay them back out of your own pocket.

The bottom line is that an artist should not expect to see much in the way of royalties, especially at the beginning. Many artists never earn royalties that aren't just *on paper.* That's why it's important to try and get a good advance. It may be the only money you get from the label, especially if recoupable expenses are high. The hotter the act, the better the potential to call some shots. But the only real money an artist may see after the advance is from doing live shows.

## CHAPTER 23

# SONGWRITING ROYALTIES: MAKING THE MOST OF YOUR PUBLISHING OPTIONS

MYTH:
*It's best not to give up any of your*
*publishing to get a record deal.*

usic publishing is an area of the music business that confuses many of my students. Over the years I've heard countless misconceptions, some of which have actually stopped young musicians and singer/songwriters from signing recording contracts that could have advanced their careers. The responses of these individuals have usually been along the lines of, "I'm not giving up 50% of my publishing to a label. I wrote the song and 50% is too much."

The issue of giving up a portion of your publishing rights is well worth your careful consideration. If your song is earning steady royalties because a record label or publishing company is doing its job, your 50% is probably worth a lot more than the royalties you might earn if you tried to market the song yourself. Remember that 50% of a substantial royalty is worth much more than 100% of nothing. Sometimes you have to give something away to get what you want in return. Keep in mind that if a label owns half of your publishing rights, it stands to make money too, and the company will work to that end. Guess who gets taken along for the ride?

It's common knowledge in the industry that publishing/songwriting royalties is where the big money is made. Songwriters generally make more money than the artist. While the artist's royalties are recoupable (the record label can pay itself back for specific expenses out of these royalties), the songwriter's royalties are not. Because a songwriter earns royalties from the first record sold, artists who write their own songs therefore stand to make more money. And, of course, if you don't write your own material, you can always try to find someone to co-write with you. A lot of big name singers have turned into songwriters by getting a good writer to work with them so they can share in the lucrative songwriting royalties.

## MUSIC PUBLISHING DEFINED

The first step to make the most of your publishing options is to understand what publishing rights are. As a songwriter, you first put your original song into a tangible form, such as on tape or on paper. This automatically copyrights it. You then register your material with the Office of Copyright in Washington D.C., which gives you proof that you own your copyright. As a songwriter you can file the PA (Performing Arts) form that copyrights the lyrics and music, or you can file an SR (Sound Recording) form, which copyrights the actual sound as well as the lyrics and music. Either way the song is yours. At this point all of the songwriter's royalties are yours as well. Your next step is to get your song published, which means it's put into a form where it's available for purchase. Once your song is available for purchase, it's considered published. That's when the royalties come into play.

My first lawyer used to say that songwriting royalties is one of the few instances where you can get 200% of 100% of something. I think this is where confusion begins. Many people think of all songwriting royalties as publishing. That's why so many don't want to give up half of it. In actuality, *publishing* usually refers to only 50% of the total writer's royalty. This is known as the *publisher's share*. The other half is the writer's share. Are you with me so far?

The *writer's share* is, not surprisingly, alloted to the writer of the song. If more than one person wrote the song, it's shared equally unless there's a separate written agreement indicating different percentages. Be careful about offering a piece of the songwriting credit to someone who makes a small contribution to your song. I used to put my engineer's name on the copyright because he helped me to put my songs together. I always write my own lyrics, and create the melody for the song. Technically, that is the song. But since I needed help, I'd put my engineer, producer, or a friend down on the copyright as a show of good faith. What I didn't realize was that this person owned 50% of the song, since I didn't specify otherwise, even though I created 90% of it. It was an expensive lesson.

The *publisher's share* of songwriting royalties is considered an administrative fee for the music publisher, for taking care of the business end of songwriting. They usually have the copyright on songs assigned to them and issue licenses for others to use these materials. They market these songs on various levels, such as trying to get people to do cover versions and getting the songs into movies, TV shows, commercials, and other places where income can be earned. Publishers know where royalties can come from. They know the going rate for licensing songs. Publishers collect the money and pay the writer.

Music publishing is a business. Established publishers have the business acumen that songwriters often don't. And for that they often get 50% of the total songwriting royalties. Remember that publishing is where the big money can be made. It's a lucrative business. Songwriters aren't always business people. Although my business skills are top notch, when I'm involved in a creative project I'd prefer not to be bothered with the business end. A publisher may split the total royalty 50/50 so that the songwriter doesn't have to be worried about business matters and can focus on what they do best—creating songs.

Music publishing today isn't what it used to be. In the past, publishers had writers creating songs which they'd then go out and sell to others. Songs were in great demand by singers. A songwriter would sit in the publisher's office and bang out songs on the piano. In fact, the noise coming down to the street from all the pianos gave New York's Tin Pan Alley its name. In those days, publishers acted as song pluggers and hustled to sell the songs wherever they could. Publishers were essential to getting songs marketed. Music publishers and songwriters did the 50/50 split on the royalties because they were both integral parts in making money from the song.

This isn't as often the case today. Artists are writing more of their own material, so songs aren't being bought as often as they were years ago. Labels now prefer artists to write their own songs. Producers often have songs available if needed. Singers have more access to songs than ever before so a publisher isn't considered as essential as it used to be. The role of a publisher has changed since the days of Tin Pan Alley. But what hasn't changed is how much money the royalties are worth!

## CO-PUBLISHING DEALS

Many record labels, especially independent ones, want what's called a co-publishing arrangement, if the artist is also the songwriter. This means the label and songwriter each get 50% of the publishing rights, larger labels sometimes take a smaller percentage. Almost all labels will want to control the copyright, though, so they can issue licenses for others to record your songs. Chances are that if you get a record deal, your label will want a piece of your publishing action.

Here's how it works when a label wants some of your publishing royalties. You start off owning the copyright of your song so all the songwriting royalties are yours. No one can take your publishing rights unless you assign it to them, in writing. Because it's the most common split, I'll show you an example of the writer and label each getting 50%.

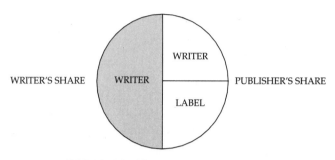

TOTAL SONGWRITER'S ROYALTIES

A *co-publishing deal* means that at least two people are sharing the publishing royalties for the song. This is a normal occurrence between a writer and record label. The writer's share of royalties should always go to the writer. Nobody should take that away. In the above diagram, the publishing is split 50/50. As you can see, the songwriter gets 50% of the publishing for a total of 75% of the total royalties. The label get 50% of the publishing, which is 25% of the total royalties. So when your friend is complaining he won't give up 50% of his publishing, explain to him that giving up 50% of his publishing means he'll still get 75% of the total songwriter's royalties. And with a label involved in the publishing, it could mean a larger royalty pot from which to get that 75%. In order to collect your share of the publishing royalties, you have to open a publishing company (more about this later in the chapter). It cannot be paid to you as an individual.

## SOURCES OF SONGWRITING ROYALTIES

There are several sources of income available to you if you are a songwriter. As a songwriter you must become familiar with the different ways in which your songs can earn songwriting royalties, and with the organizations that can help you with the collection of this income.

### MECHANICAL ROYALTIES

One source of income available to you is *mechanical royalties*. These are royalties paid by the record label to license the use of your song on their record. The publisher will issue a *mechanical license* which gives the label permission to manufacture and distribute records, tapes, and CDs with a song handled by the publisher. As of this printing, the current rate is 6.95¢ per song on each record sold. The record label isn't supposed to cross-collateralize this royalty, in other words, to use this royalty to recoup money in the same way that artist's royalties are recouped. Some smaller independent labels may try to get away with this, however. While it's not illegal if you sign a contract allowing them to, you're supposed to get paid from the first record sold. Mechanical royalties can really add up!

If you're concerned about your mechanical royalties, you can use the services of the Harry Fox Agency, which is a subsidiary of the NMPA (National Music Publisher's Association). One of the services it performs is to issue the mechanical licenses for the publisher. The agency also makes sure the correct mechanical royalties are paid, and provides an accounting for its clients. It regularly audits the record labels. The Harry Fox Agency takes a small percentage of the royalties to perform their services.

## PERFORMANCE ROYALTIES

A second potential source of income is *performance royalties*. These are royalties paid for the license to use songs in public places. Most public places that play music must pay a royalty for its use. The obvious sources of income are television and radio, although royalties are also paid by restaurants, stores, clubs (for both music being played and live performances), and other public places that play music. The three performing rights societies, ASCAP (American Society of Composers, Authors and Publishers), BMI (Broadcast Music Incorporated), and SESAC issue licences for a song's use, collect the subsequent royalties, and pay the writers and publishers.

Each society gives a *blanket license* to radio stations, T.V. stations, clubs and any other public venues where songs might be played. A fee is determined based on the establishment, and it entitles them to use all the songs that are represented by the society issuing the license. ASCAP and BMI take sample surveys to see what songs are being played or performed. SESAC is the first organization to employ BDS (Broadcast Data System) Technology to track royalties with more accuracy. For non-commercial formats where industry trade charts are utilized to determine chart position, SESAC uses the charts as a criteria for evaluating performance activity (royalties). Keep in mind that a song needs a lot of play to earn even a small royalty.

ASCAP and BMI are non-profit and any writer can join. SESAC, a much smaller society in comparison, is privately owned and is selective about who can join. ASCAP, founded in 1914, is the oldest and largest performing rights society in terms of membership. BMI was created in 1940 in response to a need from creators of certain genres of music that were not being allowed to join ASCAP. Today all three societies represent all genres of music. Both ASCAP and BMI sponsor seminars and have representatives that you can talk to for guidance. ASCAP charges $10.00 a year for a writer to be a member. BMI and SESAC don't charge anything.

Which one should you join? I can't make that decision for you. I won't say that one is better than the other. There are pros and cons for all of them. They can all benefit a songwriter. If you live close enough to a city that has offices for these societies, make an appointment with somebody at each one. Or talk with representatives on the phone. See where you feel more comfortable. Let someone at each society tell you why you should join theirs. You may like the representative at one so much that you'll choose that society. According to Frances Preston, president of BMI,

> The BMI Writer/Publisher Relations executive is often the first person a new songwriter or artist meets in his or her career and the BMI contract is often the first piece of paper the songwriter signs to prove he or she is a "professional." They come to rely on us, not just for our enthusiasm for their music, but for the good professional advice we are able to give them about the intracacies of the music business and their rights as creators. Those

relationships, begun so early, can span entire careers and we are very proud of that.

Marilyn Bergman, president of ASCAP as well as a reknowned songwriter, says

> Why join ASCAP? As a songwriter, I am with ASCAP because it excels in what matters to me most—protection, reliability and fairness. ASCAP is first in revenue collections, royalty distributions and in negotiating the best license agreements with music user groups. Just as importantly, ASCAP has championed the rights of music creators in the courts and in Congress since its inception in 1914 and continues to be the leader today as music use in cyberspace begins to take center stage. The royalties paid by ASCAP are based on uncompromising fairness—comparable performances are treated exactly the same way whether the writer is a superstar or a newcomer.

Linda Lorence, Vice President of Writer/Publisher Relations at SESAC says,

> SESAC is a sixty-five year old performing rights organization. It is a privately owned organization whose recent owners are music industry veterans who have turned the organization around with a brand new vision to the future. Being the smallest of the three, SESAC maintains its selectivity in order to offer a competitive payment structure and personalized service.

Speak to people at all three organizations and see what they offer. Since each performing rights society offers assistance to songwriters, don't hesitate to approach the people on staff to get advice on what to do with your songs. This service is free to members. Take advantage of it. Once you affiliate with (join) one of them, they'll be available to give you assistance in making money with your songs. After all, they make money when you do. The people at these societies do have good contacts with the labels, too.

Once you're a published writer (remember, this means your song is on a format that's offered for sale), you should become a member of one of these three societies. You may join before being published, though at that point there are no royalties to collect. You can only join one society as a songwriter, however, as opposed to being able to open a publishing company with all three. All your songs should be registered. Your society will send you accounting statements after each royalty period.

You've got to be getting serious airplay before seeing performance royalties. What may seem like a lot of airplay to you may not be enough to earn any money for your songs. Real publishers are better at handling these collections than you, which is why a co-publishing deal with a good company can be worth the percent you give up. They can keep a more accurate record of what monies may be due. And they know the avenues to pursue when they feel you're being short-changed.

## SYNCHRONIZATION ROYALTIES

A third source of income is *synchronization royalties*, which are paid when your song is played on televison, in movies, etc. The license issued for this kind of use is called a *synchronization license*. A synchronization license, known as a *synch* for short, is a license to use your song in a situation where it's used *in synch* with visual images. The royalties paid for these kinds of uses can vary dramatically. It's up to the publisher to negotiate a fair licensing fee. More commonly, a flat fee is paid rather than royalties based on play. Fees vary according to the budget, the length of the movie or show, and how much of the song is used. The income for songs used in T.V. commercials has been increasing. Real publishers know how to tap into these sources. The Harry Fox Agency can issue synch licenses for you.

## OPENING YOUR OWN PUBLISHING COMPANY

Writers must open their own publishing companies to collect the publishing royalties. To do this you must submit three potential company names to one of the Performing Rights Societies. You'd usually set this up with the organization you're affiliated with as a songwriter. It will check to see which of the names you've proposed haven't been used. Once a name has been cleared, you fill out the forms, wait for acceptance, and—you're a publisher. Very simple!

ASCAP charges $50.00 a year to be affiliated with them as a publishing company. BMI charges a one-time fee of $100.00. This money is supposed to come out of your royalties, but if you haven't earned any you'll still have to pay. SESAC doesn't charge a fee.

Once your publishing company is accepted, you can get a business certificate and open a bank account to prepare to receive your royalty checks. If you're going to publish other artists' songs as well as your own, it's a good idea to have a publishing company established with all the affiliates.

## SIGNING WITH AN ESTABLISHED PUBLISHING COMPANY

I'm asked all the time by songwriters who perform their own material whether it's worthwhile to sign with an established music publishing company. If you're an artist/songwriter, getting signed to a music publishing deal can be another option for getting a deal with a record label. Artists who write their own songs are in a much better position to get a label deal these days, according to Kenny MacPherson, Senior Vice President, Creative at Warner/Chappell. He says that record labels prefer to sign a complete package: singers who can write their own material. And a publisher can help market you on this level.

Publishers do take a chunk of what might otherwise be your royalty. They usually control the use of your song so they can issue licenses. But as I said before, a smaller piece of a much larger pie may still make you more money. Publishers can be more aggressive than you in getting your material in the position of earning royalties, protecting your copyright and making sure your songs are licenced properly. If you're an artist, they can help you shop a deal with a label. Publishers used to just shop songs, but they'll now try to get a label interested in an act whose songs they represent. After all, if you make an album with your songs, the publisher stands to make money. So a publisher who believes in your songs may help you get where you want to be. Publisher Julie Lipsius, president of Lipservices, says

> A publisher can help to guide your career . . . they can provide advice . . . be a back-up to your management or act instead of management if you're too new to have management. It depends on the rapport that you have with the individuals at the publishing company . . . I think to a great extent publishers and managers fill in the empty spaces of what you need.

Sometimes a publisher can also help you get your songs on other people's albums. Publishers are in a better position to know which artists are looking for songs. If someone more well-known uses one of your songs, it shows a label that you're capable of writing good material for yourself. You can make some serious money with good songwriting skills. Many famous singers write for others. If your publisher is able to place your favorite song with a known singer, you might want to let it go, even if it's the one you wanted to make a hit with yourself. It could open doors for you and you can always sing it yourself later.

Good music publishers know who's looking for material to be used in movies and on T.V. I know a group that got a tremendous record deal because they had one of their songs used in the movie of a trendy director. One of the band members told me that the only reason they got the deal was because the song would be on this sound track. Publishers are in a better position to get your songs placed where they get exposure, and earn income. So having an established publisher can be lucrative, especially when they make sure your royalties are paid in full. It's yet another option to keep in mind for getting the deal you want.

## SONGWRITING AGREEMENTS

Most often a songwriter will get a Standard Songwriter's Agreement from a publisher, though this agreement is not uniform. Each contract varies according to the publisher. The publisher will want to control your copyright and to issue the licenses. Advances for this right vary from nothing to an average of $250 to $500. Most often the total royalties are split 50/50.

The term of such an agreement is usually for a year with possible options for an additional four. During each period the publisher is entitled to a certain number of songs, often with a stipulation that they can choose not to accept songs of poor quality offered to fulfill the required number. The publisher, unless otherwise stated, is entitled to maintain ownership of the songs for the duration of the copyright. But in the case of a publisher not fulfilling their end of the agreement, or not being successful with your song in the course of a year, you can exercise a *reversion clause* and have the song revert back to you.

## FINDING THE RIGHT PUBLISHER

The most important factor in a publishing deal is who you sign with. Anyone can open a publishing company. Don't get desperate and sign with the first one offering you a contract. Having a publishing deal assures nothing. There are no guarantees the publisher will do anything with your songs. Therefore, you'll want to get the right one for your music. Ask who the publisher represents and see if their songs are being recorded. If the publisher is reputable, signing with them may be a good way to get your career going. Again, you sometimes have to give something up to get something you want, which in this case is ultimately a contract with a record label.

Approaching music publishers isn't that much easier than approaching record labels. But a publisher's prime concern is the songs. Some publishers may sign you if they believe you've got good potential for a successful recording career. Rich Ezra's directory of publishers (see the resource section) is a good listing to start with. There are many more smaller publishing companies all over the country. Sometimes someone at your performing rights society can recommend someone. Many publishers teach songwriting workshops at the different songwriting organizations. I've sat in on a few songwriting workshops at the Songwriter's Hall of Fame and they were led by established publishers. Get out there and find them if that's your chosen direction.

## CHAPTER 24

# SAMPLING: WHAT IT IS, AND WHAT IT CAN COST YOU

MYTH:
*I can legally sample from a record as long
as I take only a small amount*

ampling is using the copyrighted sound of someone else's recording for your own use. Some musicians sample beats. Some sample sounds. Some sample actual vocals. Whatever is ultimately taken, sampling is usually done by playing the original recording into a digital sampler which duplicates the sound. That sound can then be played on a keyboard so that a *sample* can be added to any part of your recording.

Authorized sampling involves getting permission from the owner of the sound recording copyright (usually the record label) to use a piece of the song. A record label can issue you a license to use the sample as a courtesy or for a fee. Unauthorized sampling is stealing, an infringement of Copyright Law. It's illegal, even if the publisher of the song gives you permission.

## WHY SAMPLE?

I've been told that sampling became popular in the days when hip hop music first began. Many young rappers couldn't afford to hire someone to come to the studio (often a home-based four track) to play an instrument or make a drum machine available. It thus became a common practice for them to sample a drum beat and loop it for the base of their rap. If they wanted some guitar chords, they'd simply sample them and put them where they were needed.

Without getting too technical, sampling opens the door to having a multitude of sounds, instruments, and beats for a minimum of money. Even talent can be inexpensive if you're able to sample all the beats, bass lines, etc. and mix them together as the base of your song. For a vocalist or DJ who can't play an instrument or program a drum machine, sampling offers options.

Many producers/writers enjoy the challenge of listening to lots of records, often old or obscure ones, to find new and interesting sounds to sample onto their own recordings. Kids listen for these sounds when recordings come out. When I was working with dance music and hip hop, the guys producing and writing for me sampled all the time, much to my chagrin. They loved doing it and refused to acknowledge the liability it involved. "Everybody does it" was what I heard in answer to my fears.

## THE HIGH COST OF SAMPLING

In my classes, I'm always asked about the minimum amount of bars/notes/seconds of other artists' recordings you can get away with using as samples without getting written permission. Zero. Nada. Not one recognizable note! I've asked several lawyers about this and have been told that if the owner of the copyright for the sound recording can recognize one second of their song, you're at risk. Of course, many musicians get away with it, as artists on my label liked to remind me. But the fact is, there are no rules about allowing the use of even small bits of a song. If it can be proven that you've stolen a sample of another artist's recording, no matter how small, you can be in serious financial hot water. Copyright infringement is a federal offense.

Yes, there are ways to camouflage samples. If they're covered and buried by other music they may not be as recognizable and you may not get caught. Yes, you may blatantly sample and still get away with it. But it's a serious risk. And it's against the law. According to musicologist Sandy Wilbur, president of Musiodata, "If someone takes a lipstick and doesn't get caught, it's still considered stealing. Sampling without permission, no matter how small or how disguised, is also stealing."

Part of this risk depends on which label you take your sample from. For example, if you get material from a record on a label that does a lot of hip hop or dance tracks where sampling is prevalent, there's more often some professional courtesy extended. But if you sample from a label that has artists who don't use a lot of sampling, they may come down harder on you. Sampling simply isn't worth the risk.

There are ways to prove that you've sampled. Wilbur says that "When someone believes a sample of their work has been taken without permission, a musicologist can often examine the two works with forensic thoroughness. Analytic skills and new technology can often be used to show if they came from the same source."

Most record labels have clauses in their artists' contracts which specify that the artist warrants there's nothing in their finished product that will infringe on anyone's copyright. The artists must sign it, leaving them legally responsible for using an uncleared sample. When I ran my record label, my artists had something similar in their contract. My lawyer included a clause stating that the artist would be responsible for any lawsuits claiming copyright infringement.

If you get caught sampling illegally, you can lose all your income, royalties, and more, if the record label holds you liable, which it probably will try to do. Since most copyright disputes are settled quietly out of court, it's hard to say what the penalty might run you if you're found guilty. But if you do get caught with an uncleared sample, lawyers alone can cost a fortune. So even if you win the case you may lose. And sometimes when you lose, you may also have to pay the legal fees for the other side. Losing the case can be an extremely expensive ordeal.

The actual penalty you may have to pay for copyright infringement can exceed $100,000. This can depend on how much money you're making from the song with the illegal sample in it. Sampling can be a dangerous gamble. While the odds may seem in your favor, if you get caught you may lose everything you own, now and in the future.

## SEEKING PERMISSION TO SAMPLE

When you use a sample there are two separate concerns. One is the owner of the copyright on the song itself; the other is the owner of the sound recording copyright. Many participants at my seminars are under the misconception that if the writer of the song says it's okay to sample, they're in the clear. The writer may not even own the copyright, and consequently might not have the power to allow you to use it. Besides, the bigger liability lies in not getting clearance from the record label. That's where so many musicians get into trouble.

The owner of the song's copyright is usually the publisher and/or writer. It may not be so much a consideration of whether you can use the sample. What needs to be worked out, preferably before the song is released, is what percentage of the songwriter royalties you're going to give them. If you use ten seconds of a song, what's it worth to you? If you negotiate this before your record is released, you've got a decent chance of giving them a fair but reasonable percentage. If you wait until your records are in the stores, they may decide they want more. At that point how do you get any leverage?

The sound coming off of a record is copyrighted as well. The copyright owner of the sound recording, usually the record label, can be the harder party with whom to negotiate. You'll have to license the use of the sound coming off the record. A flat licensing fee, rather than a percentage of royalties, is most commonly the deal. And whereas there's a limit with the publisher (the maximum usually being no more than 100% of songwriting royalties), for the sound recording there's no limit on the licensing fee. Again, it's easier to negotiate a reasonable deal if you clear it before you release the record. Once your product is for sale, you're in infringement of copyright and you'll pay a lot more, or get sued.

I cannot emphasize this enough: *Get everything cleared before the record is released!!!* The first step you may want to take is to contact the record label and ask for the legal department or the person who handles copyright clearances. Deborah Mannis-Gardner, a licensing and clearance agent with her own private clearance company, dmg, inc. recommends submitting a letter of request with recorded copies of the songs to the appropriate copyright holders. She also advises having some patience because they may not respond right away. I've actually gotten samples used on my label cleared gratis by asking politely. These samples were from labels that have a lot of rap acts and it was a professional courtesy. Otherwise they probably would have charged me a fee. Your other option is to go to a music clearance company. For a fee these companies will approach the record label for you to request the use of a sample. They know the going rates, who to ask, and how to negotiate.

If you like the way a sample sounds but don't want to go through the hassle and expense of clearing it, try reproducing the sound. You'll still have to work out an agreement with the music publisher for a percentage of royalties, but you don't have to clear it with the record label. Reproducing the sound means going into the studio and recording the track, as close to the way it is on the record, yourself. Then you'll have to sample your recording, and use that sample in your project. I know it's not quite the same as taking the original, but it's a lot safer. And cheaper.

## CHAPTER 25

# SOME FINAL WORDS

*Men can starve from a lack of self-realization*
*as much as they can from a lack of bread.*
—RICHARD WRIGHT

*Our doubts are traitors, and make us lose the good*
*we oft might win by fearing to attempt.*
—WILLIAM SHAKESPEARE

*Great works are performed not by strength, but by perseverance.*
—SAMUEL JOHNSON

*To be a good shepherd is to shear the flock, not skin it!*
—TIBERIUS

*Destiny is no matter of chance. It is a matter of choice:*
*It is not a thing to be waited for, it is a thing to be achieved.*
—WILLIAM JENNINGS BRYANT

*Even if you're on the right track, you'll get run over*
*if you just sit there.*
—WILL ROGERS

To have the best chance of getting signed to a record label, you've got to believe in yourself and your music with all your heart. Otherwise, it'll be hard to keep going when people continually put walls in your face. At a panel I attended on getting a buzz, all of the speakers agreed that the best talent will rise above the rest. They encouraged artists to keep going, believing that if the talent is there someone will find them. It was emphasized that "the cream always rises to the top." But this can take time, and patience again becomes a virtue when it comes to not giving up.

*Keep a healthy attitude about drugs and alcohol!* I don't want to get preachy here, but if you respect what I've said in the rest of the book, you'll respect what I say here too. Partying has been a partner to the pop music scene for too many years. Using drugs and alcohol has been glamourized. When I began in the music industry, I felt like a freak because I didn't do drugs and enjoyed alcohol in moderation. I've been the only one in a room who didn't share in the coke lines being passed around, as I watched talented musicians turn to mush. I've held a musician's hand while we cried together as he free-based crack, wishing he could end the pattern that was destroying his career. I've gone to rehab with musicians who struggled to get back control over their lives. I've watched many a talented musician lose their precision playing their instruments, their ability to create good songs, and their desire to have a life. I've had my heart broken when I've seen former students, once beautiful, smart, and talented, look like someone scooped out their insides because they were so hollow from their addictions. Drugs and alcohol seem exciting and cool on the surface. How glamourous and cool do you think Jimi Hendrix felt dying in his own vomit?

Chris Jones, manager of Blind Melons, did whatever he could to help Shannon Hoon get over his drug addiction and ultimately watched him die. He told me, "No matter how strong you think you are, the drugs are always stronger. The passion you have for your music will be destroyed by the drugs and the addiction to them." Chuck D added, "Underneath the streets is jail and death.

Too many times the streets are marketed as this fantastic place of creativity where we come to reflect. The streets were thrust on us. It's up to us to elevate past the status and bring our people up." More and more musicians are trying to get away from drugs and alcohol because they kill, if *only* your soul. They do not enhance your creativity on a long-term basis. They do nothing except slowly melt your brain.

I want you to know about MusiCares, a non-profit organization launched by NARAS and headed by NARAS's president, Michael Greene. Greene told me they're trying to make musicians understand that it's not cool to have a substance abuse problem.

MusiCares offers support and education within the music industy. Among their services they have a network of music professionals who've recovered and are available to give support to those who are stuggling. If you need help with substance abuse, or want more info about it, call 1-800-MUSICARES. Respect yourself by not poisoning your body with excessive use of drugs and alcohol. Trust me, the rush of the moment isn't worth the consequences of long-term addiciton which you'll pay for with the rest of your life. Pursue your career on a healthier level! More and more labels are concerned about signing acts that party too hardy. The trend is now towards a healthy attitude about drugs and alcohol. Please at least think about this the next time someone offers you something. Don't get high, get a record deal!

*Get yourself prepared on a mental level.*
You must be ready to deal with trying to get ahead in an industry that doesn't give anything easily. A healthy attitude is essential for staying on track. You'll need a lot of determination to keep yourself from quitting. You also cannot take rejection or criticism too personally. So many people in higher positions don't have a clue about what will sell. If your material is good, someone will recognize it, if you hang in there.

*Keep believing in yourself and your music.*
When people don't treat you fairly or things don't go your way, use

the energy behind your anger to work harder rather than wallowing in your obstacles. You may not feel confident enough to ask for help, intros, etc. Sometimes you may look for excuses for not succeeding, instead of forging ahead. Don't let those who don't appreciate your music discourage you. Prove to those who stand in your way that you can do it. Get that positive revenge, as I did when I opened Revenge Records. Nobody believed a schoolteacher with no experience in the industry could make a success of a record label. Nobody but me.

*Build a strong foundation.*
Do everything you can to create a buzz. The road to fame and fortune can get discouraging. I always tell people that you can never be a failure if you don't stop trying. Most artists that you may think were overnight successes paid their dues for many years. There's a process that you must go through to build a foundation. The pieces—a good recording, a large following, write-ups in music publications, radio play, industry relationships, etc.—take time to put together. It can be like climbing steps: one piece can lead to the next. The foundation needs to be very strong before you're ready to go for a record deal. Having the patience to wait until that foundation is set gives you the best chance of attracting an A & R person's attention. A strong foundation will give you the confidence to move forward. You've got to remember to keep working hard. If you keep going you will succeed, if you have talent *and* strong material.

*Be positive in your approach to life.*
I truly believe with all my heart that we attract what we give out. A negative attitude will attract negative people. Positive vibes fulfill our joys so much more. This includes always trying to be courteous. Public Relations specialist Terrie Williams believes we should always try to do the right thing, even with those who don't do unto us. Good or bad, it comes back to you. When you get turned down, thank the person anyway. Be gracious. It'll come through in your attitude, which can influence that person toward helping you on another occasion.

*Never stop having fun while doing your music!*
Sometimes you may get so fed up that you lose your perspective as to why you're doing music in the first place. Try to keep the pleasure of creating and performing at the top of your priorities. Even if the deal takes awhile, you can still enjoy the road to getting it. Didn't you get involved with your music because you love it? You can love it whether or not you have a deal.

*Be specific about what you need.*
Know your strengths for following through when you get someone's attention. Keep putting your needs and your talents out there and you'll eventually find someone who will lead you to your answers.

I'll end with this thought: Whenever you're trying to figure out the how, where, who, etc. of something you need, say to yourself "Seek and ye shall find; knock and it shall be opened unto you" (New Testament, *Matthew, VII, 7*). I live by the intention behind this quote. I've repeated it to myself at times when I didn't know where to turn for what I needed and then found the answers.

I'll again say that the only failure is someone who stops trying! Let your belief in your music guide your heart and your energy in the right direction. Keep the faith. A little spirituality won't hurt you!

I wish you all successful record deals.

# APPENDIXES

# APPENDIX 1

# ADVICE TO AN UNSIGNED ARTIST

**PHOEBE SNOW,** RECORDING ARTIST

You have to be a self-starter. This is something I've found after twenty plus years in the industry—no one's gonna do it for me. Nobody is going to really make that difference and be the special, persistent kind of force that an artist needs to keep people interested in them. Although, yeah, you do need a good team, and you do need people who are running interference for you and working for labels. But you need the belief in yourself. This is a hard lesson that I learned, but it's definitely a viable one: that no one is going to hand me my career on a silver platter. I have to really kind of be the nucleus of whatever's happening. I have to make others want to be interested in me. That's the only secret that I know. Obviously if you're talented, that's 75%. I wish it was 100%, that everybody who's talented just automatically gets settled somewhere, and gets a label gig. But, that ain't the reality. It's really belief in oneself. [There are] people who are generally regarded as not being predominantly musicians, but as being "entertainers," who are now worth tens of millions of dollars, if not hundreds, because they are self-generating. They're their own best PR people, their own best hype-machine. The minute they get out on stage or get onto a CD, what they're doing is promoting themselves. For a lot of people that's an unsavory side of the business. "I don't want to sit there and talk about myself all night. I don't want to get in people's face all the time." I'm the kind of person who really doesn't want to do that, but there are ways to do it. If you love music, you'll do anything to make music the center of your universe, if you love it that much. I finally figured it out, and for young artists, I hope it doesn't take as long.

### CHUCK D, RECORDING ARTIST, SOLO AND WITH RAP GROUP PUBLIC ENEMY

Make sure that you gather information about the different occupations that make up the music business. Learn the names of every record company and important personnel within, and submit not only a tape but a presentable package (photo and bio info). This can be obtained by acquiring trade magazines and books consisting of history, facts, and know-how of the music business.

### SHIRLEY MANSON, RECORDING ARTIST WITH ROCK BAND, GARBAGE

I can only speak from personal experience, but my advice would be as follows: If your music is your passion then guard it ferociously and do not be afraid of failure. Go forth and commit to it. Out of commitment comes surprise and magic. In relation to the industry, however—be afraid, be very afraid! Take responsibility for your business and watch it like a hawk."

### LEANN RIMES, COUNTRY RECORDING ARTIST

Sing as much as you can for experience and exposure, record a good demo album, and send it to people—friends and acquaintances who can get it into the right hands of major record companies. I sang on stages in Dallas and various sports functions, and recorded an album on a small independent label in Dallas. The album attracted attention from a couple of record executives, and they came to see me perform live. Before I knew it, I had an official recording contract.

**JOHNNY CLEGG,** INTERNATIONAL RECORDING ARTIST
FROM SOUTH AFRICA
Believe in what you do and this will win through.

**KAREN MATHESON,** RECORDING ARTIST
WITH CELTIC BAND, CAPERCAILLIE
The record company will still come to me to wear this or that. Do I listen? Never! I never felt it was relevant to our music.

**?UESTLOVE,** RECORDING ARTIST WITH RAP GROUP THE ROOTS
We (The Roots) weren't that eager to sign with anybody. Since hip-hop is definitely on the low end of the totem pole, we weren't getting the offer that we thought we deserved . . . Eventually, in December '93, Geffen Records, a label with no street credibility and a label not even knowledgeable in the fact that rap groups are even low on the totem pole, gave us a very, very decent offer, as if we were a rock band. Needless to say, we did it. That's when our troubles began. Usually groups tell you the light at the end of the tunnel is when the ink dries. Not at all! Now we're stuck in a situation in which these very artistically capable musicians are giving quality product and the label doesn't know what to do with it . . . The problem wasn't for us getting a record deal. The problem is what happens when we get it. That's when the obstacles ran into play with Geffen. I don't want to leave the impression that I'm anti-Geffen, because . . . things are better now. I'm definitely involved in every aspect of this new album that is coming out. [The label] thought 300,000 copies sold was great for an unknown band. But we shouldn't have been unknown when we signed. It scared me that the record executives were happy with the results. Usually it's the opposite. Now things are much different. I don't have any far-fetched dreams for this group. I want to do respectable numbers. I want to recoup . . . You have to have a hustler's attitude. I don't think you should prostitute yourself like some people do. Nepotism is definitely the name of the game in this industry. We're the rare exception . . . No one of note put us on. We took the back entrance.

**CHRIS SCHWARTZ,** CEO AND FOUNDER, RUFFHOUSE RECORDS
The success of a recording artist is the rare culmination of a lot of factors including the aligning of the stars in heaven. The single most driving factor for any act is HIT SONGS. Regardless if it is Rap, Rock, R & B, etc . . . The hit song is crucial in driving any project. Therefore, I feel it is important that the artist devote the majority of their time to perfecting their songwriting craft.

**KARIN BERG,** SENIOR VICE PRESIDENT
OF A & R, WARNER BROS. RECORDS
Make sure that you play live, and that you establish an audience before you make a record. Don't think of a record as the end of what you want to do. It's only a facet of what you should be doing. You should enjoy playing live and making music and a record should only be a facet of it. If you are getting into the business only to make a record, something's wrong.

**DAVE AYRES,** VICE PRESIDENT OF A & R, CAPITOL RECORDS
You need to be out there. If you're good, someone will find you.

**ROSE NOONE,** DIRECTOR OF A & R, ISLAND RECORDS
I think the best thing for an artist or band to do is to create their own foundation, wherever they happen to be located. Play out a lot, build up a nice live following . . . if you feel the need to have music to give to people or sell, manufacture a cassette, CD or 7″ . . . sell them at your gigs. Get the local press to support you. And even in some cases, radio will. There are specialty shows on some radio stations, Sunday or Monday nights, that will play local bands. Promote yourself on college radio. You can do these things by yourself and if you do take that initiative, people will notice.

**MARK PITTS**, VICE PRESIDENT OF A & R AT UNIVERSAL RECORDS, AND PRESIDENT OF MARK PITTS MANAGEMENT
I would showcase myself as much as I can. There [are] a lot of unsigned showcases out there.

**GLADYS PIZARRO,** VICE PRESIDENT OF A & R, STRICTLY RHYTHM
You have to be really good. I gave Josh Wink, Roger Sanchez, Armand Van Helden, and Erick Morillo their start. And the proof is in their music.

**KIRK BURROWES,** GENERAL MANAGER
OF BAD BOY ENTERTAINMENT
Know what it is you're looking for in your search for a career as a musician or artist. What are you trying to get out of it? Why do you want to do this?

**KATHY BAYLOR,** A & R REP FOR UNIVERSAL RECORDS
Persevere, persevere. Get a good attorney. Learn all you can about the whole industry, even if you're on the creative end. You need to know how the whole process works. Understand that this is a business . . . anyone who thinks this is not work is fooling themselves. I have never worked so hard in my life . . . Just don't be discouraged. The most difficult part of the whole thing is to continue to have the balls and the emotional wherewithal to continue to shop when you've been rejected.

**JANE BLUMENFELD,** PRESIDENT OF IN MEDIA PUBLICITY
You can have a star person in your band who's been featured elsewhere, but unless he's a team member it's going to work against you in the long run. You've got to have a team if you're gonna have a band. Nobody can be a star in the band. Everyone has to be part of the team and chip in, and if somebody in the band isn't doing their fair share, then they're the wrong person. Because what happens when you get further down the line and you're touring . . . doing thirty cities . . . across the country and you're sleeping in whatever hotel you can find . . . on the same bus with the same people day in and day out, you've really gotta be a team. You really have to like the people in the band. Automatically the media will gravitate to the lead singer as the focal point, the voice of the band. So it's important that the lead singer must pull in the band mem-

bers and never goes to an interview alone. You can rotate the members of your band.

## SHANNON O'SHEA, SOS MANAGEMENT

Your attitude is as important as the music, and the way that you approach what you do is as important as your creative aspects. The greater knowledge that you can have about how the whole business works and how you can help the system., the more successful you'll be . . . You've got to weigh the system with your personal integrity and what's right. But if you cooperate with the system and you understand how it works, it makes it a lot less frustrating. If people are asking you to do a radio show, you should find out information about the show. Find out information about it because you may be helping yourself as much as you're helping the "record company." [Once you're signed] try and approach it as a team effort. There [are] human beings inside labels. There is a big system you have to deal with, but inside that system there are people that will work with you from their heart. The best thing a band can do is to motivate them on that level.

## JERRY ADE, PRESIDENT OF FAMOUS ARTIST AGENCY

The most successful people have been the most aggressive individuals . . . the artists who are out there hustling . . . doing their groundwork. That can get the excitement of everyone else involved.

## ADAM KORNFELD, BOOKING AGENT
## WITH QBQ ENTERTAINMENT

Have a deep passion for what you're doing and play as much as you can.

## ALEX KOCHAN, PRESIDENT OF ARTISTS
## & AUDIENCE ENTERTAINMENT

You have to make the music that's true to yourself, but you can't rely on just the music to build an audience. You do have to learn some tricks along the way and you have to get the right people involved to help you develop and expand your audience. It's all not going to happen solely because you make good music. You can make great music and have bad judgments about people you get involved, and then who's ever going to hear that good music? So it's make good music but also learn about relationships with people so that you can decipher who does what they say they're gonna do . . . A lot of bands in the 60's or 70's would often just turn everything over to somebody else and say "They'll deal with it. We trust them and whatever they say." There's a lot of bands that are questioning what people say, looking to reinvent the wheel for themselves. I think that's healthy. Anybody coming along saying there's only one way for a band to do things is probably too lazy or uncreative to think about some new way . . . Always remember, if you look at people who have had the long-term success, like the Rolling Stones or the remaining members of the Beatles, they ultimately gained control of their recorded material and their tours, and everything about their shows. In the beginning a band is giving that up.

**PETER LEEDS,** LEEDS/DAVIS MANAGEMENT
Don't work with someone who makes you unhappy. You can die tonight, and with that realization, and the realization that in your life there's enough aggravation and enough bad times and unhappiness that you can't do something about, you can do something about a job that makes you crazy every day. You don't have to go back there tomorrow. You can find a new job and take that unhappiness out of your life. After a trip with Blondie, I told the head of the record label that I was getting out. Parallel Lines went on the sell about 12 million copies, over a million in the UK alone. I didn't regret it. Spend your time writing great songs. Don't believe everything that people tell you about how wonderful you are. Take seriously that which people offer you as criticism. Don't just reject it because you don't like it. Listen to what it is. Maybe it's valuable and you can learn something from it.

**DEBBIE SCHWARTZ,** PARTNER IN DSM MANAGEMENT

Work hard and get yourself out there. Be responsible. When we started managing Wanderlust, nobody knew who they were in Philadelphia at all . . . Just by sending a tape around and getting all the press interested in creating a buzz . . . (before they had a record out) we created a buzz in Philadelphia and just kept going for it. You have to keep sending things out to people . . . eventually you will get somewhere.

**LARRY RUDOLPH,** ESQ., PARTNER IN RUDOLPH & BEER

It is the music business. You have to remember the business side of it. You've got to be business oriented all around. It's not just about being talented. There are a lot of talented people sitting in their basements that don't do anything without being talented and business-like.

**MICHELINE LEVINE,** ESQ.

Do not discuss any financial terms with anybody, ever, except for your attorney and your manager. It isn't that whatever you agree to without having discussed it with your manager and lawyer will commit you necessarily, because your lawyer can undo that . . . But it makes the job much harder. Don't, based on your limited knowledge, agree to or discuss what you think will be good or bad with an A & R person who is interested in you.

**KEN GORKA,** MANAGER, BOOKER, EVERYTHING
AT THE BITTER END, NEW YORK CITY

Hang on and never get discouraged. If things don't go the way you want them to go the first time around, sometimes the waiting period only makes you better for it and makes a better presentation, so don't get discouraged.

**BOB GROSSWEINER,** NEW YORK BUREAU CHIEF
OF PERFORMANCE MAGAZINE

If you want to get signed to a label you need to have a demo tape and it should only be three tracks. If you give them a whole album's worth or seven or eight tracks, (A) they're not going to listen to it, and (B), you basically want to give them a tease and you want to get some feedback from the label. Then they'll ask you for some more songs and you have another three that you're holding onto. The key is you need the feedback whether they sign you or not. Sometimes getting a rejection is more important than getting an acceptance if they can tell you what you need your improvement in and why they didn't like it. It just might be that you're not right for the label or that you're last year's model. Or they could say they want to hear more.

**JEANNIE STAHLMAN,** BOOKING AGENT,
MERCURY RISING ENTERTAINMENT

Getting signed isn't the end-all, be-all. You can never stop working. Find an audience.

# APPENDIX 2

# RESOURCES

## BOOKS AND VIDEOS

There are many books written about breaking into the music industry. What follows are some books I've read that have been extremely useful. There are also a few video and audio tapes available, mainly by mail order, on a variety of music business topics. Check your local bookstores and catalogues to see what else is available. You can never aquire enough knowledge about the music industry.

THIS BUSINESS OF MUSIC, 7TH EDITION,
Sidney Shemel and M. William Krasilovsky, Billboard Books
When I first got into the business, this book was recommended to me as the bible of the music industry. It has retained this status over many years due to its thorough coverage of topics relating to the business end of music. It's an excellent reference for anyone wanting to fully understand the music industry's structure and standards—a must for all bookshelves.

MORE ABOUT THIS BUSINESS OF MUSIC, 5TH EDITION,
Sidney Shemel and M. William Krasilovsky, Billboard Books
This is another excellent reference and companion volume to *This Business of Music*, containing new information on trends in the music industry, including the impact of technology from CDs to DATs to VCRs.

ALL YOU NEED TO KNOW ABOUT THIS BUSINESS OF MUSIC,
REVISED EDITION,
Donald Passman, Prentice Hall Press
Passman presents a comprehensive picture of how the music industry functions on a business level, including the most important issues a musician needs to understand when seeking a deal. The writing is light, making often difficult topics more easily understood.

THE BILLBOARD GUIDE TO MUSIC PUBLICITY, 2ND EDITION,
James Pettigrew, Billboard Books
A detailed "how to" for getting that all-important media exposure. The book includes strategies for putting together publicity campaigns for acts of all levels and provides a clear-headed focus on developing the basic tool of the trade—the effective press kit.

MUSIC PUBLISHING
Randy Poe, Writer's Digest Books
If you write your own songs, this book is a good reference to have on hand. It explains the ins and outs of copyright and publishing and contains information necessary to getting your songs published. Read it through to get an overall picture of the songwriting business: use it later as a reference when marketing your songs.

THIS BUSINESS OF ARTIST MANAGEMENT, 3RD EDITION,
Xavier M. Frascogna and H. Lee Hetherington, Billboard Books
The standard reference on management in the music and entertainment business. It includes the latest information pertaining to management-related issues, and includes case studies and interviews with industry insiders and successful performers. The approach isn't sugar-coated, so you'll get a realistic view of what management is all about.

THE PERSONAL TOUCH,
Terrie Williams, Warner Books
The subtitle of this book is "What You Really Need to Succeed in Today's Fast-paced World," and Terrie Williams ought to know as she switched from a career as a social worker to become president of her own successful Public Relations agency. In this book she shares her story and her principles about developing social skills and showing personal consideration towards others. The tools Williams provides are essential in building and maintaining those all important relationships.

# RESOURCES

**THE BILLBOARD GUIDE TO HOME RECORDING, REVISED AND UPDATED,**
Ray Baragary, Billboard Books
For those of you who have or are planning to build your own home studio, this do-it-yourself reference is a *must have*. From the most basic to the most highly sophisticated technology, this guide covers equipment and recording techniques that everyone can learn from.

**HOW TO GET A RECORD DEAL**
This video, produced by Ritch Ezra, who has put out a number of resources through his company, SRS publishing, contains a series of interviews with top executives, managers, producers and leading recording artists. SRS Publishing: (800) 377-7411.

**MIX BOOKSHELF**
This mail order company has an excellent selection of books, tapes, and videos on all ends of the music industry. Call for a catalog at (800) 233-9604.

## DIRECTORIES

Here's a listing of directories that I've found to be extremely useful. I'm not including prices because they change too quickly. Call the company to get specific information. Some will take your order over the phone with a credit card.

**MUSICIAN: GUIDE TO TOURING AND PROMOTION**
Put out by *Musician* Magazine—(212) 536-5248—this is my own personal pick for the absolute best value in directories. It contains a *city-by-city* (U.S. and Canada) directory listing of clubs, music publications, radio stations, record stores, and places to buy or rent equipment. It also includes an A & R directory for both major and independent labels. As of this printing, the price was under ten bucks! It's available by mail order and in some book stores. The directory is available on disk for both PC and Mac as well, enabling you to generate mailing labels directly from it.

## SRS PUBLISHING

Ritch Ezra has compiled or made available the following directories. They can be ordered by calling (800) 377-7411. All of the SRS directories are available on disk

**A & R REGISTRY:**
This lists the entire A & R staff, with direct dial numbers and names of their assistants, for most major and independent labels in New York, Los Angeles, Nashville, and London. It's updated every eight weeks and is available by subscription. A trial issue can be purchased.

## MUSIC PUBLISHER REGISTRY:
This lists all major music publishers and significant independents in New York, Los Angeles, Nashville, and London with their direct dial numbers and names of their assistants.

## FILM/TV MUSIC GUIDE:
This is a directory for those looking to get their music into film or television.

## THE NATIONAL RAP DIRECTORY:
This lists the address, contact names, phone, and fax numbers for over 1,000 Urban Record Labels and Music Publishers, cross-referenced by region and style. Besides hip-hop, it includes Reggae, R & B, Euro-Tech, Gospel, Dance, and House music. This comprehensive directory also contains information and articles written by music industry professionals. It can be ordered from SRS Publishing.

## BILLBOARD
*Billboard* has a variety of directories and publications for sale. They can be ordered by calling (800) 247-2160.

## BILLBOARD RECORD RETAILING DIRECTORY:
This is a comprehensive directory of music stores, both the chain and those independently operated. It's published every March.

## BILLBOARD INTERNATIONAL BUYERS GUIDE:
This guide contains a listing of worldwide contacts covering every phase of the music and video industry. It's published every January.

## BILLBOARD INTERNATIONAL TALENT & TOURING DIRECTORY:
This directory has listings for U.S. and international talent, booking agencies, facilities, services, and products. It's published every October.

## BILLBOARD INTERNATIONAL LATIN MUSIC BUYER'S GUIDE:
This guide contains resources for finding contacts for breaking into the Latin music marketplace. It's published every August.

## BILLBOARD NASHVILLE 615/COUNTRY MUSIC SOURCEBOOK:
This is a comprehensive listing of resources for working the country music market, including performing artists, booking agents, managers, radio stations, and venues for the country music market. It's published every March.

## PERFORMANCE GUIDE SERIES
Besides their informative weekly publication, Performance puts out an excellent series of guides for the concert industry. I've listed the ones I feel are most relevant.

You can get a full listing of what's offered or find out how to order them by calling (817) 338-9444.

## TALENT/PM:

This guide has a listing of almost every musical act available for touring with contact information on their personal managers, booking agencies, and record labels. There's also a listing of management companies, public relations firms, and entertainment publications, including their address, phone and fax numbers, and personnel.

## BOOKING AGENCIES:

This guide contains a listing of over 350 booking agencies with their address, phone and fax numbers, agents, branch offices, and the acts they book.

## COUNTRY TALENT/VARIETY:

Country music acts and country talent buyers are listed in this guide which contains information on their agents and record companies. It also includes an assortment of information on where talent is booked, such as fairs and corporate affairs.

## PROMOTERS/CLUBS:

This guide provides a state-by-state listing of concert promoters and show producers. It includes a separate listing of showcase clubs, with their contacts, capacities, and the types of acts they book.

## INTERNATIONAL MARKETS:

This guide provides a listing of managers, promoters, booking agents, production and transportation companies, and concert venues in Canada, the U.K., Europe, Australia, South America, and the Pacific Rim.

## THE BLACK BOOK:

This guide has a state-by-state and country-by-country listing of resources needed for touring including hotels, promoters, public relations firms, lighting companies, promoters, booking agents, publications, and many, many more.

## POLLSTAR:

Beside their regular publication, Pollstar puts out a wonderful series of Contact Directories, published bi-annually. You can get a full listing of everything they have available by calling (800) 344-7383 or in California (209) 271-7900.

## RECORD COMPANY ROSTERS:

This directory contains a complete artist roster and list of executive contacts for every major and almost every independent label in the business. It includes all A&R, Artist Relations, Public Relations, legal, promotion staff & other key personnel.

AGENCY ROSTERS:
This booking contact directory contains over 6,750 artists.

TALENT BUYERS & CLUBS:
This directory lists every major concert promoter, nightclub, fair, festival, and theme park booking touring artists. It includes college buyers as well.

CONCERT VENUES:
This directory contains booking and contact information for every venue used by major touring artists.

## MUSIC CONFERENCES/TRADE SHOWS

Music conferences and trade shows are wonderful places to network and meet like-minded people. Most offer opportunities to showcase new music. Here's a list of some of the most popular ones. Most are listed in the *Billboard* calendar section. If possible, attend the ones that are targeted towards your music, rather than just a general music seminar. This way you have the best chance of meeting the most people who are involved in what you're doing. Some seminars are held in different cities from year to year. Some vary the time of year they are held. I've tried to get as specific as possible for those that have fixed times and locations. Call the ones you're interested in for a brochure.

AES (AUDIO ENGINEERING
SOCIETY) CONVENTION
(212) 661-8528
60 East 42nd street
New York, NY 10165
*Convention & exhibition for professional
audio manufacturers and engineers;
in the fall in New York or Los Angeles*

CANADIAN MUSIC WEEK
(416) 695-2553
5397 Eglinton Avenue W., Suite 106
Toronto, ON M9C 5K6
Canada
*Conference and music festival*

CMJ MUSIC MARATHON
(516) 466-6000
11 Middle Neck Road,
Suite 400
Great Neck, NY 11021
*Alternative music convention/college
radio; in New York City in the fall*

CROSSROADS MUSIC EXPO
(901) 526-4280
PO Box 41858
Memphis, TN 38174
*Includes panels, trade show, workshops,
and showcases; the last weekend of April*

CUTTING EDGE MUSIC
CONFERENCE
(504) 827-5700
710 Broad Street
New Orleans, LA 70119
*Trade show, panels, and showcases;
in August*

DETROIT REGIONAL MUSIC
CONFERENCE
(313) 963-0325
1000 Brush Avenue
Detroit, MI 48816
*Educational Conference*

F MUSIC FEST
(212) 645-1360
Concrete Marketing
1133 Broadway, Suite 1220
New York, NY 10010
*Showcases, panels and trade show;
held in Los Angeles in the fall*

GAVIN CONVENTION
(415) 495-1990
140 2nd Street
San Francisco, CA 94105
*Radio/record promoters conference.*

INDEPENDENT LABEL FESTIVAL
(312) 341-9112
600 S. Michigan Avenue
Chicago, IL 60605
*Panels, trade show, and showcases;
last weekend of July*

INTERNATIONAL DJ EXPO
(516)767-2500
25 Willowdale Drive
Port Washington, NY 11050
*For club owners, club/radio/mobile DJs*

JACK THE RAPPER
(212) 460-8012
147 Second Avenue, Suite 306
New York, NY 10010
*Black music conference; usually
held in Atlanta during August*

JAZZTIMES CONVENTION
(301) 588-4114
7961 Eastern Avenue, Suite 303
Silver Spring, MD 20910-4898
*Conference for the jazz industry*

LASS SONGWRITER'S EXPO
(213) 463-7178
P.O. Box 93759
Hollywood, CA 90093
*Educational event for songwriters/
industry professionals*

MID ATLANTIC SOUND, SURF +
SKATE SYMPOSIUM
(910) 256-4653
6766-6 Wrightsville Avenue,
Suite 214
Wilmington, NC 28403
*Panels and showcases; at the beginning
of June*

MUSIC WEST
(604) 684-9338
21 Water Street,
Suite 306
Vancouver, BC V6B 1A1, Canada

MIDEM
(212) 689-4220
475 Park Avenue S., 9th floor
New York, NY 10016
*International licensing/publishing/
distribution; held in January
at Cannes, France*

NAIRD CONVENTION
(609) 482-8999
1000 Maplewood Drive, Suite 211
Maple Shade, NJ 08052
*Convention for independent labels/
distributors*

NARM CONFERENCE
(609) 596-2221
11 Eves Drive, Suite 140
Marlton, NJ 08053
*For merchandisers, both independent
and major labels; targets issues relevant
to the larger businesses*

NORTH BY NORTHEAST
(CO-SPONSORED BY SXSW)
(512) 467-7979
P.O. Box 4999
Austin, TX 78765
*Showcases, panels, and trade show; in
Portland, Oregon*

NORTH BY NORTHWEST
(CO-SPONSORED BY SXSW)
(512) 467-7979
P.O. Box, 4999
Austin, TX 78765
*Showcases, panels, and trade show;
in Toronto, Canada*

PHILADELPHIA MUSIC
CONFERENCE
(215) 426-4109
P.O. Box 29363
Philadelphia, PA 19125-0363
*Panels and showcases for rock, urban,
and acoustic acts; in the fall*

SOUTH BY SOUTHWEST
(SXSW)
(512) 467-7979
P.O. Box 4999
Austin, TX 78765
*Music business seminar/trade/showcasing
event for industry and independent artists;
in March*

WINTER MUSIC
CONFERENCE
(954) 563-4444
3450 NE 12th Terrace
Ft. Lauderdale, FL 33334
*Industry conference featuring dance music
and rap; usually held in Miami sometime
in March*

## MUSIC BUSINESS-RELATED
## ORGANIZATIONS/ASSOCIATIONS

Joining organizations can be a great source of networking opportunities. Here are some of the more major organizations and associations. Most of them are self-explanatory. Many of the songwriter's organizations offer songwriting workshops that can be very beneficial for honing your skills as well as for making good contacts. Call any that sound interesting and get some literature.

# RESOURCES

ACADEMY OF COUNTRY MUSIC
(213) 462-2351
6255 Sunset Blvd., Suite 923
Hollywood, CA 90028

AFFILIATED INDEPENDENT
RECORD COMPANIES
(310) 208-2140
P.O. Box 241648
Los Angeles, CA 91601

AMERICAN FEDERATION
OF MUSICIANS
(212) 869-1330
1501 Broadway, Suite 600
New York, NY 10036

AMERICAN SOCIETY OF
COMPOSERS, AUTHORS, &
PUBLISHERS (ASCAP)
(212) 621-6000
One Lincoln Plaza
New York, NY 10023

ASSOCIATION OF INDEPENDENT
MUSIC PUBLISHERS (AIMP)
(818) 842-6257
P.O. Box 1561
Burbank, CA 91507

AUDIO ENGINEERING SOCIETY (AES)
(212) 661-8528
60 East 42nd Street, Room 2520
New York, NY 10165

BLACK ROCK COALITION
(212) 713-5097
P.O. Box 1054
New York, NY 10276

BROADCAST MUSIC
INCORPORATED (BMI)
(212) 586-2000
320 West 57th Street
New York, NY 10019

CANADIAN RECORDING
INDUSTRY ASSOCIATION
(416) 967-7272
300-1255 Yonge Street
Toronto, ON M4T 1W6 Canada

COUNTRY MUSIC ASSOCIATION
(615) 244-2840
1 Music Circle South
Nashville, TN 37203

COUNTRY MUSIC FOUNDATION
(615) 256-1639
4 Music Square East
Nashville, TN 37203

FLORIDA MUSIC ASSOCIATION
(813) 988-6016
P.O. Box 290005
Tampa, FL 33687

GOSPEL MUSIC ASSOCIATION
(615) 242-0303
7 Music Circle North
Nashville, TN 37203

HEARING EDUCATION AND
AWARENESS FOR ROCKERS
(415) 773-9590
P.O. Box 460847
San Francisco, CA 94146

HOME RECORDING RIGHTS
COALITION
(800) 282-TAPE
1145 19th Street NW
Box 33576
Washington DC 20033

INDEPENDENT MUSIC ASSOCIATION
(201) 818-6789
76 North Maple Avenue, Suite 371
Ridgewood, NJ 07450

INDEPENDENT MUSIC
RETAILERS ASSOCIATION
(201) 818-6789
76 North Maple Avenue, Suite 371
Ridgewood, NJ 07450

INTERNATIONAL BLUEGRASS
MUSIC ASSOCIATION
(502) 684-9025
326 Saint Elizabeth Street
Owensboro, KY 42301

JAZZMOBILE INC.
(212) 866-4900
154 West 127th Street
New York, NY 10027

LIFEBEAT
(212) 245-3240
810 7th Avenue, 8th floor
New York, NY 10019

LA WIM (LOS ANGELES WOMEN
IN MUSIC)
(213) 243-6440
P.O. Box 1817
Burbank, CA. 91507

LOS ANGELES MUSIC NETWORK
(818) 769-6095
P.O. Box 8934
Universal City, CA 91618-8934

MUSIC DISTRIBUTORS ASSOCIATION
(212) 924-9175
38 West 21st Street
New York, NY 10010

MUSICIANS AGAINST
RACISM-SEXISM
(212) 685-MARS
P.O. Box 1039, Murray Hill Station
New York, NY 10156

MUSICIANS CONTACT SERVICE
(818) 347-8888
P.O. Box 788
Woodland Hills, CA 91365

NATIONAL ACADEMY OF
POPULAR MUSIC/SONGWRITER'S
HALL OF FAME
(212) 957-9230
330 West 58th Street,
Suite 411
New York, NY 10019

NATIONAL ACADEMY OF
RECORDING ARTS & SCIENCES
(NARAS)
(310) 392-3777
3402 Pico Blvd.
Santa Monica, CA 90028

NATIONAL ACADEMY OF
SONGWRITERS
(213) 463-7178
6381 Hollywood Blvd.,
Suite 780
Hollywood, CA 90028

NATIONAL ASSOCIATION
FOR CAMPUS ACTIVITIES
(800) 845-2338
13 Harbison Way
Columbia, SC 29212-3401

NATIONAL ASSOCIATION
OF INDEPENDENT RECORD
DISTRIBUTORS & MANUFACTURERS
(NAIRD)
(609) 482-8999
1000 Maplewood Drive,
Suite 211
Maple Shade, NJ 08052

NATIONAL ASSOCIATION OF
RECORDING MERCHANDISERS, INC.
(NARM)
(609) 596-2221
11 Eves Drive, Suite 140
Marlton, NJ 08053

NORTHERN CALIFORNIA
SONGWRITERS ASSOCIATION
(415) 327-8296
855 Oak Grove Avenue,
Suite 211
Menlo Park, CA 94025

RAP COALITION
(718) 622-1964
366 Lafayette Avenue, Suite #1
Brooklyn, NY 11238

RECORDING INDUSTRY
ASSOCIATION OF AMERICA (RIAA)
(202) 775-0101
1020 Nineteenth Street NW, Suite 200
Washington D.C. 20036

RECORDING MUSICIANS
ASSOCIATION
(213) 462-4RMA
817 Vine Street, Suite 209
Hollywood, CA 90038

ROCK FOR CHOICE
(213) 651-0495
8105 West Third Street, Suite 1
Los Angeles, CA 90048

SONGWRITERS GUILD OF AMERICA
(212) 768-7902
1560 Broadway, Suite 1306
New York, NY 10036

SESAC, INC.
(212) 586-3450
421 West 54th Street
New York, NY 10019

WASHINGTON AREA MUSIC
ASSOCIATION (WAMA)
(703) 237-9500
1510 Forest Lane
McClean, VA 22101

WOMEN IN MUSIC, INC.
(212) 459-4580
P.O. Box 441
Radio City Station
New York, NY 10101

*Many of these organizations have local chapters in other large cities. Call them to find out.*

## ORGANIZATIONS TO PROTECT YOUR RIGHTS

There are organizations all over the country that provide free or low-cost legal assistance for people involved in the arts. They all vary in their fees, or lack of fees, and their criteria as to eligibility for their services. Some of these groups offer seminars. Some have publications available. All are dedicated to providing help with legal matters. Rather than just listing a few, I'm putting in the major organizations with their city and phone number. Call the one nearest you for more information. They may know of more. Many of these organizations are run by volunteers and the people I've spoken to in doing research for this book have all been sincerely supportive. There's a nice vibe throughout the staffs, one of wanting to help those in need of legal assistance as much as they can. I'd like to congratulate the efforts of all the good people who make this list possible!

ALBANY/SCHENECTADY
LEAGUE OF ARTS, INC.
Albany, New York, (518) 449-5380

ARTIST'S LEGAL ADVICE SERVICES
Toronto, Canada, (416) 340-7791
Ottawa, Canada, (613) 567-2690

ATLANTA LAWYERS FOR THE ARTS
Atlanta, Georgia, (404) 524-0606

CALIFORNIA LAWYERS FOR THE ARTS
Santa Monica, California,
(310) 998-5590
San Francisco, California,
(415) 775-7200
*There are several other branches in California. Call one of the above for more numbers.*

COLORADO LAWYERS FOR THE ARTS
Denver, Colorado, (512) 338-4458

CONNECTICUT VOLUNTEER
LAWYERS FOR THE ARTS
(203) 566-4770
Hartford, Connecticut

DISTRICT OF COLUMBIA LAWYERS
COMMITTEE FOR THE ARTS
(202) 429-0229
Washington, DC

GEORGIA VOLUNTEER LAWYERS
FOR THE ARTS
(404) 873-3911
Atlanta, Georgia

LAWYERS FOR THE ARTS/
NEW HAMPSHIRE
(603) 224-8300
Concord, New Hampshire

LAWYERS FOR THE CREATIVE ARTS
(312) 944-ARTS Chicago, Illinois
(800) 525-ARTS (Illinois only)

LOUISIANA VOLUNTEER LAWYERS
FOR THE ARTS
(504) 523-1465
New Orleans, Louisiana

MAINE LAWYERS AND
ACCOUNTANTS FOR THE ARTS
(207) 799-9646
South Portland, Maine

MARYLAND LAWYERS FOR THE ARTS
(410) 752-1633
Baltimore, Maryland

MID-AMERICA ARTS RESOURCES
(913) 227-2321
Lindsborg, Kansas
*Serving Kansas, Nebraska, Oklahoma*

MONTANA VOLUNTEER LAWYERS
FOR THE ARTS
(406) 721-1835
Missoula, Montana

NORTH CAROLINA VOLUNTEER
LAWYERS FOR THE ARTS
(919) 990-2575
Raleigh, North Carolina

NORTHWEST LAWYERS
AND ARTISTS, INC.
(503) 295-2787
Portland, Oregon

OCEAN STATE LAWYERS
FOR THE ARTS
(401) 789-5686
Saunderstown, Rhode Island

PHILADELPHIA VOLUNTEER LAWYERS
FOR THE ARTS
(215) 545-3385
Philadelphia, Pennsylvania
*Serves Pennsylvania, Delaware, and
New Jersey*

RESOURCES & COUNSELING
FOR THE ARTS
(800) 546-2891
St. Paul, Minnesota
*Serves Minnesota, western Wisconsin,
Iowa, North Dakota, South Dakota*

ST. LOUIS VOLUNTEER
LAWYERS AND ACCOUNTANTS
FOR THE ARTS
(314) 652-0011
St. Louis, Missouri

TEXAS ACCOUNTANTS AND
LAWYERS FOR THE ARTS
(713) 526-4876
Houston, Texas
*They are also located in Austin, Dallas,
El Paso, and San Antonio. This office will
give you the information.*

TOLEDO VOLUNTEER LAWYERS
FOR THE ARTS
(419) 255-3344
Toledo, Ohio

UTAH LAWYERS FOR THE ARTS
(801) 482-5373
Salt Lake City, Utah

VOLUNTEER LAWYERS FOR THE ARTS
(954) 462-9191
Ft. Lauderdale, Florida

VOLUNTEER LAWYERS FOR THE ARTS
(212) 319-ARTS
Law line: (212) 319-2910
New York City, New York

VOLUNTEER LAWYERS FOR THE ARTS
OF MASSACHUSETTS, INC.
(617) 123-0648
Boston, Massachusetts
(800) 864-0476 (in Massachusetts only)

# INDEX

# INDEX

baby bands, touring, importance of, 102
Baylor, Kathy, 65, 109, 152, 153, 154, 155, 234
BDS (Broadcast Data System), 212
Beats Per Minute (BPMs), 76
belief in yourself, importance of, 16–17
Berg, Karin, 139, 142, 153, 233
Bergman, Marilyn, 213
*Billboard Guide to Home Recording*, 241
*Billboard Guide to Music Publicity*, 240
*Billboard International Buyers Guide*, 242
*Billboard International Latin Music Buyers Guide*, 242
*Billboard International Talent & Touring Directory*, 242
*Billboard Magazine*, 132, 182, 242
  *Executive Turntable*, 183
*Billboard Nashville 615/Country Music Sourcebook*, 242
*Billboard Record Retailing Directory*, 242
bios, importance of, in press kits, 89
Black Rock Coalition, 247
blanket license, 211
Blumenfeld, Jane, 84, 160, 166, 184, 190, 191, 234
BMI (Broadcast Music Incorporated), 109, 211
*Booking Agencies*, 243
books and videos, reference, list of, 239–241
Boyd, Gail, 169
BPMs (Beats Per Minute), 76
breakage; See also: royalties
Broadcast Data System (BDS), 212
Broadcast Music Incorporated (BMI), 211, 247
Burrowes, Kirk, 56, 66, 109, 141, 152, 234
business cards, importance of, 166
buzz, creating, 11

California Lawyers for the Arts, 250
Canadian Music Week, 244
Canadian Recording Industry Association, 247
CD rate; See also: royalties
*Certain Damage*, 117
Chuck D, 231
Ciaccia, Peter, 20, 22, 23, 24
Clegg, Johnny, 232
clubs and concert circuit, uses of, 120–124
  preplanning, importance of, 122

*CMJ (College Music Journal)*, 115–118, 132
*CMJ Music Conference*, 107
*CMJ Music Marathon*, 244
*CMJ Music Marathon & Musicfest*, 116
*CMJ New Music Monthly*, 117
*CMJ New Music Report*, 116
co-publishing deals, 209–210
Cohen, David, 33, 38, 40
college markets
  power of, 114–115
  reaching, ways of, 115–124
    club and concert circuit, 120–124
    CMJ, 115–118, 132
    college radio, 118–120
    student activities director, 114, 115
  targeting, 113–124
*College Music Journal* (CMJ), 115–118, 132
college radio, 118–120
  interviews on, 122
Collins, Wallace, 45, 46, 170, 171, 173, 174, 175, 176, 177
Colorado Lawyers for the Arts, 250
*Concert Venues*, 244
Connecticut Volunteer Lawyers for the Arts, 250
consignment, of self-pressed discs, 134
contacts; See also: networkingcontract
  commitment, details of, 194–198
contract, terms of, 194
  commitment, definition of, 195
  record labels, long-term contracts, 197–198
  record labels, options to record, 196–197
  rushing into signing, drawbacks of, 197
  shorter contracts, benefits of, 195–198
copyright law, infringement of, 219, 220
Copyright Office, 207
Country Music Association, 247
Country Music Foundation, 247
*Country Talent/Variety*, 243
cover letters, description of, 87
criticism, constructive
  negative sources of, 61–62
  open mindedness, benefit of, 64
  positive sources of, 63–64
  uses of, 60–61Crossroads Music Expo, 244
Cutting Edge Music Conference, 245

# BillboardBooks

### THE BILLBOARD BOOK OF AMERICAN SINGING GROUPS:
A History, 1940-1990 by *Jay Warner*
The definitive history of pop vocal groups, from the doo wop of Dion and the Belmonts, to the Motown hits of the Supremes, to the surf sound of the Beach Boys, to the country rock of Crosby, Stills and Nash. More than 350 classic acts spanning five decades are profiled here, with fascinating information about each group's career, key members, and musical impact as well as extensive discographies and rare photos. A one-of-a-kind reference for vocal group fans and record collectors alike. 544 pages. 80 photos. Paperback. $21.95. 0-8230-8264-4.

### THE BILLBOARD BOOK OF NUMBER ONE ALBUMS:
The Inside Story Behind Pop Music's Blockbuster Records
*by Craig Rosen*
A behind-the-scenes look at the people and stories involved in the enormously popular records that achieved Number One album status in the Billboard charts. Inside information on over 400 albums that have topped the chart since 1956, plus new interviews with hundreds of superstar record artists as well as a wealth of trivia statistics and other facts. 448 pages. 425 photos. Paperback. $21.95. 0-8230-7586-9.

### THE BILLBOARD BOOK OF NUMBER ONE HITS,
Third Edition, Revised and Enlarged
*by Fred Bronson*
The inside story behind the top of the charts. An indispensable listing of every single to appear in the top spot on the Billboard Hot 100 chart from 1955 through 1991, along with anecdotes, interviews, and chart data. 848 pages. 800 photos. Paperback. $21.95. 0-8230-8297-0.

### THE BILLBOARD BOOK OF TOP 40 ALBUMS,
Third Edition, Revised and Enlarged *by Joel Whitburn*
The complete guide to every Top 40 album from 1955 to 1994. Comprehensive information on the most successful rock, jazz, comedy, country, classical, Christmas, Broadway, and film soundtrack albums ever to reach the top of the Billboard charts. Includes chart positions, number of weeks on the chart, and label and catalog number for every album listed. 416 pages. 150 photos. Paperback. $21.95. 0-8230-7631-8.

## THE BILLBOARD BOOK OF TOP 40 COUNTRY HITS:
### Country Music's Hottest Records, 1944 to the Present
*by Joel Whitburn*
From the classic recordings of Hank Williams and Bob Wills, to enduring artists Patsy Cline and Tammy Wynette, to today's young superstars Garth Brooks and Shania Twain, the rich history of country music is documented in this comprehensive compilation of Billboard's Country Singles charts. Provides exhaustive data on every record to score at least one Top 40 hit. 562 pages. 96 photos. Paperback. $21.95. 0-8230-8289-X.

## THE BILLBOARD BOOK OF TOP 40 HITS,
### Sixth Edition, Revised and Enlarged
*by Joel Whitburn*
A perennial favorite, listing every single to reach the Top 40 of Billboard's weekly Hot 100 charts since 1955. Includes new chart data and expanded biographical information and trivia on artists listed. 800 pages. 300 photos. Paperback. $21.95
0-8230-7632-6.

## THE BILLBOARD BOOK OF ONE-HIT WONDERS,
### Second Edition, Revised and Expanded
*by Wayne Jancik*
A one-of-a-kind rock and roll reference guide that charts the flip side of the pop music story. Uncovers the fascinating circumstances surrounding the rise to fame—and occasional rapid return to obscurity—of performers who had only one hit in Billboard's Top 40 charts. Contains over 100 new entries and a wealth of data and entertaining information that just can't be found elsewhere. A must for pop music fans and record collectors. 512 pages. 235 photos. Paperback. $21.95. 0-8230-7622-9.

## THE BILLBOARD GUIDE TO HOME RECORDING,
### Second Edition, Revised and Updated
*by Ray Baragary*
The complete do-it-yourself reference to recording techniques and equipment options. Provides a step-by-step approach to producing high-quality tapes, demos, and CDs in a home studio. Includes information on recorders, mixers, microphones, and signal processors; recording basic tracks and overdubbing; expanding the home studio with MIDI; the development of General MIDI standards; and the use of computers in sequencing. 272 pages. 97 illustrations. Paperback. $19.95. 0-8230-8300-4.

## THE BILLBOARD GUIDE TO MUSIC PUBLICITY,
### Revised Edition *by Jim Pettigrew, Jr.*
A clear-headed reference providing career-minded musicians and their representatives with key information about such vital activities as getting media exposure, preparing effective publicity materials, and developing short-term and long-range publicity. New to the revised edition is coverage of desktop publishing, compact disks, basic copy-editing tips, and a recommended reading list. 176 pages. 16 illustrations. Paperback. $18.95. 0-8230-7626-1.

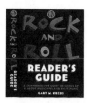

## THE ROCK AND ROLL READER'S GUIDE
*by Gary M. Krebs*
An indispensable consumer guide for book collectors and music fans alike. The first comprehensive bibliography of books about, and by, rock and pop stars in addition to works written about the music scene itself. Focuses on both selected general reference works—such as artist profiles, chart data, pictorials, concert events, women and rock, and magazines—and all publications on artists A-Z. 464 pages. Paperback. $21.95. 0-8230-7602-4.

## THIS BUSINESS OF ARTIST MANAGEMENT,
Revised and Enlarged Third Edition
*by Xavier M. Frascogna, Jr. and H. Lee Hetherington*
Firmly established as the standard reference work in the field of artist management in music, and winner of the 1980 Deems Taylor Book Award, this new edition of the title formerly known as Successful Artist Management offers the wise guidance and authoritative professional information required to develop an artist's career. Now revised and updated to include interviews with top record executives, coverage of new forms of business, updates on the legal framework of the music business, and contemporary investment and money management advice. 304 pages. Hardcover. $21.95. 0-8230-7705-5.

## THIS BUSINESS OF MUSIC,
Seventh Edition *by M. William Krasilovsky and Sidney Shemel*
The bible of the music business, with over 250,000 copies sold. A practical guide to the music industry for publishers, writers, record companies, producers, artists, and agents. Provides detailed information on virtually every economic, legal, and financial aspect of the complex business of music. 736 pages. Hardcover. $29.95. 0-8230-7755-1.

## BILLBOARD'S HOTTEST HOT 100 HITS,
Revised and Enlarged Edition *by Fred Bronson*
The ultimate music trivia book. An illustrated compendium of 40 years of Billboard's chart data broken down into 175 categories, including artists, writers, producers, and record labels. Plus, a definitive list of the Top 5000 hits from 1955 through 1995. 512 pages. 250 photos. Paperback. $21.95. 0-8230-7646-6.

## BLACK & WHITE BLUES:
Photographs by Marc Norberg, *edited by B. Martin Pedersen*
From Graphis Publications, portraits of 60 of the finest blues musicians of all time, accompanied by the artist's personal statement about the blues. A CD-ROM disc is packaged with the hardcover edition. 192 pages. 60 photos. Hardcover (with CD): $69.95. 0-8230-6471-9. Paperback: $45.95. 0-8230-6480-8.

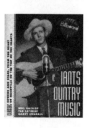

## GIANTS OF COUNTRY MUSIC
Classic Sounds and Stars, from the Heart
of Nashville to the Top of the Charts
*by Neil Haislop, Tad Lathrop, and Harry Sumrall*
An inside view of country's biggest names, drawing upon dozens of never-before-published interviews with such stars as Garth Brooks, Mary Chapin Carpenter, and Willie Nelson. Each entry focuses of the artist's career in detail and explains how their work has fit into the surrounding musical landscape. 288 pages. 100 photos. Paperback. $21.95. 0-8230-7635-0.

## GRAPHIS MUSIC CDS
### edited by B. Martin Pedersen
This wide-ranging international collection from Graphis Publications includes innovative covers, foldouts, inner sleeves, and compact disk surfaces created by graphic designers specializing in cover and packaging design for music CDs. 224 Pages. Over 300 illustrations. Hardcover. $75.95. 0-8230-6470-0.

## KISS AND SELL:
### The Making of A Supergroup by C.K. Lendt
A riveting expose of the machinations and manipulations of what's involved in making it to the top of the rock world, written by the man who traveled with Kiss for 12 years as their business manager. Both a case study of the harsh realities of how the business of music works and a unique perspective on the lives, lifestyles, and indulgences of rock stars. 352 pages. 18 photos. Paperback. $18.95. 0-8230-7551-6.

## MORE ABOUT THIS BUSINESS OF MUSIC,
### Fifth Edition, Revised and Enlarged
### by Sidney Shemel and M. William Krasilovsky
A completely updated companion to This Business of Music, this book presents a practical guide to areas of the music business such as jazz, religious music, live performances, the production and sale of printed music, background music and transcriptions, and the impact of technology from CDs and DATs to VCRs. 224 pages. Hardcover. $18.95. 0-8230-7642-3.

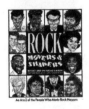

## ROCK MOVERS AND SHAKERS:
### An A-Z of the People Who Made Rock Happen, Revised and Enlarged by Dafyyd Rees and Luke Crampton
An entertaining reference work identifying the most influential and popular artists of the past 40 years. Documents the events of artists' musical careers and personal lives chronologically. More than 750 entries reveal what happened and when. 608 pages. 125 photos. Paperback. $19.95. 0-8230-7609-1.

The above titles should all be available from your neighborhood bookseller. If you don't find a copy on the shelf, books can also be ordered either through the store or directly from Watson-Guptill Publications. To order copies by phone or to request information on any of these titles, please call our toll-free number: 1-800-278-8477. To order copies by mail, send a check or money order for the cost of the book, with $2.00 postage and handling for one book and $ .50 for each additional book, plus applicable sales tax in the states of CA, DC, IL, OH, MA, NJ, NY, PA, TN, and VA, to:

WATSON-GUPTILL PUBLICATIONS
PO Box 2013
Lakewood, NJ 08701-9913